Contributions to Economics

The series *Contributions to Economics* provides an outlet for innovative research in all areas of economics. Books published in the series are primarily monographs and multiple author works that present new research results on a clearly defined topic, but contributed volumes and conference proceedings are also considered. All books are published in print and ebook and disseminated and promoted globally.

The series and the volumes published in it are indexed by Scopus and ISI (selected volumes).

More information about this series at http://www.springer.com/series/1262

Alexandra Horobet · Persefoni Polychronidou ·
Anastasios Karasavvoglou
Editors

Business Performance and Financial Institutions in Europe

Business Models and Value Creation Across European Industries

Springer

Editors
Alexandra Horobet
Bucharest University of Economic Studies
Bucharest, Romania

Persefoni Polychronidou
Department of Economics
International Hellenic University
Serres, Greece

Anastasios Karasavvoglou
International Hellenic University
Kavala, Greece

ISSN 1431-1933 ISSN 2197-7178 (electronic)
Contributions to Economics
ISBN 978-3-030-57516-8 ISBN 978-3-030-57517-5 (eBook)
https://doi.org/10.1007/978-3-030-57517-5

This Springer imprint is published by the registered company Springer Nature Switzerland AG
The registered company address is: Gewerbestrasse 11, 6330 Cham, Switzerland

Preface

Exploring business performance is a challenging endeavour now as ever, but recent times have brought into the business landscape more diversity and complexity of information, as well as micro- and macroeconomic volatility. Europe has been the scene of interesting developments in the last decades, fundamentally driven by the creation of the European Union and its further enlargement towards Central and Eastern Europe. Businesses from all sectors, industries and countries have quickly acknowledged friendlier and open economic environments, as well as profit-generating expansion opportunities, and have consolidated their value chains across the wide European region. But the last decades have brought serious challenges and new opportunities for businesses all over the world, such as the "Internet of things" and the digital technology-based economy, on the one hand, but also demographic changes, migration and climate change, on the other hand. All these create genuine sources of revenues and cash flows, increased efficiency and better performance for shareholders and stakeholders alike. Nevertheless, they expose businesses to higher specific and market risks, which require superior risk management strategies. More recently, distressful events such as Brexit or the US-China trade war continue to test businesses' resilience abilities and their capabilities in terms of restructuring for performance betterment.

The European business landscape is multifaceted and intricate, regardless of whether one refers to the financial or non-financial corporations. Thus, a collection of studies that explores how companies respond to the challenges they face and manage risks with the aim of increasing business value and performance offers an insightful look at business models and value creation across European industries and countries. Academics and professional researchers whose works are included in this volume investigate the facets and performance of various European industries and companies, thus demonstrating that this is a fertile ground for research development. Many of the authors are working in Central and Southeastern European universities and institutions, which shows that there is a significant progress in research and research methods in this part of Europe, particularly if we add the innovative quantitative approaches proposed in the volume by several authors, many based on neural networks and artificial intelligence tools.

The international conference "Economies of the Balkan and Eastern European Countries (EBEEC)", through its eleven previous editions, has become a recognized forum where the knowledge and experiences gained by academics specialized in economics and business in the region of Central and Southeastern Europe are exchanged, debated and validated. Moreover, the research results presented and discussed at the conference and included in the various publications supported by EBEEC are disseminated by making them available to interested parties—academics, the business community, political decision-makers—all over the world. In this framework, significant help and contribution come from renowned publishers such as Springer.

The 11th International Conference "Economies of the Balkan and Eastern European Countries" was organized jointly in Bucharest, Romania, by the International Hellenic University, Department of Accounting and Finance (Kavala, Greece), The Bucharest University of Economic Studies—through the Faculty of International Business and Economics and the Center of Research in International Business and Economics—and the Romanian Academy of Sciences, represented by the Institute for Economic Forecasting and the Center for Financial and Monetary Research "Victor Slavescu", between 11 and 13 May 2019. The conference aimed at presenting academic papers and exchanging theoretical and empirical research results on recent evolutions at micro- and macroeconomic level in the Balkans and the Eastern European countries, but also understood in the framework of the influences they receive from both wider European and global challenges. The conference brought together more than 120 papers authored by more than 150 authors from 16 countries from Europe and all over the world.

The conference offered a platform for discussions and debates on a broad range of issues—knowledge economics, management and innovation; multinational enterprises and foreign direct investments; regional integration with special reference to the EU; economic growth, development and stability; management and marketing; finance, banking and insurance; corporate governance and corporate performance; business information systems and entrepreneurship, micro- and macroeconomics; labour markets; artificial intelligence use; international and European political economy, etc.

The volume is one of the publications resulting from the 11th International Conference "Economies of the Balkan and Eastern European Countries (EBEEC)"—Bucharest, May 2019, and makes available to readers insightful research into the development and performance evolution of financial and non-financial businesses across Europe. The volume includes 10 contributions selected from the papers prepared and presented at the 11th EBEEC Conference, which make a solid contribution to the business and financial services fields, as well as to the application of econometric models and innovative quantitative analysis tools. All the papers proposed for the volume have been thoroughly peer-reviewed and edited. The selection process of these papers was confidential and methodical, as book editors studied all of them and decided on the final selection after in-depth discussions among them. They show that the research undertaken by scientists in

Central and Southeastern Europe is worth acknowledging and reading, given its thorough understanding of the many-sided financial and non-financial business in Europe.

The papers included in this volume cover a wide performance and business model analysis spectrum, from the banking to pharmaceutical industries, from business services to airline companies and from research and development to efficiency. Moreover, the understanding of European business is complemented by comprehensive analyses on the diversity of economic activities in Europe, on the energy deficiency and growth in the European Union, but also on lessons that one may extract from the Chinese approaches on business development between local companies and peers from other developing countries. The papers are independent, but they may be included into three distinctive parts, as follows:

- European Business Competitiveness and Performance: A Critical Assessment
- Decision-Making Approaches in Financial Institutions: The Case of European Banks
- Economy-Wide Risks and Opportunities for Business Development: Lessons from Europe and Abroad.

First Part: European Business Competitiveness and Performance: A Critical Assessment

The book opens with the paper written by Alexandra Horobet (The Bucharest University of Economic Studies, Romania), Oana Popovici (The Bucharest University of Economic Studies and the Romanian Academy of Sciences, Romania) and Lucian Belascu ("Lucian Blaga" University of Sibiu, Romania), which proposes a new method for analysing the structure and dynamics of economic activity undertaken by locally and foreign-owned companies within the European Union. The authors implement an unsupervised learning algorithm that generates a neural network that is depicted on Kohonen's self-organizing map (SOM) that offers a clustering of companies with a different ownership (local and foreign) from various industries and countries of the European Union. Each type of company (locally owned and foreign-owned) from a specific industry and country is characterized by a series of performance indicators that are included in the SOM algorithm, i.e. indicators at the average enterprise and employee level (turnover, value added at factor cost, gross operating surplus, personnel costs, gross investments) and comprehensive indicators, such as labour productivity and profitability (the latter through the gross operating rate). Various clusters of companies based on Euclidian distances that provide similarities and differentiation between companies' common production activities by taking into account their ownership (foreign versus local), industry and country of location, and related performance results, as well as their interrelationships, are identified in the paper. The resulting classification can be used to understand the linkages between European Union companies and the different branches of economic activities across EU countries, as well as to investigate the performance gap between locally owned and foreign-owned companies.

The second paper of the volume, co-authored by Özcan Karahan (Bandırma Onyedi Eylül University, Turkey) and Olcay Colak (Uşak University, Turkey), aims at determining the driving forces of business R&D expenditures in the Eastern European region, given that identifying the driving forces of enterprise R&D spending is important for achieving long-term economic growth. The chapter uses panel data regression models to determine the impact of human capital, high-technology density and public R&D expenditures on the business R&D intensity of the Eastern European countries. The empirical results show that all three factors have a significant and positive effect on the business R&D intensity of the Eastern European area. More specifically, the high-tech industrial structure is seen as the most significant factor of influence on business R&D expenditures, while human capital is second and public R&D expenditures come on the third place. The authors argue that, within the framework of innovation policies aiming to increase business R&D expenditures, priority should be given to boosting the share of the manufacturing sector that uses advanced technology. Moreover, higher investments in human capital and public R&D activities are suggested as other significant options for effective innovation policies to be implemented in Eastern European countries with the aim of increasing R&D expenditures and eventually enhance economic growth.

The next paper, prepared by Vasiliki Kounnou and Dimitris Kyrkilis (University of Macedonia, Greece), studies the Greek pharmaceutical industry that has emerged as one of the major drivers for the Greek manufacturing sector growth. The value added generated by the industry at the economy-wide level is observable through its impact on the gross value-added production, employment, exports, innovation and global competiveness. Greek pharmaceutical firms have some of the highest shares of investment in innovation and R&D activities in the total Greek economy. The purpose of the papers resides in investigating the potential causal relationship between industry-level competitiveness, profitability and R&D intensity in the Greek pharmaceutical industry. Thus, the authors select specific financial ratios from a sample of Greek pharmaceutical firms with in-house Research and Development departments and implement a regression analysis between 2004 and 2015. They find that return of equity (ROE), capital intensity and firm size are significant determinants of profitability. On the other hand, there is no statistical significance of the influence of the R&D intensity on profitability, which indicates that further analysis should be conducted on this respect. Moreover, while the use of capital, the effective management of firm's assets and the company size are important factors for the profitability of Greek companies from the pharmaceutical industry, the results do not suggest any relation of profitability with business age and financial leverage.

The first part of the volume closes with the paper written by Leyla Adiloglu-Yalcinkaya (Özyeğin University, Turkey) and Senem Besler (Anadolu University, Turkey) that addresses the evolution of Pegasus Airlines (the second

Turkish carrier after Turkish airlines) business model, building on the substantial attention towards it in the strategic management and airline management literature in recent years. For this purpose, a single case study approach was designed to allow in-depth analysis of business model evolution of Pegasus Airlines. The authors conducted semi-structured interviews with executives of Pegasus Airlines in 2019, which were furthermore supported by data gathered from multiple sources. From its beginnings in 2005, Pegasus Airlines adopted a charter airline business model, but the economic crises and regulations forced the company to make changes into this initial setting. In 2005, the acquisition of Pegasus by ESAS Holding AS and the government's support of private airlines in the Turkish civil aviation sector motivated Pegasus to enter the market with a new business model, called the "low-cost-network business model". The chapter presented in the volume identifies that regulations, country conditions and government support were critical for Pegasus success and are among the most important factors that affect a business model.

Second Part: Decision-Making Approaches in Financial Institutions: The Case of European Banks

The second part of the volume, dedicated to European banks, opens with the paper of Ivana Marjanović and Zarko Popović (both from Faculty of Economics, Niš, Serbia). The authors build on the significance and role of the banking sector for the development of national economy that defines the need for continuous monitoring of banks' performance. The banking sector in the Republic of Serbia has undergone considerable changes in recent decades, and its liberalization enabled the entry of foreign capital, which led to an increase in competition; consequently, the issue of banks' financial performance received significant attention in Serbia. An adequate assessment of banks' financial performance may provide useful guidelines to bank managers during the decision-making process and may be supported by a multi-criteria decision-making (MCDM) framework, given the bank's needs to check and oversee an extensive set of performance indicators. Therefore, the authors propose MCDM techniques as a useful tool for the evaluation of banks' financial performance. In the paper, the financial performance of all banks that operated in the Republic of Serbia between 2012 and 2017 is assessed using an integrated model combining the CRITIC and TOPSIS methods, which gives a unique measure of financial performance obtained through the integration of several financial ratios. The analysis consists of two steps: in the first step criteria weights are obtained by the CRITIC method, while in the second step the ranking is performed using TOPSIS method. The results show that liquidity and financial soundness indicators are becoming increasingly important for the assessment of banks' financial performance. Therefore, the results of this study offer useful guidelines to bank managers, as well as government authorities. Bank managers may improve the bank's financial performance by adequate risk management, particularly by controlling liquidity and solvency risks. Furthermore, government authorities should continue efforts to create and maintain a stable macroeconomic environment in which banks will operate profitably and sustainably and thus help further stabilization of the economy.

The digitalization of the banking sector, as a direct consequence of the digitization of the economy, is the topic of the paper prepared by Stavros Valsamidis (International University of Greece, Greece), Lambros Tsourgiannis (Directorate of Public Health and Social Care of Regional District of Xanthi, Greece), Dimosthenis Pappas (International University of Greece, Greece) and Eirini Mosxou (International University of Greece). The authors consider that today's demand is anytime and anywhere banking, which requires innovative, robust, secure, optimized and ready-to-meet-the-expectations of empowered and tech-savvy customer approaches. As a result, it is important to capture the new reality in relation to the banking environment, through the views of customers. The study aims to explore customers' attitudes towards the use of digital services and applications in the banking sector. In particular, it aims to identify the factors that affect customers' attitudes towards those applications, to classify them into groups according to their similar behaviour patterns and to profile each group of customers according to their demographic characteristics and other factors. Principal component analysis (PCA) is conducted to identify the main factors that affect consumers' attitudes towards the use of digital services and applications in banking sector. Cluster analysis is implemented in order to classify customers into groups with similar behaviour, while discriminant analysis is conducted to check for cluster predictability. Nonparametric tests performed to profile each group of customers according to their demographic characteristics and other factors are also performed. The authors identify three main factors that shape customers' attitudes towards those applications: better service, cautiousness and timelines/directness. Cluster analysis classifies customers into three groups according to their purchasing behaviour towards the use of those digital services/applications in those that are in favour of, opportunists and sceptical. Statistical chi-square tests indicate that demographic characteristics such as gender, age, education, marital status and income have an impact on customers' particular behaviour. Furthermore, the use of the Friedman nonparametric test finds that some other opinion of customers regarding the use of digital applications compared to those on traditional banking services is also related to their behaviour towards those digital banking applications.

Sotirios J. Trigkas and Konstantinos J. Liapis (both from Panteion University of Social and Political Sciences Athens, Greece) aim in their paper to test the effect of using the artificial neural networks (ANNs) nonparametric methodology for enhancing decision-making procedures in Greek banks, compared to a classic multivariate regression model. The authors implement ANNs and regression for decision-making regarding loan allowances and collateral valuation of collaterals using data from a small-to-medium Greek bank. Using sensitivity analysis, they also identify the key points where decision-making results change. All the needed estimations, as well as a comparable matrix, are produced in order to point out the similarities and differences between the two methodologies. Also, the key points in decision-making approach are presented. From the presentation of comparison between the two methodologies, the authors provide also the relationship between independent variables along with decision-making options. The paper contributes to the academic debate between theoretical and non-theoretical approaches in decision-making procedures and demonstrates a practical tool for decision roles and units who are trying to define the best practice for decision-making procedures.

Third Part: Economy-Wide Risks and Opportunities for Business Development: Lessons from Europe and Abroad

A multinational team of authors—Tatiana Corejova (University of Zilina, Slovakia), Roman Chinoracky (University of Zilina, Slovakia), Birgit Franken (DHBW, Fakultät Wirtschaft, Karlsruhe, Germany) and Maria Rostasova (University of Zilina, Slovakia)—authors the first paper in the third part of the volume, which deals with the trends and structure of the trade with other business services among the Visegrad countries (e.g. Czech Republic, Poland, Hungary and Slovak Republic), also in the context of trade in EU28 and in Eurozone. Visegrad countries are classified as high-income countries, but they are all transition economy countries. They have significantly changed their economic structure in the transition period, and now a new economic structure based on high value-added services is emerging. They have to move to the new structure by the sectors to the economy based on the services with high value added. The development of business services in these countries is related to changes in the business environment, fuelled by rapid changes in technology, changing regulations and increased market volatility, which further intensify the motives for trade and lead to a stronger integration into the world trading system. The authors find that there is an anticipated strong market dynamics for three groups of business services (accounting, auditing, bookkeeping and tax consulting services; advertising, market research and public opinion polling services; and business and management consulting and public relations services), but R&D's growth in trade in services in the investigated countries is associated with different levels of R&D support at the national level and is observable in the values of these countries in the Global Innovation Index. The authors suggest that the key to growth in business services' trade is the strategic positioning of the business services portfolio in the each country and a specialization based on comparative advantages of Visegrad countries in terms of their localization and available labour resources.

The next paper, written by Tania Muñoz Remos (University of Veracruz, Xalapa, Mexico), Edgar Juan Saucedo Acosta (University of Veracruz, Xalapa, Mexico) and Jesús Diaz Pedroza (Metropolitan Autonomous University—Iztapalapa, Mexico City, Mexico), aims to evaluate the decoupling of the gross domestic product and greenhouse gas emissions and to analyse the effects of population growth and gross domestic product on increase of greenhouse gas emissions and energy inefficiency in the members of the European Union. The climate change is a global externality that requires international efforts. The European Union have subscribed to international agreements and internally have launched the European Union 2020 Strategy, with specific environmental targets. In this context, it is important to measure the environmental damage and economic growth relationship in the European Union. The authors use data envelopment analysis models, which were applied to analyse the inefficiency levels and the population growth and gross domestic product decoupling of the 28 member countries of the European Union using data from the years 1995, 2000, 2005, 2010 and 2014. Their results show that Luxembourg, Austria, Denmark, Malta, UK and Italy are the economies that turn out to be the most decoupled, and there is a reduction of inefficiency rates from 2010 to 2014 that could be affected by the global economic and financial crisis in 2007–2009.

The last paper included in the volume, authored by David Morris (Corvinus University of Budapest, Hungary), addresses the issue of political risk, which refers to non-market risks that may affect business outcomes as a result of changing political, security, social, cultural, environmental or other factors. These are risks that require strategies for understanding, mitigation, management or sometimes avoidance by firms investing in foreign business environments but are also important for governments which promote outward foreign investment or seek to attract inward foreign investment. China's programme for inter-regional economic connectivity, the Belt and Road Initiative (BRI), aimed to develop new trade routes and production chains linking predominantly developing world economies with the Chinese market, will make a unique contribution to global economic development but will be disrupting power relativities. At the same time, problems with debt servicing, corruption and a range of other political risks such as the role of Chinese state-owned enterprises have emerged in some BRI partner countries and with some projects, which have encouraged an increasingly negative commentary, particularly since the shift of the US rhetoric since 2017 characterizing China as a strategic competitor. Conventional geopolitical, realist and liberal internationalist analysis appears to have reached foregone conclusions that the BRI will generate zero sum benefits to China and costs to others, yet there is a significant research gap in empirical case studies of what is actually taking place on the BRI. To date, firms engaged in BRI projects have been overwhelmingly Chinese but it is likely that there will be future internationalization of BRI projects and firms (and governments) will need to assess the full range of political risks of participation. While most political risk analysis has usually taken place at the national (country) level or at the firm (project) level, this paper utilizes a political risk framework to identify political risks generated by the BRI at the geopolitical and transnational level, as well as at the country and project levels. Under each of these categories, this paper discusses how risks are constructed, assesses available evidence and agency of stakeholders and identifies where further empirical investigation and theoretical development are required.

Hoping that the paper selection included in the volume confirms the research quality standards needed for addressing the business performance in the financial and non-financial sectors in Europe and offers insightful look at how new business models support value-creation activities, we leave to the readers the final assessment of their quality, as well as of their ability to disseminate new approaches and ideas that may be further used by academics, practitioners and public decision-makers alike.

Bucharest, Romania Alexandra Horobet
Serres, Greece Persefoni Polychronidou
Kavala, Greece Anastasios Karasavvoglou

Introduction

The volume is one of the publications resulting from the 11th International Conference "Economies of the Balkan and Eastern European Countries (EBEEC)"—Bucharest, May 2019, and makes available to readers insightful research into the development and performance evolution of financial and non-financial businesses across Europe. The volume includes 10 papers selected from the papers prepared and presented at the 11th EBEEC Conference, which make a solid contribution to the business and financial services fields, as well as to the application of econometric models and innovative quantitative analysis tools.

There were 161 papers proposed for the 11th EBEEC Conference, of which 124 were presented at the conference. After the conference, the papers were divided into two categories. The first category was formed of the papers to be published in the conference proceedings, while the second category included 10 papers to be published as a Springer volume (book). All the papers proposed for the volume have been thoroughly peer-reviewed and edited. The selection process of these papers was confidential and methodical, as book editors studied all of them and decided on the final selection after thorough discussions among them. The quality of the research presented in the papers has been the first criteria of selection, but this was complemented by the overall paper quality and the contribution made to the domain development.

The EasyChair system was used for paper submission at the conference. The system ensures the confidentiality and the transparency of all submission and evaluation procedures. The authors were asked after the conference to submit camera-ready versions of their papers that have been uploaded in the same EasyChair system. All the uploaded papers were included in the blind peer-review process, and reviewers prepared their evaluation reports online. The evaluation was formed of an overall assessment of the paper, reviewer's recommendations for paper improvement and a recommended decision, on a scale from "strong reject" to "strong accept" (specifically, reviewers had to choose the following decisions: reject, weak reject, borderline paper, weak accept, accept, strong accept). The overall evaluation provided a detailed review of the paper, including scores' reasoning. Reviewers were required to provide both a score and a review text, as well as their level of expertise regarding the topic of the paper being reviewed: expert, high, average, low and non-expert. All reviewers had at least an average level of expertise in the reviewed fields.

The number of papers evaluated with “weak reject” or “strong reject” is very small. The remaining papers were evaluated with “accept” and “strong accept”. The latter reviews were sent to authors, and the final decision of acceptance of a paper has been taken only after all concerns raised by reviewers were considered by the authors. Next, the authors were asked by the volume editors to apply the Springer editorial standards to be found at the following links: https://www.springer.com/cda/content/document/cda_downloaddocument/manuscript-guidelines-1.0.pdf and https://www.springer.com/cda/content/document/cda_downloaddocument/Manuscript+Key+Style+Points?SGWID=0-0-45-1410203-p175157688.

All the 10 papers proposed for the Springer volume, which are the best papers prepared for and presented at the 11th EBEEC Conference, were made ready according to the above-mentioned standards.

We hope that the above description meets your expectations.

Alexandra Horobet
Persefoni Polychronidou
Anastasios Karasavvoglou

Contents

About the Editors

Alexandra Horobet is Full Professor at the Bucharest University of Economic Studies (BUES) and holds a Ph.D. in international business and economics (since 2003). Since 2001, she is Professor in the Romanian-Canadian MBA Program of BUES, teaching corporate finance and international finance. She is specialized in international investments, international finance, risk management and corporate finance. She is Doctoral Scientific Advisor since 2011 and participated in various research projects on topics related to international finance, risk management, higher education and regional development as team leader or member. She is author/co-author of books and chapters in books published in Romania and abroad by prestigious publishing houses and of more than 60 peer-reviewed articles in academic journals.

Persefoni Polychronidou is Assistant Professor of applied econometrics in the Department of Economics at the International Hellenic University. Her research focuses on statistical and data analysis, and she has published numerous papers on empirical economic data. She is the Co-editor of the International Journal of Business and Economic Sciences Applied Research.

Anastasios Karasavvoglou is Professor of economics and President of the annual international conference "Economies of the Balkan and Eastern European Countries". He has published numerous books and papers on immigration, regional development and the labour market.

European Business Competitiveness and Performance: A Critical Assessment

Mapping Economic Activity in the European Union: Do Ownership, Industry and Location Matter?

Alexandra Horobet, Oana Popovici, and Lucian Belascu

Abstract The paper proposes a new method for analysing the structure and dynamics of economic activity undertaken by locally owned and foreign-owned companies within the European Union. We employ an unsupervised learning algorithm that generates a neural network depicted on Kohonen maps and offering a clustering of companies with a different ownership (local and foreign) from various industries and countries of the European Union during 2009–2016. The research methodology, based on a self-organizing map (SOM) algorithm, belongs to a class of neural networks trained to organize data so that unknown patterns may be discovered, thus leading to results that cannot be attained by more traditional clustering methods. Each type of company (locally owned and foreign-owned) from a specific industry and country is characterized by a series of performance indicators that are included in the SOM algorithm, i.e. indicators at the average enterprise and employee level (turnover, value added at factor cost, gross operating surplus, personnel costs, gross investments) and comprehensive indicators, such as labour productivity and profitability (the latter through the gross operating rate). We detect various clusters of companies based on Euclidian distances that provide similarities and differentiation between companies' common production activities by taking into account their ownership (foreign versus local), industry and country of location, and related performance results, as well as their interrelationships. The resulting classification can be used to understand the linkages between European Union companies and the different branches of economic activities across EU countries, as well as to investigate the performance gap between locally owned and foreign-owned companies.

A. Horobet (✉)
Bucharest University of Economic Studies, 6 Piata Romana, Bucharest, Romania
e-mail: alexandra.horobet@rei.ase.ro

O. Popovici
Bucharest University of Economic Studies and Institute for Economic Forecasting, Romanian Academy, 6 Piata Romana, Bucharest, Romania
e-mail: oana.popovici@rei.ase.ro

L. Belascu
"Lucian Blaga" University of Sibiu, 17 Calea Dumbravii, Sibiu, Romania
e-mail: lucian.belascu@ulbsibiu.ro

A. Horobet et al. (eds.), *Business Performance and Financial Institutions in Europe*, Contributions to Economics, https://doi.org/10.1007/978-3-030-57517-5_1

Keywords Economic performance · European Union · Foreign enterprises · Neural networks · Self-organizing maps

JEL Classification Codes C45 · F23 · L25

1 Introduction

Explaining companies' performance continues to be as difficult today as decades ago but due to completely different reasons. While lack of data is not a problem anymore, the complexity and diversity of information risk affecting the capacity of analysis. The use of neural networks, such as the self-organizing maps (SOMs), able to cluster large amount of data without affecting their multidimensionality and to provide friendly visualization outputs is indicated in these cases. The literature acknowledged the attractiveness of SOM as a tool for organizing data given the effectiveness in visualizing and interpreting vast amounts of data, which also extends the analysis capabilities (Eklund et al. 2003). The SOM procedure provides better outcomes than factor analysis and clustering in market segmentation (Kiang et al. 2006) and is superior to traditional cluster analysis techniques (Mingoti and Lima 2016; Budayan et al. 2009; Kiang and Kumar 2001).

Initially, SOM was used for reducing the large financial data sets and for identifying unusual financial behaviour which could lead to bankruptcy (Resta et al. 2018). Therefore, the procedure started to be used in predicting business failures, in which case proved high accuracy (Tsai 2014; Kirkos et al. 2007). Other types of artificial neural networks are increasingly used in forecasting stock market indexes (Niaki and Hoseinzade 2013; O'Connor and Madden 2006; Altay and Satman 2005). The performance of SOM was also revealed in dealing with complex data sets without reducing multidimensionality (Back et al. 2001; Eklund et al. 2003) and in providing reliable grouping of companies based on their similar financial characteristics (Back et al. 1998; Di Tollo et al. 2012). The use of SOM was extended to establishing the profile of EU countries related to their macroeconomic financial imbalances (Itturiaga and Sanz 2013), but in general SOM is marginally used in other areas. Additionally, even if the field of financial analysis usually employed SOM, the method was less used for analysing companies' performance.

Riva and Lucchini (2018) used the SOM method for grouping European companies according to their performance and obtained six prototypical clusters based on the assessment of their outcomes in terms of financial situation, work climate and personnel issues, such as labour productivity, employee motivation, absenteeism, recruiting and retaining staff. Eklund et al. (2003) appreciated the procedure for allowing them to deal with a large amount of financial data describing 91 companies for the period 1995 to 2001 and to establish patterns based on their performance. An early study of Severin (2001) deeper investigated the ownership structure of the company related to the members of Board of Directors for explaining the performance in 199 French firms. To these variables, the author added proxies for the external discipline, organizational structure and control and size.

Our objective resides in investigating the differences in the economic performance of companies from the European Union, resulting in proposing a new method for analysing the structure and dynamics of economic activity undertaken by business with different attributes. Specifically, the EU companies are characterized by their location—Western versus Eastern EU—ownership—foreign versus locally owned—and sector of operations, which have the potential to represent sources for the differences in their economic performance. Using an unsupervised learning algorithm from the field of neural networks, we attempt a clusterization of these companies depending on their attributes that will offer insight into their activity. The paper is organized as follows: Sect. 2 provides a brief presentation of the most important results in the existing academic literature related to the topic of our research, Sect. 3 outlines the data and methodologies employed, Sect. 4 discusses our results, and Sect. 5 concludes, sets the limits of our research and offers guidance for future research.

2 Literature Review

The literature dealing with company performance is complex and diversified. Starting with the "structure–conduct–performance" model in 1950 for explaining the profitability of a company (Porter 1981), the basic framework was extended and enriched thanks to studies in different sectors and improved methodologies. The patterns of companies' performance used to be described in terms of industry-specific influences and market environment (Porter 1979; Schmalensee 1985; Rumelt 1991), firm own resources and decisions (Ramsay 2001; Hawawini 2003) or location influence due to their endowments and created assets (Dunning (2004, 2010). Brouthers (1998) indicated towards clusters of excellence that could emerge in different countries based on the characteristics of the host locations which interact with that of the companies, thus emphasizing the role of both country and industry as determinants of performance. The topic of interactions continues to draw a similar interest today. In questioning about the superstar effect in global economy, Manyika et al. (2018) investigate the linkages between the firm, sector and location (most specifically, cities) characteristics. Also, Horobet et al. (2018) draw the attention that the framework for assessing companies' performance is large and complex. The results of the studies in the field continue to stir scholar's indecision related to the importance attributed to the industry, location or external factors in explaining corporate performance.

Studies disclose that the sector of activity (therefore a particular industry) is relevant in determining performance. High-tech sectors prove better productivity performance when they are enhanced by research and development (Ortega-Argiles et al. 2011), while government and business investments in this area significantly affect the labour performance in medium- to high-tech industries (Varum and Cibrao 2008).

In addition, discriminating on the type of industry is important in the interaction with location determinants. In this respect, the performance of high-tech industries is heavily influenced by locations endowed with knowledge, research and development or technological inputs (Cantwell and Piscitello 2005; Arvanitis and Hollenstein 2009; Eickelpasch et al. 2015; Belderbos et al. 2017).

The distinction between industry and firm characteristics is not that clear-cut. The results of the studies are very diverse, without giving the possibility of establishing an explicit pattern depending on the type, sector or other characteristics of the companies. Rumelt (1991) and Hawawini et al. (2003) conclude that industry's characteristics are significant for the profitability of the manufacturing firms, while Fernandez et al. (2018) find that the same is available for medium-sized enterprises. On the contrary, firm effects prove to be more important during the economic crisis (Bamiatzi and Bozos 2016), for large and small companies (Fernandez et al. 2019) or during the years 1995–1999, according to Hough (2006) analysis. Barbosa and Louri (2005) reach inconclusive results, depending on the country in which the companies are present. Goldszmidt et al. (2011) and Karabang and Berggren (2014) explain that the level of development of the host country matters in determining performance. Brouthers (1998) demonstrates that there is an interaction between country- and industry-specific effects which directly and indirectly influence the profitability of foreign companies, but he does not take into account what happens with domestic companies.

Other authors emphasize that the ownership of the company is, in fact, contributing to differences in the competitiveness of foreign and domestic companies (Bellak 2004; Barbosa and Louri 2005; Chacar et al. 2010), as foreign companies have a specific advantage which allow them to act internationally (Weche Gelubcke 2011), such as the benefits of performing inside a network of affiliates. Cantwell and Sanna-Randaccio (1993) find that multinationality has an important impact on the performance of the company expressed as the rate of growth within the same industry. Better performance of foreign companies is found in terms of employees, wages and export orientation (Weche Gelubcke 2011), indebtedness (Grasseni 2010), capital intensity (Hintosova and Kubikova 2016), research and development expenditure (Notta and Vlachvei 2008), higher- and long-term commitment (Douma et al. 2006), financial soundness, size and profitability (Bentivogli and Mirenda 2016), but lower profitability (Weche Gelubcke 2011) and similar labour productivity (Weche Gelubcke 2011; Grasseni 2010), number of research and development employees or leverage intensity (Hintosova and Kubikova 2016) as compared to the domestic ones. Prochazka (2017) finds that domestic companies in the Czech Republic, Hungary, Poland and Slovakia usually have a similar or even a better performance than that of other countries, except for those with Anglo-Saxon corporate shareholders, which perform better. Ferreira et al. (2017) reflect the fact that domestic companies have a better performance when location is confronted with corruption, low protection for investors and poor stock markets.

Grasseni (2010) does not find any difference related to ownership between high-tech and other type of sectors, while earlier Thomsen and Pedersen (1996) concluded that ownership modes do not have an influence on company performance in six developed countries in Europe, but the nation-specific differences should be taken into account. The advantage of foreign ownership or of multinationality has a higher impact on performance for the technologically advanced industries in the tertiary sector (services), according to Lopez-Gamero et al. (2009) and Weche Gelubcke (2011).

3 Data and Research Methodology

Our analysis covers the period 2009–2016 and includes twenty European Union countries with the highest level of data availability on firms' performance at industry level. Data was collected from inward FATS—Foreign Affiliates Statistics, published by Eurostat, where FATS are foreign direct investment (FDI) companies in which the share of foreign capital is at least 50% of the subsidiary's capital. Thus, we have extracted data on industries' performance for two categories of companies, as follows: (i) "controlled by the reporting country" category, which includes data on the performance of companies controlled by local capital—denoted in our study as "L" companies; and (ii) "world total except for the reporting country", which includes data on the performance of companies controlled by foreign capital—denoted by "F" in our study.

The twenty countries were separated in two categories, based on their development levels and shared economic and political history. Thus, eleven countries are mature market economies and, at the same time, older EU members—Austria (AU), Denmark (DE), France (FR), Germany (GE), Greece (GR), Italy (IT), Netherlands (NE), Portugal (PT), Spain (SP), Sweden (SW) and the United Kingdom (UK)—while the remaining nine countries are emerging economies that shared a communist past in the twentieth century and are newer EU members (after 2004)—Bulgaria (BG), Czech Republic (CZ), Hungary (HU), Latvia (LV), Lithuania (LT), Poland (PL), Romania (RO), Slovenia (SL) and Slovakia (SK). To simplify the notations, we have labelled the first category of countries as "Western" (W) and the second category of countries as "Eastern" (E).

Although our intention was to investigate the link between business performance and companies' location and ownership by considering all industries and sectors in the European Union, we have included in our analysis 27 industries from nine NACE sectors based on data availability.[1] At the same time, though, the sample of industries and countries included in our research is representative at EU level, as they generate 72.03% of EU turnover and 66.62% of EU value added in 2016, despite differences from one sector to another; as such, our sample covers on average 74.87% of sector's turnover and 75.87% of sector's value added—the highest coverage is for sector I—information and communication (95.71% for turnover and 97.89% for value added),

[1]In making the decision on the number of countries versus the number of industries included in the analysis, we have opted for a higher number of countries to be investigated, thus increasing the locational factor relevance for our results.

while the lowest coverage is for sector M—professional, scientific and technical activities (34.44% for turnover and 31.50% for value added). All industries included in our analysis, as well as turnover and value added, are presented in Table 1.

We describe the attributes and the performance of foreign-owned and locally owned businesses in the selected industries by a set of comprehensive indicators, available from Eurostat FATS, by using the simple averages the period 2009 to 2016—see Table 2. As observed, there are five raw indicators included in the analysis—turnover, value added, gross operating surplus, personnel costs and gross investments—and two derived indicators for labour productivity (SWALP) and operational profitability (GOR). In order to adjust for differences across industries, we have computed the values of the raw indicators for the "average" enterprise—by dividing the total value to the number of enterprises—and for the "average" employee—by dividing the total value to the number of persons employed. Overall, the performance of each type of company from a specific industry (business unit—BU) is described by twelve indicators, which refer to the "input" and "output" values at enterprise and employee level, but also to the aggregate performance in terms of labour productivity and profitability. It should also be noted that each BU is defined by three main characteristics—location (Western or Eastern EU), ownership (foreign or local) and industry/sector. The total number of BUs included in our investigation is 1080.

Table 3 shows the distribution of these BUs depending on location, ownership and sector of activity across the raw indicators used in our research. The sample of BUs is dominated, as expected, by Western-located companies that hold shares between 82.67% in the number of enterprises and 93.86% in personnel cost. Moreover, locally owned companies hold the most important part of our sample, with a total share of 95.44% in the number of enterprises, 85.48% in employees and shares around 70–80% for the other indicators. In terms of sector distribution, almost a third of all enterprises and employees are from the G-wholesale and retail trade sector (31.58% and 30.37%, respectively), but other sectors are also well represented, such as C-manufacturing and F-construction. On the other hand, although BUs from the trade sector hold the largest shares in all the other indicators, followed by the manufacturing sector (C), we notice the higher shares in value added, GOS and also personnel costs in sectors such as F-construction, H-transportation and storage and J-information and communication. On the other hand, the importance of different sectors in the total amount of GI demonstrates a higher intensity of capital investments in the manufacturing, real estate and trade sectors. The last three columns in Table 2 show a different perspective on these indicators, which sheds some light into the sectors' particularities across EU when location, ownership and sector are taken into account. As such, the ratio between GOS and turnover, which might be considered a measure of profitability, does not indicate significant differences between Eastern and Western BUs or between foreign to local BUs, but the differences are clear at a sectoral level—the ratio varies between 4.84% in sector G and 42.87% in sector L. Furthermore, the importance of personnel costs in turnover is higher for Western compared to Eastern BUs and for local- compared to foreign-owned BUs, but important differences exist when sectors are considered (the ratio takes values between 4.57% for sector D and 29.20% for sector I). The values of the last ratio between GI and turnover, which may

Table 1 Shares of sectors and industries in EU turnover and value added, 2016

Sectors and industries—NACE codes	Turnover			Value added		
	Value (million euro)	Share in EU sector value (%)	Share in EU AH sector value (%)	Value (million euro)	Share in EU sector value (%)	Share in EU all sector value (%)
C—manufacturing	*4,673,045*	*62.99*	*17.11*	*1,203,739*	*62.94*	*16.79*
C10—Manufacture of food products	954,395	12.86	3.49	192,746	10.08	2.69
C13—Manufacture of textiles	72,503	0.98	0.27	21,950	1.15	0.31
C16—Manufacture of wood and products of wood and cork; except furniture; manufacture of articles of straw and plaiting materials	121,772	1.64	0.45	32,426	1.70	0.45
C18—Printing or reproduction of recorded media	75,957	1.02	0.28	27,216	1.42	0.38
C20—Manufacture of chemicals and chemical products	505,382	6.81	1.85	126,648	6.62	1.77
C22—Manufacture of rubber and plastic products	307,551	4.15	1.13	93,225	4.87	1.30
C25—Manufacture of fabricated metal products, except machinery and equipment	471,749	6.36	1.73	172,157	9.00	2.40
C27—Manufacture of electrical equipment	305,829	4.12	1.12	89,288	4.67	1.25
C28—Manufacture of machinery and equipment n.e.c	676,054	9.11	2.47	205,515	10.75	2.87
C29—Manufacture of motor vehicles, trailers and semi-trailers	1,081,414	14.58	3.96	210,988	11.03	2.94
C31—Manufacture of furniture	100,440	1.35	0.37	31,580	1.65	0.44
D—Electricity, gas, steam and air-conditioning supply	*1,308,582*	*97.66*	*4.79*	*215,730*	*96.74*	*3.01*
D35—Electricity, gas, steam and air-conditioning supply	1,308,582	97.66	4.79	215,730	96.74	3.01
F—Construction	*1,558,819*	*95.05*	*5.71*	*521,108*	*96.50*	*7.27*

(continued)

Table 1 (continued)

Sectors and industries—NACE codes	Turnover			Value added		
	Value (million euro)	Share in EU sector value (%)	Share in EU AH sector value (%)	Value (million euro)	Share in EU sector value (%)	Share in EU all sector value (%)
*F*41—Construction of buildings	566,952	34.57	2.08	149,001	27.59	2.08
*F*42—Civil engineering	253,068	15.43	0.93	76,538	14.17	1.07
*F*43—Specialized construction activities	738,799	45.05	2.70	295,570	54.74	4.12
G—Wholesale and retail trade; repair of motor vehicles and motorcycles	*8,367,919*	*84.43*	*30.63*	*1,159,618*	*85.71*	*16.17*
*G*46—Wholesale trade, except of motor vehicles and motorcycles	5,591,218	56.42	20.47	653,281	48.29	9.11
*G*47—Retail trade, except of motor vehicles and motorcycles	2,776,701	28.02	10.16	506,337	37.42	7.06
H—Transportation and storage	*1,095,090*	*73.01*	*4.01*	*424,826*	*77.24*	*5.92*
*H*49—Land transport and transport via pipelines	561,727	37.45	2.06	241,415	43.89	3.37
*H*52—Warehousing and support activities for transportation	533,363	35.56	1.95	183,411	33.35	2.56
I—Accommodation and food service activities	579,613	95.71	2.12	258,796	97.89	3.61
*I*55—Accommodation	180,164	29.75	0.66	87,414	33.06	1.22
*I*56—Food and beverage service activities	399,448	65.96	1.46	171,382	64.83	2.39
J—Information and communication	*1,072,436*	*78.46*	*3.93*	*473,874*	*79.29*	*6.61*
*J*58—Publishing activities	132,818	9.72	0.49	56,649	9.48	0.79
*J*61—Telecommunications	382,529	27.99	1.40	157,574	26.37	2.20
*J*62—Computer programming, consultancy and related activities	557,089	40.76	2.04	259,650	43.45	3.62
L—Real estate activities	*499,766*	*95.34*	*1.83*	*284,954*	98.99	*3.97*
*L*68—Real estate activities	499,766	95.34	1.83	284,954	98.99	3.97

(continued)

Table 1 (continued)

Sectors and industries—NACE codes	Turnover			Value added		
	Value (million euro)	Share in EU sector value (%)	Share in EU AH sector value (%)	Value (million euro)	Share in EU sector value (%)	Share in EU all sector value (%)
M—Professional, scientific and technical activities	520,895	34.44	1.91	234,250	31.50	3.27
*M*71—Architectural and engineering activities; technical testing and analysis	355,154	23.48	1.30	174,021	23.40	2.43
*M*73—Advertising and market research	165,741	10.96	0.61	60,229	8.10	0.84
Total	19,676,165	–	72.03	4,776,893	–	66.62

Source Eurostat and authors' calculations

indicate BUs' investment propensity, are higher for Eastern companies compared to Western ones, higher for local- compared to foreign-owned BUs, with significant variation across sectors—not surprisingly, the L-sector shows the highest investment intensity (a ratio of 31.68%), followed by H-sector (10.35%), but there are sectors with a ratio value even lower than 5% (C, F, G and M).

Our research uses the Kohonen self-organizing map (SOM) algorithm to cluster the 1080 BUs from various sectors and industries of the EU in a two-dimensional space, based on a number of 12 economic performance variables considered at enterprise and employee level, as well as at the aggregate level. In order to generate the SOMs, we add to this set of variables other three dummy variables that describe the BUs in terms of their belonging to one of the two regions of EU considered (1 for Eastern EU and 0 for Western EU), of their ownership (1 for foreign ownership and 0 for local ownership) and of their sector of operation (from 0 to 8, moving from C to M). Before including them in the SOM algorithm, all data has been standardized. Moreover, since none of the variables was favoured against all the others, we have allocated the same weight to all variables in building the topological grid.

The methods for analysing data have multiplied in recent years, driven by the technological advances that allow for better data manipulation and for work with larger amounts of information. Besides data analysis methods, visual techniques that provide data organization and pattern recognition have also proliferated, in a univariate or multivariate framework. Although univariate representations, such as histograms, box-and-whisker plots and dot plots, are quite common, multivariate representations have grown in frequency and performance, given their ability to produce extremely useful visualization of the data. Among these multivariate representations, self-organizing maps (SOMs) were proposed as a tool by Teuvo Kohonen in a paper published in 1982 (Kohonen 1982) and further developed (Kohonen 1984,

Table 2 Indicator variables across industries and countries, 2009–2016

Variable	Description and measurement unit	Mean	Median	Range	Standard deviation
Turnover (Turn)	The totals invoiced by the observation unit during the reference period, and this corresponds to market sales of goods or services supplied to third parties; it includes all duties and taxes on the goods or services invoiced by the unit with the exception of the VAT invoiced by the unit to its customer and other similar deductible taxes directly linked to turnover; it also includes all other charges (transport, packaging, etc.) passed on to the customer. Price reductions, rebates and discounts as well as the value of returned packing must be deducted. *Million euro*	16,285.49	2,587.31	768,853.42	52,994.18

(continued)

Table 2 (continued)

Variable	Description and measurement unit	Mean	Median	Range	Standard deviation
Value added at factor cost (VA)	Gross income from operating activities after adjusting with operating subsidies and indirect taxes. *Million euro*	3,780.66	737.12	83,575.69	8,874.53
Gross operating surplus (GOS)	The additional amount generated by the company's activities after paying for labour costs. It represents the capital available to the company for the payment of creditors, taxes and possibly investment financing, either totally or partially. *Million euro*	1,531.20	286.60	4,9929.29	3,783.66
Personnel costs (Peiscost)	The total remuneration, in cash or in kind, provided by the employer to all employees. *Million euro*	2,250.17	405.67	58,021.21	5,686.07

(continued)

Table 2 (continued)

Variable	Description and measurement unit	Mean	Median	Range	Standard deviation
Gross investment in tangible goods (GI)	Investment in all tangible goods. Includes the new and existing tangible capital goods, whether bought from third parties or produced for own use (i.e. capitalized production of tangible capital goods), having a useful life of more than one year including non-produced tangible goods such as land. Investments in intangible and financial assets are excluded. *Million euro*	648.77	120.29	33,916.92	1,937.52
Enterprises	The number of enterprises active during at least a part of the reference period. *Number of units*	13,417.26	661.19	631,132.67	47,095.22

(continued)

Table 2 (continued)

Variable	Description and measurement unit	Mean	Median	Range	Standard deviation
Persons employed	The total number of persons who work in the observation unit (inclusive of working proprietors, partners working regularly in the unit and unpaid family workers), as well as persons who work outside the unit who belong to it and are paid by it (e.g. sales representatives, delivery personnel, repair and maintenance teams). It excludes manpower supplied to the unit by other enterprises, persons carrying out repair and maintenance work in the enquiry unit on behalf of other enterprises, as well as those on compulsory military service. *Number of persons*	80,958.72	18,979.29	326,0997.00	221,029.33

(continued)

Table 2 (continued)

Variable	Description and measurement unit	Mean	Median	Range	Standard deviation
Simple wage-adjusted labour productivity (SWALP)	Apparent labour productivity (or gross value added per person employed) by average personnel costs. *Percentage*	195.84	158.92	3,272.04	152.63
Gross operating rate (GOR)	Gross operating surplus to turnover. *Percentage*	11.91	9.74	96.03	8.72
Turnover per enterprise (turn en)	Turnover divided by the number of enterprises. *Million euro*	15.8611	3.0616	480.3065	37.0010
Value added per enterprise (VA en)	Value added at factor cost divided by the number of enterprises. *Million euro*	3.9524	0.8093	108.9967	8.4889
Gross operating surplus per enterprise (GOS en)	Gross operating surplus divided by the number of enterprises. *Million euro*	1.8166	0.2801	87.1455	5.4230
Personnel cost per enterprise (Perscost en)	Personnel cost divided by the number of enterprises. *Million euro*	2.1370	0.4944	37.8737	3.8908
Gross investment per enterprise (GI en)	Gross investment in tangible goods divided by the number of enterprises. *Million euro*	0.7589	0.1316	28.1264	2.2644

(continued)

Table 2 (continued)

Variable	Description and measurement unit	Mean	Median	Range	Standard deviation
Turnover per employee (turn emp)	Turnover divided by the number of persons employed. *Million euro*	0.2321	0.1483	4.5736	0.3589
Value added per employee (VA emp)	Value added at factor cost divided by the number of persons employed. *Million euro*	0.0590	0.0426	1.4435	0.0728
Gross operating surplus per employee (GOS emp)	Gross operating surplus divided by the number of persons employed. *Million euro*	0.0283	0.0126	1.4068	0.0632
Personnel cost per employee (Perscost emp)	Personnel cost divided by the number of persons employed. *Million euro*	0.0307	0.0253	0.1314	0.0212
Gross investment per employee (GI emp)	Gross investment in tangible goods divided by the number of persons employed. *Million euro*	0.0140	0.0052	0.4822	0.0338

Source Eurostat and authors' calculations

Table 3 Distribution of BUs on location, ownership and sector, based on averages, 2009–2016

Indicators	Enterprises	Turnover	VA	GOS	Personnel cost	GI	Employees	GOS/turnover	Personnel costs/turnover	GI/turnover
West to East										
E (%)	17.24	9.02	7.53	9.57	6.14	12.83	16.88	9.97	9.41	5.67
W (%)	82.76	90.98	92.47	90.43	93.86	87.17	83.12	9.35	14.25	3.82
Total (%)	100.00	100.00	100.00	100.00	100.00	100.00	100.00	9.40	13.82	3.98
Foreign to local										
F (%)	4.56	26.05	22.32	23.67	21.43	19.86	14.52	8.54	11.37	3.04
L (%)	95.44	73.95	77.68	76.33	78.57	80.14	85.48	9.71	14.68	4.32
Total (%)	100.00	100.00	100.00	100.00	100.00	100.00	100.00	9.40	13.82	3.98
Sector										
C (%)	11.58	23.19	25.15	20.58	28.26	19.94	22.26	8.35	16.84	3.43
D (%)	0.48	7.48	4.90	8.49	2.48	12.22	1.32	10.66	4.57	6.50
F (%)	19.60	8.24	11.61	9.71	12.90	7.70	13.53	11.08	21.65	3.72
G (%)	31.58	43.27	24.00	22.30	25.16	14.22	30.37	4.84	8.03	1.31
H (%)	5.73	5.24	8.92	8.71	9.03	13.61	8.61	15.64	23.82	10.35
I (%)	11.11	2.71	5.00	3.93	5.72	4.17	11.28	13.67	29.20	6.14
J (%)	4.39	4.82	9.51	10.27	8.99	6.53	5.18	20.06	25.80	5.40
L (%)	8.06	2.50	5.92	11.39	2.23	19.86	3.03	42.87	12.36	31.68
M (%)	7.47	2.57	4.98	4.62	5.23	1.76	4.43	16.93	28.15	2.73
Total (%)	100.00	100.00	100.00	100.00	100.00	100.00	100.00	9.40	13.82	3.98

Source Eurostat and authors' calculations

2001). The SOM is based on an unsupervised learning algorithm that generates a neural network that helps visualize high-dimensional data (i.e. data described by multiple characteristics or variables). The categorical advantage of SOM resides in the compression of high-dimensional data into a low-dimension representation where neurons are found. The SOM orders neurons in two layers: the input layer is formed of N neurons, one for each input variable, and a competition layer, formed of a topologically grid of geometrically ordered neurons; the grid is low-dimensional, usually two-dimensional. The number of neurons to be found in the competitive or output layer depends on the data that is being organized, and it increases with the complexity of the problem being addressed. The two layers are connected, in the sense that each neuron in the input layer is connected to a neuron in the competition layer (the reverse is not necessarily true, given that some output neurons may be empty) and an N-dimensional vector of weights is associated with each unit or neuron in the competition layer. The SOM algorithm finds the models or patterns to describe the underlying data in an optimal manner, and these models are organized in the grid so that models with a higher similarity are closer to each other and those with a higher dissimilarity are farther away from each other. Thus, SOM identifies a neighbourhood relation between the initial high-dimensionality data and the resulting low-dimensional topological grid.

When generating the topological grid, the researcher has to decide the map type and the number of neurons that will be generated by the SOM algorithm. For what concerns the map type, it can be rectangular or hexagonal, but the literature seems to favour the hexagonal type, given its better ability to result in smoother maps and preferable to the human eye (Kohonen 1999; Brabazon et al. 2015). The number of neurons defines the dimension of the grid and is based on the number of units to be included in the algorithm; although some indication exists in the literature concerning the optimal number of neurons (see, e.g., Tian et al. 2014; or Valova et al. 2013), the "trial and error" process applied to map initialization is frequently applied (including by us) so that it minimizes as much as possible the number of empty neurons.

Once the map type and the number of neurons have been decided, the associated weights to each output neuron are calculated by the unsupervised learning algorithm using an iterative procedure. At the beginning, the weights are initialized randomly (this is the usual approach), but through the iterations they are approached to optimum values by the use of a distance measurement (in most cases, Euclidian distances are used). Specifically, in each iteration a random input observation is chosen and the algorithm calculates the minimum distance within its N-dimensional space and the vectors of weights connected to each of the output neurons; the resulting neuron whose vector of weights is the closest to the input observation is called the "winning neuron" or the "best-matching unit" (BMU). All the BMU's neighbours on the grid are treated in a similar manner, and through weight updates, the final topological map is constructed.

For generating the SOM fitted to our data, we have decided to generate a hexagonal grid based on 156 neurons (12 × 13) and a bubble neighbourhood function (after trial and error, whose goal was to minimize the number of empty neurons in the

SOM[2]). The distance measure we used is Euclidian distance. The R software and the "Kohonen" package in R 3.6.0 have been used in order to generate the SOM and the associated statistics.

4 Main Results and Discussion

4.1 Brief Examination of BUs Performance Across EU

The sample of BUs included in our research demonstrates a high diversity across EU in terms of their attributes at enterprise and employee level, as well as aggregated performance. At the same time, though, specific patterns of BUs' characteristics emerge from the data used that support a mapping of business activities within EU on three main axes: ownership, location and sector.

Figure 1 presents box plots of all variables based on median values and ranges, grouped by the sector of activity and categorized depending on ownership (horizontal axis) and region (vertical axis).[3] A few observations are noteworthy based on our results. First, foreign- and Western-located BUs have higher turnover value added, gross operating surplus, gross investments and personnel costs compared to local- and Eastern-located BUs, in both mean and median terms and considering the enterprise and employee levels. Second, the same foreign- and Western-located BUs show more heterogeneity for all indicators compared to local- and Eastern-located BUs. Third, for all indicators, means are higher than medians, which suggests the presence of higher-sized BUs, regardless of the category. Fourth, SWALP and particularly GOR distributions across BUs differ compared to the other indicators, showing more similarity both depending on ownership and location. Fifth, differences across sectors are obvious and expected, with significant variability based on ownership and locations at the same time. Sixth, the performance gap observable at enterprise level is reduced at employee level, which suggests a better adjustment of local- and Eastern-located BUs to work use in business.

Table 4 shows the ratios of medians between foreign-owned and locally owned BUs depending on region and sector, as well as the same ratios for Western- to Eastern-located BUs based on ownership and sector. The most striking observation is that, except for SWALP and GOR, all ratios are above one, which indicates the superior performance of foreign-owned versus locally owned companies regardless of their location and sector of activity, as well as the pre-eminence of Western- versus Eastern-located business, regardless of their ownership and sector of activity.

[2]It should be noted that there is no agreement between researchers on a specific way of determining the size of the SOM. We have started from the formula $5\sqrt{N}$, where N is the number of BUs in our study, proposed by Vesanto (2005), and performed trial and error to find the optimal size of 12 × 13 neurons.

[3]More descriptive statistics of the variables and BUs included in our study may be requested from the authors.

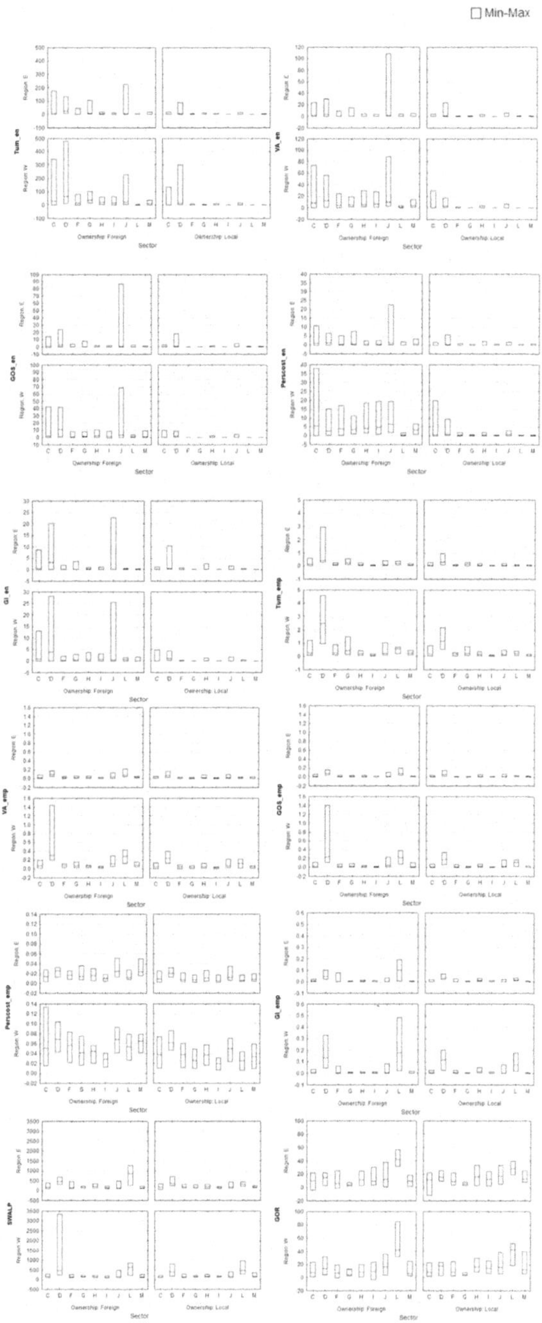

Fig. 1 Box plots of variables based on median and range, grouped by sector and categorized by ownership and region. *Source* Authors' calculations

Table 4 Ratios of medians between foreign-owned to locally owned BUs and for Western- to Eastern-located BUs

Indicators	Turn_en	VA_en	GOS_en	Perscost_en	GI_en	Turn_emp	VA_emp	GOS_emp	Perscost_emp	GI_emp	SWALP	GOR
Foreign to local by region												
West	8.235	9.263	9.383	9.171	7.717	1.716	1.522	1.647	1.424	1.459	1.081	0.878
East	8.677	7.795	8.108	7.387	6.289	2.099	1.812	1.939	1.686	1.964	1.142	0.926
Foreign to local by sector												
C	13.333	12.835	12.253	11.300	10.502	1.791	1.552	1.645	1.293	1.600	1.068	0.996
D	4.871	4.149	5.315	3.377	3.557	1.806	1.300	1.577	0.930	1.358	1.217	0.864
F	15.245	11.557	9.553	12.787	8.034	1.819	1.740	1.346	1.627	1.137	0.925	0.680
G	23.566	26.221	19.422	27.301	19.769	1.528	1.666	1.658	1.753	1.440	0.995	0.868
H	15.920	8.272	6.190	10.442	3.829	1.512	1.101	0.841	1.322	0.561	0.859	0.569
I	25.819	21.876	14.190	24.521	31.173	1.430	1.371	1.021	1.648	1.436	0.892	0.732
J	24.044	23.223	16.652	24.009	19.974	1.752	1.572	1.429	1.477	1.552	0.880	0.814
L	6.620	8.394	9.486	3.873	8.018	2.963	4.051	4.929	2.498	4.281	2.053	1.165
M	28.006	19.866	10.771	24.689	12.664	2.014	1.778	1.216	2.612	1.331	0.769	0.628
West to East by ownership												
Foreign	4.656	6.305	4.416	6.414	2.424	2.335	2.741	2.280	3.324	1.324	0.826	0.826
Local	3.365	4.191	2.972	4.600	1.457	2.880	3.450	2.427	4.330	1.571	0.840	0.834
West to East by sector												
C	3.664	3.936	2.661	4.994	1.833	3.117	3.490	2.483	4.208	1.628	0.825	0.792
D	1.552	1.767	1.940	1.996	1.161	4.230	2.913	3.046	2.998	2.974	1.039	0.960
F	2.368	3.257	3.386	3.811	1.776	2.474	3.236	2.474	3.747	1.545	0.851	1.023
G	2.664	3.836	3.075	4.623	2.317	1.537	2.253	1.566	3.324	1.280	0.854	0.911

(continued)

Table 4 (continued)

Indicators	Turn_ en	VA_en	GOS_en	Perscost_en	GI_en	Turn_emp	VA_emp	GOS_emp	Perscost_emp	GI_emp	SWALP	GOR
H	6.725	7.021	4.072	8.074	2.735	2.132	2.521	1.788	3.131	1.327	0.786	0.960
I	3.557	5.605	4.409	4.346	3.031	2.450	2.952	2.102	3.384	1.184	0.950	0.972
J	5.039	4.937	7.127	3.813	5.397	2.895	2.908	2.654	2.933	1.535	0.910	1.005
L	3.335	3.670	3.581	4.808	1.833	3.083	4.355	4.456	4.287	3.447	1.315	1.269
M	2.595	2.787	2.288	3.380	1.896	2.055	2.644	1.578	2.892	1.086	0.855	0.922

Source Authors' calculations

At the same time, though, when ownership is considered, the ratios have higher values when indicators are presented at the enterprise compared to employee level—when the location is considered, ratios calculated at enterprise level vary between 6.289 (for GI) and 9.383 (for GOS), but ratios at employee level vary only between 1.424 (for personnel cost) and 2.099 (for turn); when various sectors are taken into account, enterprise-based ratios vary between 3.377 (for personnel cost in sector D) and 31.173 (for GI in sector I), while employee-based ratios vary between 0.561 (for GI in sector H) and 4.929 (for GOS in sector L). SWALP and GOR, on the other hand, show a different picture of BUs' performance depending on ownership, as the ratios of median SWALP for Western to Eastern BUs for both foreign and local businesses are above one, but below one for GOR. Moreover, when the sector of activity is considered, the ratios of median SWALP do not indicate a clear superior performance of foreign versus local BUs, as well as of Western- versus Eastern-located companies; this suggests that, after adjusting labour productivity to wage levels, locally owned BUs perform better that the foreign-owned ones. In the case of GOR, all ratios have values below one, with very few exceptions (sector L for both foreign to local and Western to Eastern BUs), but this should not come as a surprise, given that from a theoretical and empirical perspective smaller entities (as is the case with locally owned and Eastern-located BUs) generate higher profitability ratios, but not higher cash flows (see, e.g., Brealey et al. 2013; Berk and DeMarzo 2016; Ramezani et al. 2002).

When location is the discriminant factor, foreign ownership generates higher medians than Local ownership for all variables, at both enterprise and employee levels, with the notable exceptions of SWALP and GOR. At the same time, the ratios of medians are higher at enterprise level compared to the employee level, as in the case of ownership as discriminant factor, and this suggests a more a more intense labour utilization in the locally owned BUs, as well as in the Western-located BUs. At sector level, ratios of medians are also above one and also higher when the enterprise compared to the employee level is considered. In the case of SWALP and GOR, though, the ratios of medians are mostly below one (in six out of nine sectors for each variable), which confirms the previous statement related to wage-adjusted labour productivity and business size.

4.1.1 A Tentative Map of Economic Activity Within the EU

The topological two-dimensional grid based on 156 neurons is presented in Fig. 2. At this point, it should be noted that visualizations provided by the SOM are formed of multiple "nodes", where each node vector has the following attributes: (i) a fixed position on the grid; (ii) a vector of weights that had the same size (dimension) as the input space—in our case, each node will have values for our 15 variables; and (iii) a number of associated samples of the input data in the algorithm and each node may represent several samples of the data. A crucial feature of the SOM is that similar samples from the input data (similarity is defined in terms of the variables that are

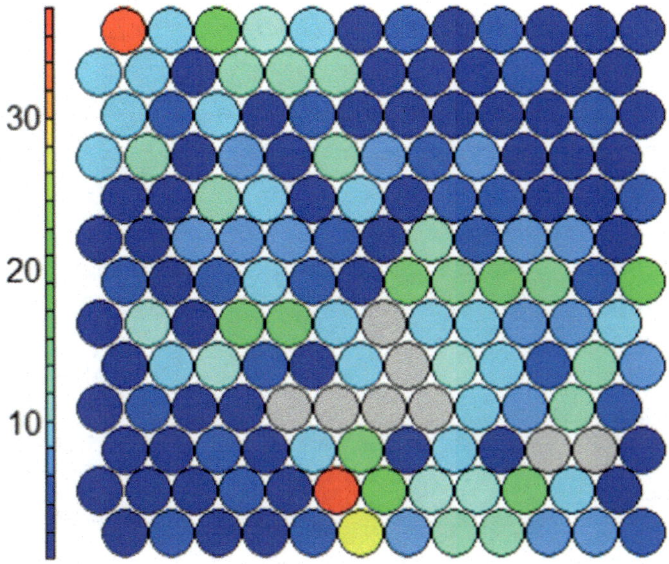

Fig. 2 Topological map (12 × 13) of 1080 BUs, based on 15 variables. *Source* Authors' calculations; *R* output

used) are placed closer together on the resulting grid; thus, BMUs that are closer on the grid are more similar to BMUs that are located farther away on the grid.

The mean distance to the closest unit in the map is 0.826, which shows a rather degree of similarity between the inputted 1080 units. The map in Fig. 2 shows that the neurons located to the left include, generally, a lower number of BUs, while the ones located to the right and particularly towards the north-west include a higher number of observations. Overall, the presence of at least two main clusters is observed in Fig. 2: one cluster located towards the left of the map, with neurons that include fewer observations, and one located towards the right, with more heterogeneous neurons and including more observations.

The visualization of the distance between each node and its neighbours, called the "neighbour distance plot" or the "U-matrix", shows areas of low or high distance that indicate groups of nodes that tend to be more similar. Thus, areas with low distances between the nodes indicate that the nodes are more similar, while areas with high distances indicate more dissimilarity between the nodes. In our case, the neighbour distance plot (see Fig. 3) suggests that all the BMUs are rather similar, as distances between them are low; the only exceptions are the BMUs located in the south-western low part of the map, in whose case the distances are higher, indicating a lower similarity between the respective neurons. We will further investigate the neurons located in the down-left part of the map.

Another interesting output related to the SOM grid is the "codes" map or the node weight vectors, made up of normalized values of the initial variables included in the algorithm. The weight vector attached to each node is representative of the samples

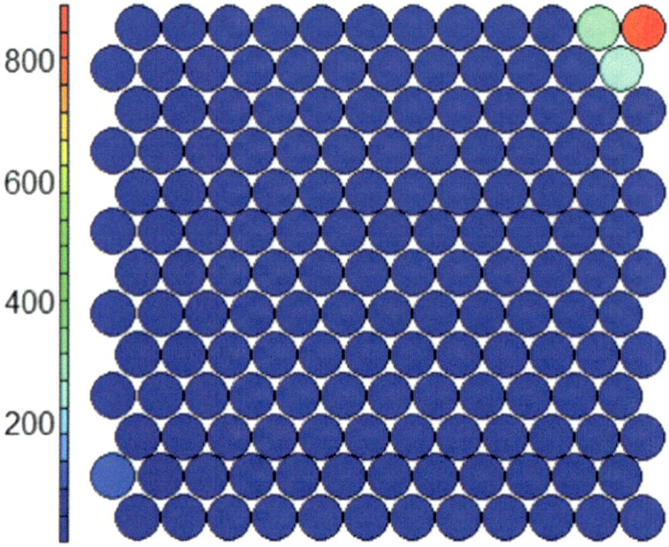

Fig. 3 Neighbour distance plot (right) of 1080 BUs, based on 15 variables. *Source* Authors' calculations; *R* output

included in the node, and the visualization of the weight vectors' distribution across the SOM grid allows for the observation of patterns (if any) in the distribution of input samples and variables in the map. Figure 4 shows the "codes" map generated by our algorithm in the "default" fan diagram visualization—here, individual fan representations show the magnitude of each of our 15 variables in the weight vectors attached to each node in the SOM grid. The "codes" map generated by our algorithm shows that the neurons located in the lower-left part of the grid are formed with the more important contribution of the gross operating surplus, personnel cost and gross investments per enterprise, while the neurons in the right-upper part of the grid incorporate to a higher extent the contribution of aggregate performance variables, SWALP and GOR.

By far, the most interesting output of the SOM is represented by the so-called heatmaps, which help decipher and interpret the componence of the clusters identified above. A heatmap is a representation of a variable distribution across the SOM grid, where the positions of the individual samples are the same from a heatmap to another and compared to the grid. Heatmaps are very useful for exploring the potential relationships between the variables used to generate the SOM grid and for understanding the attributes of the inputted data.

Figure 5 shows the division of the neurons by taking into account the BUs' regional origin (West or East), their ownership and sector. It is easy to notice that there is rather clear-cut separation of the neurons based on region and ownership, and somehow less obvious when the sector is considered. From the regional perspective, the upper-left and bottom part of the map hosts the BUs from Eastern Europe, while the neurons

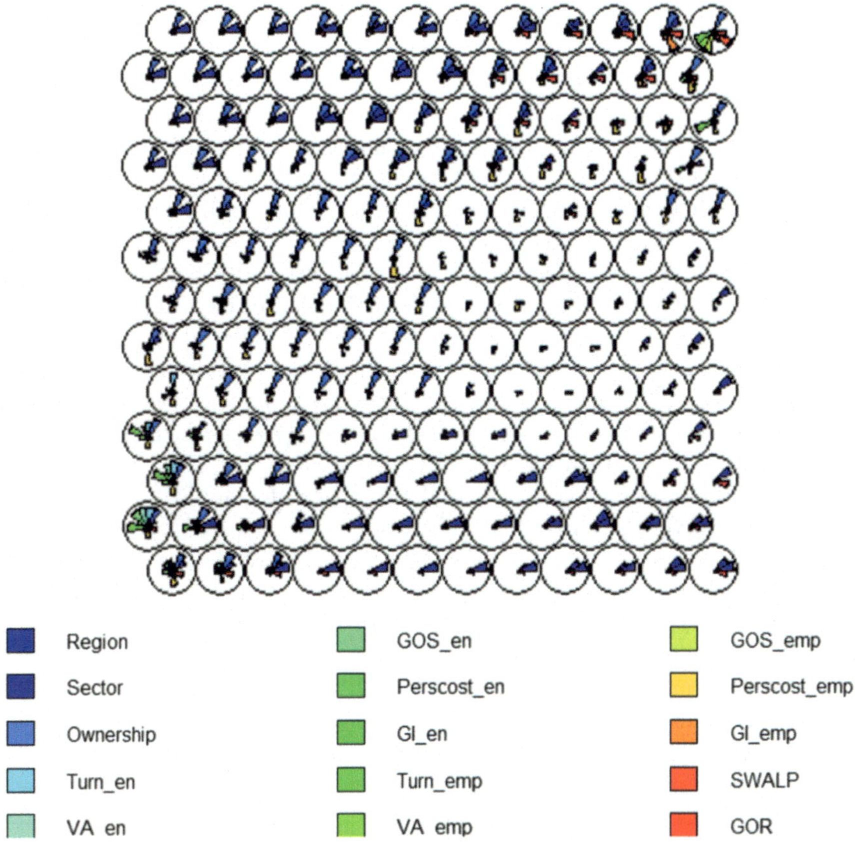

Fig. 4 "Codes" or weight vector map of 1080 BUs, based on 15 variables. *Source* Authors' calculations; *R* output

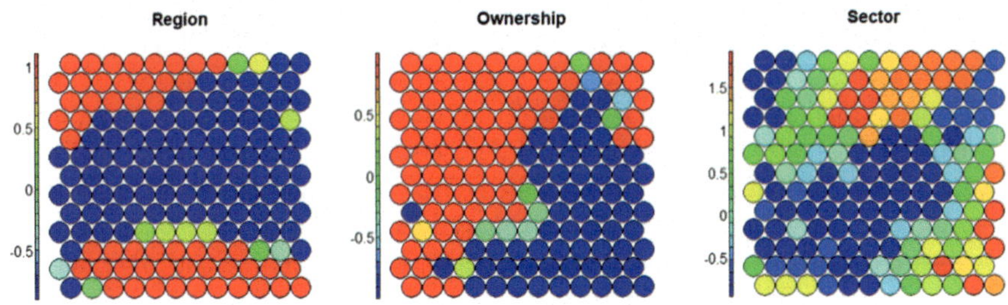

Fig. 5 SOM heatmaps based on region, ownership and sector. *Source* Authors' calculations; *R* output

in the remaining of the map include mostly Western-located BUs. An interesting observation is that there are only seven neurons that include BUs from both regions, which indicates a consistent "segregation" of performance across the EU at a regional level. Of them, four neurons include only foreign-located BUs, while the remaining three also host locally owned companies; it should also be noted that almost all sectors are present in these seven neurons, with the exception of sector M. At the same time, the seven neurons are rather well defined, since the number of BUs included in each varies between 4 and 7.

Ownership is a differentiating variable as well, as observed in Fig. 5; mostly on the right part of the map, we see the foreign-owned BUs, while on the left side we have the neurons including the locally owned BUs. As in the case of the regional perspective, the BUs are well "discriminated" on an ownership basis across the neurons, as only seven neurons include foreign and locally owned BUs; of them, four neurons hold only Western-located BUs, one neuron includes only Eastern-located BUs and the remaining two neurons are mixed from the regional perspective. These seven neurons include BUs from all sectors, again with the exception of sector M.

The sectorial view of the SOM grid is less divided compared to the region and ownership views. Still, despite the visual heterogeneity, we observe that more than half of the neurons include BUs from only one sector—the favourite is C; at the same time, 8 neurons include BUs from three sectors and 2 neurons from 4 sectors. By far, the BUs from the manufacturing sector (C) are mostly clustered together in the SOM neurons, while, at the other end, all BUs from the accommodation and food services sector (I) share the neurons where they are placed with other sectors (mostly with BUs from sector L—real estate activities). Moreover, sectors H (transportation and storage) and J (information and communication) share eleven neurons, while sectors C (manufacturing) and F (construction), G (wholesale and retail trade) and H (transportation and storage), and J (information and communication) and M (professional, scientific and technical activities) share nine neurons. These results suggest that business performance at sector level is more homogeneous within the European Union; at the same time, it should be noted that mostly services sectors tend to be present in the same neurons, while sectors C and F tend to produce their own neurons.

Figure 6 continues the presentation of heatmaps depending on economic performance variables of the 1080 BUs. When we consider the performance at enterprise level, we observe that BUs included in the neurons from the left-bottom part of the map enjoy higher turnover, value added, gross operating surplus, gross investments, but also pay higher overall personnel costs. These neurons include BUs that are mostly foreign-owned and Western-located, operating from almost all sectors. This indicates, in our opinion, that the higher values of the business performance are not necessarily explained by the industry and/or the sector where the BUs activate, but rather by their location and ownership. When performance and employee level are considered, it is interesting to observe that the BUs located in the left-bottom part of the SOM grid do not enjoy higher performance in terms of turnover, value added and gross operating profit; nevertheless, they do pay higher personnel costs per employee. At the same time, we notice a number of neurons located in the extreme right-upper

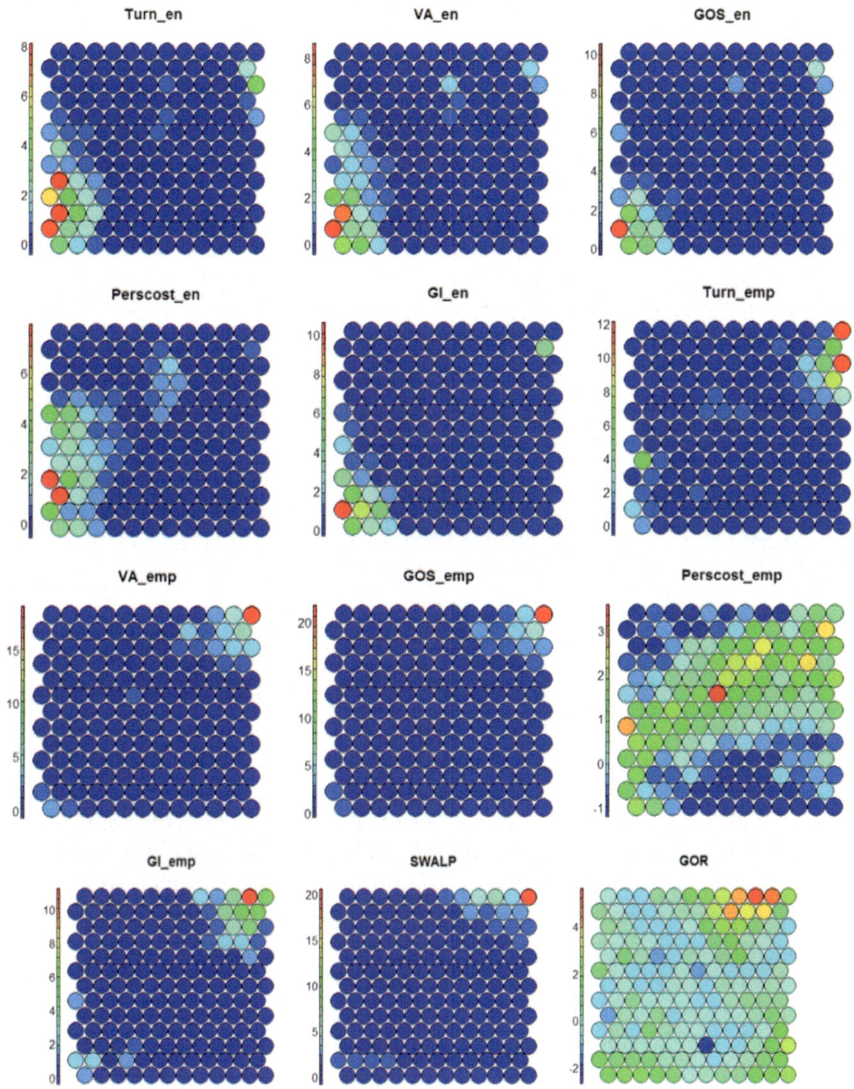

Fig. 6 SOM heatmaps based on economic performance variables. *Source* Authors' calculations; *R* output

part of the grid in whose case the turnover, value added and gross operating surplus per employee are higher. These neurons host BUs that are mostly foreign-located, Western-based and originating from sectors D, F, G, J and L—with the exception of sector D, all the others are services sectors. On the other hand, when we analyse the heatmap for personnel cost per employee, it almost replicates the same map for the region, which indicates, with no surprise, that Western-based companies pay higher personnel costs per employee. In terms of aggregate performance, depicted by the heatmaps for SWALP and GOR, the obvious observation is that BUs are rather homogeneous across EU, maybe with the exception of the BUs located in the extreme right-upper part of the maps.

5 Conclusion

Our paper introduced a new method that helps analysing the structure and dynamics of economic activity within the European Union, which is based on an unsupervised learning algorithm that generates a neural network that is further depicted on self-organizing (Kohonen) maps. The maps are built by taking into account various measures of EU companies' economic performance and by considering the fundamental attributes of businesses in terms of location—Western versus Eastern EU—based, ownership—foreign versus local—and sector of operations. The main research interested resided in observing whether location, ownership and/or sector of activity are linked to companies' performance and may be understood as discriminatory attributes at EU level.

The results we obtained point towards the presence of performance gaps between companies within EU, although with nuances that need to be properly understood. We find, with no surprise, that foreign-owned and Western-located business outperform the locally owned and Eastern-located ones, at both enterprise and employee levels, but the gap at employee level is lower compared to the gap at enterprise level. Moreover, the performance of foreign-owned and Western-located businesses is more heterogeneous compared to the performance of locally owned and Eastern-located companies, which suggests higher in-sample performance differences between companies. At the same time, differences across sectors are obvious and expected, but ownership and location contribute to these differences as well. The Kohonen maps show a rather clear-cut grouping of economic performance within the EU, with location and ownership providing easily observable differentiation between companies; at the same time, sector-induced performance differences are less heterogeneous across EU companies. Overall, the better business performance within EU is less explained by the industry and/or the sector where companies activate, but rather by their location and ownership. This points towards the need for increasing the performance convergence within the EU, since the maintenance of such gaps between the Western and Eastern parts of the EU is damaging over the long-run for business equilibrium. On the other hand, locally owned companies should engage more in the learning process from the foreign-owned ones, with positive effects on the former performance.

Certainly, our research has limits that might impact our results and conclusions. The most important limit is, in our opinion, related to data availability, since we were not able to use performance measures for all sectors and industries within the EU. Second, the data used in our research, although useful, fails to deliver the specific differences between Western and Eastern companies, on the one hand, and foreign-owned versus locally owned ones, on the other hand. The foreign versus local ownership dichotomy is taken into account only at the 50% ownership cut-off rate, which excludes from the foreign-owned companies the ones that have a lower stake for foreign ownership, but with significant influence over the business performance. On the other hand, the Western versus Eastern division is realized at a geographical level, but many companies are part of multinational groups that operate at a regional or global level and adjust their strategies accordingly. As a result, this might impact the performance gaps identified in our research.

More investigation is needed in order to have a proper image of performance gap across EU, including here the dynamics of this gap. At the same time, an analysis at the industry, not only sector level, might be more appropriated, as this would take into account other dissimilarities within the main sectors that are not easily accounted for here. Moreover, a research at company level is also useful, given that differences between individual companies are present and they are difficult to explore when employing performance measure at an aggregate level.

References

Altay E, Satman MH (2005) Stock market forecasting: artificial neural network and linear regression comparison in an emerging market. J Finan Manag Anal 18(2):18–33

Arvanitis S, Hollenstein H (2009) How do different motives for R&D investment in foreign locations affect domestic firm performance? An analysis based on swiss panel micro data. WIFO working papers No 375

Back B, Irjala M, Sere K, Vanharanta H (1998) Competitive financial benchmarking using self-organizing Maps. In: Vasarhelyi MA, Kogan A (eds) Artificial intelligence in accounting and auditing: towards new paradigms. Rutgers series in accounting information systems, 69–81

Back B, Toivonen J, Vanharanta H, Visa A (2001) Comparing numerical data and text information from annual reports using self-organizing maps. Int J Account Inf Syst 2(4):249–269

Bamiatzi V, Bozos K, Cavusgil ST, Hult GTM (2016) Revisiting the firm, industry, and country effects on profitability under recessionary and expansion periods: a multi-level analysis. Strat Manag J 37(7):1448–1471

Barbosa N, Louri H (2005) Corporate performance: does ownership matter? A comparison of foreign- and domestic-owned firms in Greece and Portugal. Rev Indus Organ 27:73–102

Bellak C (2004) How domestic and foreign firms differ and why does it matter? Vienna University of Economics and B.A., Department of Economics working paper series No. 87

Bentivogli C, Mirenda L (2016) Foreign ownership and performance: evidence from a panel of Italian firms. Paper presented at IFC-ECCBSO-CBRT Conference on "Uses of Central Balance Sheet Data Offices' information", Ozdere-Izmir, Turkey

Berk J, DeMarzo P (2016) Corporate finance, 4th edn. Pearson Series in Finance, Pearson, Harlow

Brabazon A, O'Neill M, McGarraghy S (2015) Natural computing algorithms. Springer , Berlin, Germany

Brealey RA, Myers SC, Allen F (2013) Principles of corporate finance, 11th edn. The Mcgraw-Hill/Irwin Series in Finance, Insurance, and Real Estate. McGraw-Hill, New York

Brouthers LE (1998) Explaining MNC profitability: country-specific, industry-specific and country-industry. Manage Int Rev 38(4):345–361

Budayan C, Dikmen I, Birgonul MT (2009) Comparing the performance of traditional cluster analysis, self-organizing maps and fuzzy C-means method for strategic grouping. Expert Syst Appl 36(9):11772–11781

Cantwell JA, Sanna-Randaccio F (1993) Multinationality and firm growth. Weltwirtschaftliches Archiv 129(2):275–299
Cantwell J, Piscitello L (2005) The recent location of foreign R&D activities by large MNCs in the European regions. The role of different sources of spillovers. ERSA 2003 congress
Chacar AS, Celo S, Thams Y (2010) The performance of multinational affiliates versus domestic firms. J Manage Policy Pract 11(4):47–59
Di Tollo G, Tanev S, Ma Z (2012) Neural networks to model the innovativeness perception of co-creative firms. Expert Syst Appl 39(16):12719–12726
Douma S, Rejie G, Rezaul K (2006) Foreign and domestic ownership, business groups, and firm performance: evidence from a large emerging market. Strateg Manag J 27:637–657
Dunning JH (2004) Institutional reform, FDI and European transition economies. Economics & management discussion papers. Henley Business School, Reading University
Dunning JH (2010) Foreign direct investment and the locational competitiveness of countries. In: Dunning JH (ed) New challenges for international business research. Back to the future. Edward Elgar, Cheltenham
Eickelpasch A, Hirte G, Stephan A (2015) Firm's evaluation of location quality: evidence from East Germany. DIW Discussion papers, No, p 1497
Eklund T, Back B, Vanharanta H, Visa A (2003) Using the self-organizing map as a visualization tool in financial benchmarking. Inf Visual 2:171–181
Fernandez E, Iglesias-Antelo S, López-López V, Rodríguez-Rey M, Fernandez-Jardon CM (2019) Firm and industry effects on small, medium-sized and large firms' performance. BRQ Bus Res Q 22(1):25–35
Goldszmidt RGB, Brito LAL, de Vasconcelos FC (2011) Country effect on firm performance: a multilevel approach. J Bus Res 64(3):273–279
Grasseni M (2010) Domestic multinationals and foreign-owned firms in Italy: evidence from quantile regression. Eur J Comp Econ 7(1):61–86
Hawawini G, Subramanian V, Verdin P (2003) Is performance driven by industry or firm-specific factors? A new look at the evidence. Strateg Manag J 1:1–16
Hintosova AB, Kubikova Z (2016) The effect of the degree of foreign ownership on firms' performance. Rev Econ Persp 16(1):29–43
Horobet A, Popovici O, Belascu L (2018) Drivers of competitiveness in European high-tech industries. Paper presented at the 10th international conference EBEEC 2018, Warsaw, Poland, 11–13 May
Hough JR (2006) Business segment performance redux: a multilevel approach. Strateg Manag J 1:45–61
Itturiaga FJL, Sanz IP (2013) Self-organizing maps as a tool to compare financial macroeconomic imbalances: the European Spanish and German Case. Span Rev Finan Econ 11:69–84
Karabag SF, Berggren C (2014) Antecedents of firm performance in emerging economies: business groups, strategy, industry structure, and state support. J Bus Res 67:2212–2223
Kiang M, Kumar A (2001) An evaluation of self-organizing map networks as a robust alternative to factor analysis in data mining applications. Inf Syst Res 12:34–41
Kiang MY, Hu MY, Fisher DM (2006) An extended self-organizing map network for market segmentation—a telecommunication example. Decis Support Syst 42:36–47
Kirkos E, Spathis C, Manolopoulos Y (2007) Data mining techniques for the detection of fraudulent financial statements. Expert Syst Appl 32(4):995–1003
Kohonen T (1982) Self-organized formation of topologically correct feature maps. Biol Cybern 43:59–69
Kohonen T (1984) Self-organization and associative memory. Springer, Berlin
Kohonen T (1999) Comparison of SOM point densities based on different criteria. Neural Comput 11(8):2081–2095
Kohonen T (2001) Self-organizing maps. Third extended edition. Springer Series in Information Sciences, vol 30. Springer, Berlin

Lopez-Gamero MD, Molina-Azorin JF, Claver-Cortes E (2009) The whole relationship between environmental variables and firm performance: competitive advantage and firm resources as mediator variables. J Environ Manage 90(10):3110–3121
Manyika J, Ramaswamy S, Bughin J, Woetzel J, Birshan M, Nagpal Z (2018) 'Superstars': the dynamics of firms, sectors, and cities leading the global economy. McKinsey Global Institute, October 2018, discussion paper
Mingoti SA, Lima JO (2016) Comparing SOM neural network with Fuzzy c-means, K-means and traditional hierarchical clustering algorithms. Eur J Oper Res 174(3):1742–1759
Niaki STA, Hoseinzade S (2013) Forecasting S&P 500 index using artificial neural networks and design of experiments. J Indus Eng Int 9:1–9
Notta O, Vlachvei A (2008) Foreign-owned versus domestically-owned firms: evidence from Greece. New Medit 4:13–19
O'Connor N, Madden MG (2006) A neural network approach to predicting stock exchange movements using external factors. Knowl-Based Syst 19:371–378
Ortega-Argiles R, Piva M, Vivarelli M (2011) Productivity gains from R&D investment: are high-tech sectors still ahead? IZA Discussion paper no. 5975
Porter ME (1979) The structure within industries and companies' performance. Rev Econ Stat 61(2):214–227
Porter ME (1981) The contributions of industrial organization to strategic management. Acad Manage Rev 6(4):609–620
Prochazka D (2017) The impact of ownership and other corporate characteristics on performance of V4 companies. J Int Stud 10(2):204–218
Ramezani CA, Soenen L, Jung A (2002) Growth, corporate profitability, and value creation. Finan Anal J 58(6):56–67
Ramsay J (2001) The resource based perspective, rents, and purchasing's contribution to sustainable competitive advantage. J Supply Chain Manage 3:38–47
Resta M, Garelli R, Dameri RP (2018) Mapping financial performances in Italian ICT-related firms via self-organizing maps. In: Lamboglia R et al (eds) Network, smart and open. Lecture notes in information systems and organisation, vol 24, pp 271–281
Riva E, Lucchini M (2018) Firm performance: taxonomy of European companies using self-organizing maps. Qual Quant 52(1):457–477
Rumelt RP (1991) How much does industry matter? Strateg Manag J 3:167–185
Schmalensee R (1985) Do markets differ much? Am Econ Rev 3:341–351
Severin E (2001) Ownership structure and the performance of firms: evidence from France. Eur J Econ Soc Syst 15(2):85–107
Thomsen S, Pedersen T (1996) Nationality and ownership structures: the 100 largest companies in six European nations. Manage Int Rev 36(2):149–166
Tian J, Azarian MH, Pecht M (2014) Anomaly detection using self-organizing maps-based K-nearest neighbor algorithm. In: Second European conference of the prognostics and health management society 2014. https://www.phmsociety.org/sites/phmsociety.org/files/phm_submission/2014/phmce_14_077.pdf
Tsai CF (2014) Combining cluster analysis with classifier ensembles to predict financial distress. Inf Fus 16:46–58
Valova I, Georgiev G, Guerguieva N, Olson J (2013) Initialization issues in self-organizing maps. Proc Comput Sci 20:52–57
Varum CA, Cibrao B (2008) On R&D, medium and high-tech industries and productivity: an application to the Portuguese case. Universidade de Aveiro
Vesanto J (2005) SOM implementation in SOM toolbox. SOM toolbox online help. https://www.cis.hut.fi/projects/somtoolbox/documentation/somalg.shtml
Weche Gelubcke JP (2011) Foreign ownership and firm performance in German services: first evidence based on official statistics. University of Lüneburg. https://www.etsg.org/ETSG2011/Papers/Geluebcke.pdf.

The Driving Forces of Business R&D Intensity in Eastern European Countries

Özcan Karahan and Olcay Çolak

Abstract Identifying the driving forces of enterprise R&D spending, which is important for achieving long-term economic growth, has become an important research topic for economists. Accordingly, our study aims to determine the driving forces of business R&D expenditures in the Eastern European region. In this context, panel data regression models have been used to determine the impacts of human capital, high technology density and public R&D expenditures on the business R&D intensity of the Eastern European countries. The empirical results show that all three factors have a significant and positive effect on the business R&D intensity of the Eastern European area. More specifically, high-tech industrial structure is seen as the most impressive factor for business R&D expenditures, while human capital is second and public R&D expenditures play a third role. Therefore, within the framework of innovation policies aiming to increase business R&D expenditures, priority should be given to increase the share of manufacturing sector that makes production based on the advanced technology in the economy. Besides, to invest more in human capital and public R&D activities may be other significant options for effective innovation policies that will be implemented in Eastern European countries.

Keywords R&D expenditure · Eastern European countries · Panel data models

1 Introduction

Modern economies have moved from a factor-driven production process to an efficiency-driven production process over the last decades. Thus, innovation has been recognized as an important driver of economic growth today. Together with this

Ö. Karahan (✉)
Faculty of Economics and Administrative Sciences, Bandırma Onyedi Eylül University, Bandırma-Balıkesir, Turkey
e-mail: okarahan@bandirma.edu.tr

O. Çolak
Faculty of Economics and Administrative Sciences, Uşak University, Merkez-Uşak, Turkey
e-mail: ocolak@usak.edu.tr

A. Horobet et al. (eds.), *Business Performance and Financial Institutions in Europe*, Contributions to Economics, https://doi.org/10.1007/978-3-030-57517-5_2

process, Research and Development (R&D) expenditure has become a key factor in innovation-driven economy. Romer (1986) has clearly indicated that R&D investment is a significant factor enhancing long-term economic growth in the framework of Endogenous Growth Model. Some others economists advocating Endogenous Growth Model have also argued that R&D activities have expanded over the last decades and hence accounts for a significant dynamic of economic growth. In the literature, there are many empirical studies indicated that R&D activities resulting in innovation process are the basic dynamic of productivity growth at the firm and country levels (Cameron et. al. 2005; O'Mahony and Vecchi 2009; Bravo-Ortega and Marin 2011; Liik et al. 2014; Gümüş and Celikay 2015). As a result, it has been widely recognized that increasing national innovation capacity by supporting enterprise R&D expenditures is important for achieving long-term economic growth.

In the light of the importance of R&D investments in productivity increase, it has become an important research subject to investigate the determinants of business R&D expenditures. Therefore, the most important question that should be answered for economists today is related to which factors increase the volume of business R&D activities. The relevant literature has identified many driving factors for business R&D investments based on firm characteristics and non-firm but country specific. The factors based on firm characteristics determining the volume of R&D activities consist of factors such as financial restriction, financial autonomy, profitability, size and intangible resources. Economists have also touched on factors affecting the dynamics of business R&D expenditures related to the non-firm but country specific. These factors include macro-indicators such as public R&D policy, the education and health system supporting human capital, financial opportunities and the level of advanced technology industrialization of the economy.

Based on the above consideration, the main objective of this paper is to analyse the drivers of business R&D activities based on country-specific factors for Eastern European area which consists of the countries like Estonia, Latvia, Lithuania, Poland, Czech Republic, Slovakia, Hungary, Croatia, Slovenia, Romania and Bulgaria. Accordingly, human capital accumulation, public R&D intensity and the share of high-tech and medium-high-tech manufacturing have been taken as the drivers of business R&D expenditures. Based on panel data regression models, empirical analysis covers the yearly data set between 2004 and 2016 for 11 Eastern European countries. The remainder of the paper is organized as follows. Section 2 reviews the related literature. Section 3 provides data, methodology and empirical results. Final section concludes and makes some significant policy implications.

2 Literature Review

Since it is broadly accepted that business R&D activities are the most important sources of innovation and productivity growth, economists and policymakers today mostly attempt to find the factors affecting the business RD expenditures. Accordingly, a number of recent empirical studies have estimated the effect of various factors on business R&D expenditures. In general terms, these factors can be identified based on firm and non-firm characteristics. In the literature, there are many studies determining how both firm and non-firm characteristics affect the business R&D activities. Thus, there is no consensus on which factors related to firm and non-firm characteristics are outweighed. Studies focusing on non-firm characteristics use the National System of Innovation approach and indicate the determinants of factors affecting business R&D activities within the institutional context. On the other hand, a plenty of studies also indicate firm-specific factors as the dynamic of business R&D activities. In this literature, firm-specific factors can be classified in two separate groups according to whether they are related to the financial conditions of the firm or not. Thus, the factors arising from firm characteristics that affect R&D expenditures can be grouped under two subtitles as "financial firm-specific factors" and "non-financial firm-specific factors".

The literature shows that the determinants of business R&D activities related to "financial firm-specific factors" generally consist of liquidity constraint, internal finance and firm profitability. Regarding liquidity constraint, it is stated that the probability of a firm to invest in R&D activities is reduced by financial constraints. Therefore, strong cash flow seems to be import to increase the level of business R&D expenditures (Bougheas et al. 2003; Savignac 2008; Silvia and Carreira 2012; Guariglia and Liu 2014). The related literature also examined the relationship between internal financing sources and R&D expenditure. Empirical findings generally suggest that increased R&D investments are positively related to the availability of internal financing sources. This means that firms do not prefer external sources (debt and capital) to finance R&D activities. In other words, high corporate financial autonomy positively affects the investment decision of R&D activities (Czarnitzki and Hottenrott 2011; Brown et al. 2012; Sasidharan et al. 2015). Regarding financial factors, some researchers have also worked on the relationship between the expectation of entrepreneurs' profit and the volume of R&D activities. Given that R&D activities involve a high degree of risk and therefore require large and long-term capital, the high profitability expectation that entrepreneurs must have is determined as another important factor for investing in R&D (Lev and Sougiannis 1996; Coad and Rao 2010).

Concerning with the "non-financial firm-specific factors", researchers consider the firm size, intangible assets that firm has, and firm's export activities. Related to size of firm as a determinant of R&D investment, it is generally argued that larger companies are more willing to invest in R&D activities since larger companies have more capital with better management capabilities for R&D activities (Fishman and Rob 1999; Tsai and Wang 2004; Park et al. 2010; Lai et al. 2015). Researchers also consider the impact of intangible assets like human capital and patents on R&D activities. It is indicated that better enterprise human resources lead to a higher degree of R&D activities (Fleming 2001; Coad and Rao 2010). Similarly, empirical studies also showed that higher degree of accumulated patent leads to higher engagement in R&D investments (Weerawardena et al. 2006; Arora et al. 2008). With regard to firms' export activities, there is a large literature indicating that firm's export activities positively affect the business R&D activities. A capacity of firm's exports impacts positively on R&D investment since exporters must innovate rapidly to remain viable in competitive foreign markets. This also means that investing in R&D is not a profitable strategy in industries with a low competitive. Thus, encouraging more domestic firms to export is one way to boost their R&D activity (Tomiura 2007; Girma et al 2008; Harris and Trainor 2011; Yang and Chen 2012).

In order to advance the understanding of the drivers of business R&D also needs to focus on non-firm characteristics based on country-specific factors. National System of Innovation approach framed innovation activities within the national context and thus indicated a number of country-specific factors (Nelson 1993; Freeman 1995; Lundvall 2016). These country-specific factors mainly include the factors like the high-tech specialization of industrial structure, human capital capacity and density of public R&D activities.

The literature, which focuses on the link between the structure of the industrial sector and business R&D expenditures, emphasizes that advanced technology specialization of the industrial structure is the main driving force of business R&D activities. Therefore, it is best to consider the high-tech transformation of the manufacturing sector in order to capture the dynamics of business R&D intensity. Falk (2006) examined empirically the determinants of the R&D intensity of the business sector using a panel of data on OECD countries for the period 1970–2002. Analysis using a system GMM estimator shows that expertise in high-tech industries contributes significantly to the R&D intensity of the business sector. This finding shows that countries with a large proportion of technology-oriented sectors also have a high R&D intensity. Mathieu and Potterie (2010) also examined the panel data set for the USA, Japan, Korea and the EU-15 to investigate the link between business sector R&D intensity and industrial structure. They concluded that the business R&D intensity is closely related to the degree of technological expertise in the manufacturing sector. Cavalcante (2013) analysed the relationship between the share of high-tech production and the degree of business R&D expenditure for the Brazilian economy. The findings clearly show that the increased R&D intensity has increased with the growth of the high-tech industries in Brazil. Thus, focus should be directed to expanding the share of high-tech sectors to increase the volume of enterprise R&D activities in the economy.

The studies aiming to investigate the drivers of business R&D intensity have also intended to clarify how the R&D investment can be stimulated by the human capital accumulation. It is generally accepted that there is a strong link between the business R&D activities and human capital accumulation since human capital affects the rate of return to private investment in R&D. Becker and Pain (2008) identified the factors affecting the R&D intensity in the UK manufacturing industries. Using a panel data model over the period 1993–2000, they found that highly qualified human capital resources have important effects on business R&D. Therefore, it has been clearly indicated that R&D activities mainly depends on the availability and quality of science and technology workers. Garcia and Mohnen (2010) examined the various sources effecting R&D based on the micro-data from the Community Innovation Survey covering the years 1998–2000. Empirical findings have shown that the share of the number of workers with higher education in the total number of workers have significant impact on private R&D. Neagu (2011) examined how the investment in business R&D is related to the human capital accumulation in Romania. Empirical findings demonstrated that human capital accumulation stimulates both inputs and outputs of the R&D investment. It has been especially indicated that there is a strong connection between the quality of the human capital and the volume of private R&D investment. This result has implied that Romania has to design a policy focused on raising the quality of human capital in order to stimulate private R&D.

Looking at the literature examining the impact of public R&D on business R&D activities, it is generally argued that publicly managed R&D produce basic (scientific) knowledge which is intensively used by private R&D in order to make innovation. Thus, R&D activities performed by public laboratories and universities increase the private return on investment in R&D and hence trigger higher expenditure on R&D by firms. A large number of studies have detected that public spending on R&D spillovers affect firm's decision about R&D spending. Verbeek and Lykogiann (2008) analysed the impact of public R&D activities on private R&D investments for 27 European countries along with the USA and Japan by using a panel data regression model. Findings showed that public R&D activities have a positive impact on R&D spending by providing input at a significant level for the private sector. According to this, because of public R&D activities, both the number of qualified personnel and the volume of scientific knowledge significantly increase for private sector usage. Sameti et al. (2010) also examined the impact of government R&D expenditure on business R&D intensity by using panel data analysis for 30 OECD countries during the period from 1996 to 2008. Empirical results indicated that government R&D expenditures have positive effect on business R&D intensity. Thus, government indirectly supports private R&D since publicly funded research centres produce scientific knowledge that is the basic source of private R&D activities to generate technological knowledge. Finally, Coccia (2012) analysed the impact of publicly financed R&D activities in universities between 1990 and 2000 for the USA, Japan and member states of the European Union. Empirical findings demonstrated that private sector R&D activities benefited positively from R&D activities in the public universities.

As seen from the literature review above, empirical studies differ in terms of the sample period, country coverage as well as estimation technique. However, the results for the impacts of high-tech specialization of industrial structure, human capital capacity and density of public R&D activities on the business R&D investment are consistent with the theory. Thus, an analysis based on these factors in Eastern European countries constitutes an important research framework for understanding the dynamics of R&D activities and thus contributing to the innovation policy design process. Accordingly, the next part of the study is devoted to the empirical analysis of the roles played by the high-tech specialization of industrial structure, human capital and the intensity of public R&D activities in the development of business R&D in Eastern Europe.

3 Data, Methodology and Empirical Results

In this part of our study, the dynamics of national R&D expenditures in 11 Eastern European countries (EEC) have been determined using panel regression analysis. Depending on the availability of the data, the countries analysed consisted of Estonia, Latvia, Lithuania, Poland, the Czech Republic, Slovakia, Hungary, Croatia, Slovenia, Romania and Bulgaria. The country-specific factors of business R&D expenditures have been determined by the factors such as human capital accumulation, public R&D intensity and the share of advanced technology and medium-advanced technology production. The empirical analysis has included annual data for EEC-11 countries between 2004 and 2016. All variables have been taken from the Science, Technology and Innovation section of EUROSTAT.

The country-specific factors affecting business sector R&D intensity are specified like below:

$$\mathrm{BERD_{it}} = \alpha_0 + \alpha_1 \mathrm{HCA_{it}} + \alpha_2 \mathrm{HTM_{it}} + \alpha_3 \mathrm{PERD_{it}} + e_{\mathrm{it}} \quad (1)$$

where indexes (i) and (t) indicate, respectively, country and year. The left-hand side dependent variable (BERD) is defined as business R&D intensity and measured as a ratio of total business expenditures on R&D to gross domestic product (GDP). The variable of human capital accumulation (HCA) is taken into account, by including the ratio of total public expenditure on education and health to GDP. Thus, the proportion of the expenditure on education and health in GDP is used as an indicator of human capital accumulation. Industrial structure (HTM) is modelled by a country's share of high-tech and medium-high-tech manufacturing production in total manufacturing production. We use the share of high-tech and medium-high-tech sector in total manufacturing sector in order to evaluate the effect of industrial structure on business R&D intensity. The public R&D intensity (PERD) is considered by the ratio of government performed R&D expenditure to GDP. The rationale behind the inclusion of this variable is to assess whether public funding to R&D stimulus for business R&D or crowding out effects prevails.

Consequently, three major hypotheses regarding the business R&D investment are of particular interest. The first is the human capital hypothesis, which states that the rate of business R&D intensity is positively correlated with the strength of human capital accumulation. The second is the industrial structure hypothesis, which argues that intensive high-tech manufacturing structure positively affects the business R&D intensity. The last is the public R&D intensity hypothesis, which argues that the intensity of business R&D intensity is closely related to density of public investment in R&D.

Before running an econometric analysis, in order to avoid the problem of "spurious regression" we tested whether time series of BERD, HCA, HTM and PERD are stationary or not. Table 1 presents the results of panel unit root tests of Im, Pesaran and Shin (IPS), Augmented Dickey Fuller (ADF) and Phillips–Perron (PP) for all variables. Results of panel unit root tests show that first differences of the series are

Table 1 Results of panel unit root tests

Variables	IPS	ADF	PP
BERD	1.4240 (0.89)	12,2510 (0.92)	10,918 (0.88)
ΔBERD	−2.8173 (0.00)*	43,6512 (0.00)*	56,278 (0.00)*
HCA	0.7657 (0.81)	25.1121 (0.14)	14,8941 (0.75)
ΔHCA	−40,176 (0.000)*	44,7543 (0.00)*	56,453 (0.00)*
HTM	0.6123 (0.70)	142,561 (0.78)	13,356 (0.081)
ΔHTM	−4.5310 (0.000)*	43.4791 (0.000)*	58,259 (0.00)*
PERD	1.9258 (0.94)	123,321 (0.90)	11,343 (0.93)
ΔPERD	−15.671 (0.048)**	31,181 (0.040)**	31,101 (0.038)**

*, ** indicate significant level at % 1 and % 5 levels, respectively, whereas Δ denotes the first differenced form of relevant variable. Values in brackets are *p*-values

stationary at the 1 and 5% significance levels. Therefore, panel regression analysis should be implemented for the first differences of the series.

Estimation results of panel regression analysis for EEC-11 countries are shown in Table 2. Coefficients of variables in pooling estimation model have expected sign, but p-values in parenthesis show that all coefficients are statistically insignificant. However, p-values related to coefficients of fixed and random models are generally statistically significant. This indicated that group effect is strong in panel data. Although F_{group} test results indicate the group effects in panel data, it does not show that this group effect is fixed or random. Thus, F_{group} test does not let us choose between fixed effect and random effect models. For this aim, we should look at the results of Hausman test in Table 2. Hausman Test statistics indicate that fixed effect model is better than random effect model since Hausman test value is big enough to reject of null hypothesis that random effect is consistent.

Looking at the results of fixed effects model, it is clearly indicated that, in explaining business R&D intensity, high-tech specialization of industrial structure, human capital and public R&D intensity have to be significantly considered. Thus, this paper empirically investigates that all three factors have a significant and positive impact on business R&D intensity. Furthermore, by comparing among three effective factors on business R&D intensity, our results show that industrial structure matters most to business R&D spending since coefficient of country's share of high-tech and medium-high-tech manufacturing (HTM) is higher than others. We also find modest empirical support to the positive role of human capital in business R&D investment. In addition, it is observed that the R&D performed by the government has a positive

Table 2 Results of panel data analysis for EEC-11 countries

Variables	Pooling estimation	Fixed effects	Random effects
C	0.610 (0.341)	2.135 (0.000)*	0.207 (0.023)
HCA	0.234 (0.198)	0.318 (0.004)*	0.908 (0.167)
HTM	0.302 (0.211)	0.486 (0.025)**	1.302 (0.067)
PERD	0.199 (0.134)	0.279 (0.010)*	0.732 (0.023)
R^2	0.450	0.748	0.364
F-test	6.543 (0.088)***	9.302 (0.000)*	9.127 (0.000)
F_{group}-test		21.302 (0.000)*	
Hausman Test		41.641 (0.000)*	

*, **, *** denote significance at the levels of 1%, 5% and 10%, respectively. Values in brackets are p-values

effect on the R&D of the enterprise, but has the lowest impact compared to other factors.

Consequently, the empirical results confirm that industrial structure is strongly linked to business R&D intensity. This indicates that countries with a large share of technology-driven industries also have high business R&D intensity. In other words, the share of high-technology manufacturing in total manufacturing is significantly positive effect on business R&D intensity. The results also confirm the view that business R&D intensity is closely related to the human capital accumulation. The ratio of total education and health expenditures to GDP called human capital is significantly positively related to business-sector R&D. In other words, the positive role of the human capital contribution via expenditure on education and health expenditure has been found as a significant factor in explaining the business R&D intensity. This is mainly because R&D investment demands for "knowledge intensive" workers, in other words, high-quality human capital. Lastly, the results also show that government-performed R&D has a significant positive impact on R&D intensity. This indicates that public-funded R&D is a complement to private R&D in the business sector rather than crowding out them. The main reason is probably related to the fact that the public sector acts as a complement to the private sector by lowering cost of some part of business R&D since R&D conducting by public sector produces mostly basic (scientific) knowledge and presents the results freely available for private sector usage.

4 Conclusion

The investment in business R&D has been identified as the main engine of productivity growth with new endogenous models. For this reason, it became a very important issue for economists to investigate the determinants of business R&D expenditures. From this point of view, the aim of this study is to determine the factors affecting the R&D intensity of the enterprise at national level for Eastern European countries during the period of 2004–2016. Based on panel data analysis of 11 Eastern European countries, this article determines the impacts of human capital, public R&D intensity and high-tech share of industrial structure on the business R&D intensity. The main result of the empirical analysis is that all three factors have a significant and positive effect on enterprise R&D intensity. More specifically, the high-tech industrial structure is seen as the most impressive factor for R&D expenditures, while human capital is the second and public R & D expenditures play the third main role.

The findings of this paper give significant insights for country-specific factors driving business R&D investment. It is clearly confirmed that business R&D intensity is mainly associated with the high-tech density of industrial structure. Empirical findings also show that human capital and public R&D intensity have positive impact in the fostering of business R&D. More specifically, this paper indicates that business R&D expenditures in the Eastern European countries are basically determined by the high-tech specialization of manufacturing sector, while human capital and public R&D intensity have second and third roles in developments of business R&D expenditures. These results regarding the determinants of business R&D investment also give significant policy implications. Accordingly, this study presents a strong rationale for the public policies to promote high-tech specialization of manufacturing sector in order to promote the volume of business R&D expenditures in the Eastern European countries. Besides, it would be also effective to invest on more on human capital and enhance R&D activities performed by public sector in order to stimulate business R&D activities.

References

Arora A, Ceccagnoli M, Cohen WM (2008) R&D and the patent premium. Int J Ind Organ 26:1153–1179

Becker B, Pain N (2008) What determines industrial R&D expenditure in the UK? Manchester School 76(1):66–87

Bougheas S, Gorg H, Strobl E (2003) Is R&D financial constrained? Theory and evidence from Irish manufacturing. Rev Ind Organ 22(2):159–174

Bravo-Ortega C, Marin AG (2011) R&D and productivity: a two-way avenue? World Dev 39:1090–1107

Brown JR, Martinsson G, Petersen BC (2012) Do financing constraint matter for R&D? Eur Econ Rev 56:1512–1529

Cameron G, Proudman J, Redding S (2005) Technological convergence, R&D, trade and productivity growth. Eur Econ Rev 49:775–807

Cavalcante LR (2013) An analysis of the business enterprise research and development expenditures composition in Brazil. Rev Bras Innov Campinas (SP) 13(2):433–458
Coad A, Rao R (2010) Firm growth and R&D expenditure. Econ Innov New Technol 19(2):127–145
Coccia M (2012) Political Economy of R&D to support the modern competitiveness of nations and determinants of economic optimizations and inertia. Technovation 32:370–379
Czarnitzki D, Hottenrott H (2011) R&D investment and financing constraints of small and medium-sized firms. Small Bus Econ 36(1):65–83
Falk M (2006) What drives business R&D intensity across OECD countries? Appl Econ 38(5):533–547
Fishman A, Rob R (1999) The size of firms and R&D investment. Int Econ Rev 40(4):915–931
Fleming L (2001) Recombinant uncertainty in technological search. Manage Sci 47:117–132
Freeman C (1995) The national innovation systems in historical perspective. Camb J Econ 19(1):5–24
Garcia A, Mohnen P (2010) Impact of government support on R&D and innovation. UNU-MERIT working paper series. 2010-034
Girma S, Görg H, Hanley A (2008) R&D and exporting: a comparison of British and Irish firms. Rev World Econ 144:750–773
Guariglia A, Liu X, Song L (2014) Internal finance and growth: microeconometric evidence on Chinese firms. J Dev Econ 96(1):79–94
Gümüş E, Celikay F (2015) R&D expenditure and economic growth: new empirical evidence. J Appl Econ Res 9(3):205–217
Harris R, Trainor M (2011) A matching analysis of why some firms in peripheral regions undertake R&D whereas others do not. Econ Innov New Technol 20:367–385
Lai Y, Lin F, Lin Y (2015) Factors affecting firm's R&D investment decisions. J Bus Res 68:840–844
Lev B, Sougiannis T (1996) The capitalization, amortization and value relevance of R&D. J Account 21(1):107–138
Liik M, Jaan M, Ukrainski K (2014) The contribution of R&D to production efficiency in OECD countries: econometric analysis of industry-level panel data. Baltic J Econ 14(1–2):78–100
Lundvall BA (2016) National innovation systems: towards a theory of innovation and interactive learning. In: Lundvall BA (ed) The learning economy and the economics of hope. Anthem Press, London, pp 85–116
Nelson RR (1993) A retrospective. In: Nelson RR (ed) National innovation systems: a comparative analysis. Oxford University Press, New York, pp 505–523
Mathieu A, Potterie BP (2010) A note on the drivers of R&D intensity. Res World Econ 1(1):56–65
Neagu O (2011) How the investment in R&D is related to the human capital accumulation? The case of Romania. Ann Univ Apulensis Ser Oecon 13(2):539–548
O'Mahony M, Vecchi M (2009) R&D, knowledge spillovers and company productivity performance. Res Policy 38:35–44
Park Y, Jaeun S, Kim T (2010) Firm size, age, industrial networking and growth: a case of the Korean manufacturing industry. Small Bus Econ 35:153–168
Romer PM (1986) Increasing returns and long-run growth. J Polit Econ 94(5):1002–1037
Sameti M, Ranjbar H, Anaousheh S (2010) Determinants of R&D investment: a study of OECD countries. J Knowl Econ Knowl Manag 5:35–42
Sasidharan S, Lukose PJ, Komera S (2015) Financing constraints and investments in R&D: evidence from Indian manufacturing firms. Q Rev Econ Fin 55:28–39
Savignac F (2008) Impact of financial constraints on innovation: what can be learned from a direct measure? Econ Innov New Technol 16–7(6):553–569
Silvia F, Carreira C (2012) Does financial constraint threat the innovation process? Evidence from Portuguese firms. Econ Innov New Technol 21(8):701–736
Tomiura E (2007) Effects of R&D networking on the export decision of Japanese firms. Res Policy 36:758–767
Tsai KH, Wang JC (2004) The R&D performance in Twain's electronics industry: a longitudinal examination. R&D Manag 34(2):179–189

Verbeek A, Lykogianni E (2008) A time series analysis of the development in national R& intensities and national public expenditures on R&D. Final Study Report for Specific Assignment 4 (SPA4), Brussels.
Weerawardena J, O'Cass A, Julian C (2006) Does industry matter? Examining the role of industry structure and organisational learning in innovation and brand performance. J Bus Res 59:37–45
Yang C-H, Chen YH (2012) R&D, productivity and exports: plant-level evidence from Indonesia. Econ Model 29:208–216

Competitiveness, Profitability and R/D Intensity: The Case of the Domestic Pharmaceutical Industry in Greece

Vasiliki Kounnou and Dimitrios Kyrkilis

Abstract Greek pharmaceutical industry has been emerged as one of the major drivers for the Greek manufacturing sector mostly from 2000 until 2011. The value-added of the industry in the overall economy is indicated through its impact on the gross value-added production, employment, exports, innovation and global competiveness. Greek pharmaceuticals firms have one of the highest shares of investment in innovation and R&D activities in the total Greek economy. The purpose of this study is to investigate the potential causal relationship between industry-level competitiveness, profitability and R/D intensity. Specific financial ratios have been selected for the regression analysis using a sample of Greek pharmaceutical firms with in-house Research and Development department. The period of the analysis has been defined between 2004 and 2015. According to the existing literature, it is expected that R/D intensity plays a significant role on the profitability for pharmaceutical firms.

Keywords Greek pharmaceutical industry · R/D intensity · Competitiveness · Profitability

JEL Classification Codes L1 · L65

1 Introduction

The pharmaceutical industry is considered as one of the fastest growing sectors globally. Recent data for European pharmaceutical industry show the importance of the sector to overall economy. It contributes to social welfare by improving public health and quality of life. It is a research-based sector and the biggest investor in

V. Kounnou (✉) · D. Kyrkilis
University of Macedonia, Thessaloniki, Greece
e-mail: vasi14nou@gmail.com

D. Kyrkilis
e-mail: kyrkilis@uom.edu.gr

A. Horobet et al. (eds.), *Business Performance and Financial Institutions in Europe*, Contributions to Economics, https://doi.org/10.1007/978-3-030-57517-5_3

health research, leading to positive economic results and reducing a considerable amount of healthcare cost. It is a key asset for European Economy and one of the Europe's top performing high-technology sectors (EFPIA 2018).

The European pharmaceutical industry can play a critical role for boosting growth and innovation in Europe. It can ensure future competiveness in an advancing global economy. In 2017, the sector invested approximately €35,200 million in R&D in Europe. In addition, it employs directly around 750,000 people and generates four times more employment indirectly (EFPIA 2018).

Based on the existing literature on the pharmaceutical sector, pharmaceutical industry is one of the industries that present the highest incidence of R&D performers and gain significant returns (Jefferson et al. 2006). Generally, investment activity is regarded to be a source of motive power for firms (Chirinko 1993).

More specifically, Greek pharmaceutical sector is considered one of the most dynamic sectors of the Greek manufacturing industry and an essential asset to the Greek economy. As reported by a survey conducted by the Foundation for Economic and Industrial Research, in the beginning of 2000 decade the pharmaceutical expenditures have been increased faster than GDP and so domestic production has risen continuously in conjunction with the investments in the sector.

There is a considerably development for the Greek domestic pharmaceutical industry from the beginning of 2000 until 2007, where the global financial crisis affected the Greek economy and austerity measures and cuts in healthcare expenditure have been adopted by the Greek government. The domestic pharmaceutical sector has been lost a considerably part of their production in terms of value. Since then there was a noticeable increase until 2016.

Although the Greek economy has experienced an unprecedented decrease of its growth because of the financial crisis, pharmaceutical sector realized the lowest decreased in employment comparing the sector of plastics and chemicals. It is obvious that pharmaceutical sector is a dynamic and promising one in Greece and it is vital for the Greek economy to be encouraged.

Although the contribution and the value of Greek pharmaceutical industry for the economy is important, the sector faces considerably challenges. The considerable reduction of the pharmaceutical expenditure, policy measures, clawbacks, rebates and the low percentage of R&D spending on the domestic pharmaceutical industry prevents the industry from further development.

Therefore, the country needs urgently policies that will contribute to restart its economic activity. Pharmaceutical is considered a sector with an important exporting activity boosting that way the Greek economy. The issue of competitiveness and its relation to profitability and innovation has become increasingly important for firms.

The scope of this paper is to identify the potential relationship between the profitability and R&D intensity in the Greek pharmaceutical industry with in-house Research and Development department during the period 2004–2015.

2 Theory and Literature Review

The issue of competitiveness of manufacturing sector has been assessed both at industrial and firm levels. Nevertheless, there has been recently an increasing attention on firm level since the competitiveness of firms affects considerably the ability of each country to grow (Voulgaris and Lemonakis 2014).

According to Schumpeterian theory, the ability of firms to compete depends on their innovative activity allowing them to gain monopoly power. Porter (1980 and 1990) defines competitiveness as the ability of a firm to compete in a defined business environment successfully. Based on other empirical research, productivity is the source for competitiveness so they define competitiveness using productivity. Other studies use as a proxy for competitiveness market share and profitability (Fischer and Schornberg 2007). Generally, it can be assumed that when a firm increases its market share and in parallel realizing high profitability, it can be considered as competitiveness. In the present study, profitability is used as a main indicator for competitiveness.

Innovative activity and R&D are regarded to be crucial factor for firm growth and prosperity. They affect both directly and indirectly economic process by increasing profitability, turnover and employment (OECD 2013). Moreover, R&D intensity varies between industry and countries. Regarding to the empirical research, investments in innovation result in improvement on productivity (Hashi and Stojcic 2010).

Kafouros (2005) shows that innovative process is positively correlated with productivity growth and sales. Koellinger (2008) examines the link between technology, innovation and firm performance in e-business in Europe resulting that innovators are more likely to grow than non-innovators.

There is a remarkable empirical research on the relationship between innovative process and firm's competitiveness which support mainly that R/D procedure has a positive impact on firm competitiveness (Makris 2015). It is very demanding for a firm to succeed in a competitive and tough environment; therefore, Research and Development is an emerging issue needed for every firm.

Chao-Hung Wang, 2011, claims that firms that allocate higher R&D expenditure are expected to have higher profits than those which do not. The costs of R&D are outweighed by received benefits when the firm reaches the equilibrium. Therefore, the increased firm's performance compensates the costs for R&D.

Investments in R&D play a significant role to gain an advantage over current and future competitors of the firm. R&D expenditures and innovation allow firms to prevent imitation by rivals and gaining above-average profits (Erickson and Jacobson 1992). According to Hayes and Abernathy (1980), the firms, in order to succeed, should compete on technological ground so they have to offer innovative and superior products for their long-run profits.

In accounting literature, there is a positive relation between investments in R&D and future returns (Michael 2008). Donelson and Resutek (2012) argued that there is no relation of higher future returns realized by R&D. According to them, neither the level of R&D investment nor the change in R&D investment explains future returns. However, Cooper (2008) supports the view that there is a positive linkage between R&D expenses and profits in accounting theory.

Regarding Griliches study (1986), a higher R&D investment results to higher rates of productivity growth among firms using data for US firms between 1972 and 1977. In addition, Goto and Suzuki (1989) support the theory of productivity growth positively correlated to the growth of R&D investment in firm's core activity conducting a study using a sample of Japanese manufacturing firms in 1982. Finally, Wakelin (1998) finds that R&D intensity had a positive and significant effect on productivity growth testing a sample of British firms between 1988 and 1992.

Turning our interest to the European area, it can be said that R&D intensity in Eurozone presents a considerably differentiation after 2007 across economies and sectors leading to a different performance and development at firm level (Makris 2016). The period between 2000 and 2007 shows a slight convergence at the field of innovation and R&D spending between the countries of the Eurozone periphery and Eurozone core. After 2008, countries of Eurozone periphery are affected heavily by the financial crisis and because of the economic distress, spending on R&D has been reduced considerably. On the other side, countries of Eurozone core are characterized as research intensive and innovation leads to the increase of gains in performance at both micro- and macro-level (Makris 2016).

Pharmaceutical sector is one of the most value-added sectors globally. Pharmaceutical industry is the most R&D intensive based on OECD report, 2017. However, the existing literature for the investigation of the relationship between the R&D expenditure and firm performance is limited in this sector. The pharma industry is a particularly interesting industry for exploring the controversial relationship between innovation and firm growth since both R&D spending and patents are increasing considerably, but the number of new molecular entities is staying relatively flat.

Empirical studies conducting in Greece indicate that innovative activity appears to be a critical factor for restarting economic activity in Greece. More precisely, Voulgaris and Lemonakis (2014) addressed a survey to investigate the relationship between firm-level competitiveness, firm profitability and financial factors, using a sample of Greek manufacturing firms by three different sectors. Their results support the theory that profitability affects positively firm growth and R&D has been found to play a significant role on the profitability for the firms in pharmaceutical sector.

The empirical study of Makris (2008) conducting in Greek pharmaceutical industry shows that real innovative activity appears to be a critical issue in the survival and growth of the sector. Results of the survey indicate that firms in the sector should focus on in-house R&D activity.

Ghaffar and Khan (2014) tested the impact of R&D expenditure on firm profitability and growth conducting a survey on Pakistan drug companies. They concluded that there is a positive effect of R&D investments on business asset profitability, equity return and profitability per share.

In addition, the study of Vurur and Ilarslan (2016) found that there is a one-way causality relationship from R&D expenditures towards operational profit in the largest pharmaceutical firm in Turkey.

The aim of this paper is to contribute to the limited empirical literature at this context and give some insight about the Greek pharmaceutical industry.

3 Methodology and Variables Selection

The research in based on financial data of balance sheets of 14 domestic pharmaceuticals firms with in-house Research and Development department between the period of 2004 until 2015. All those firms are members of the Hellenic Association of Pharmaceutical Industry. The Association expresses the position of Greek interest of domestic pharmaceutical companies, a dynamic sector with a specific strategic importance for the Greek economy. The domestic pharmaceutical firms produce mainly branded generics.

The data were extracted from the financial database of ICAP Group, a private research company in Greece. The choice of the sample included the firms which have expenditure in R&D between the period 2004 and 2015. Although the members of the Association include 46 firms, we selected only 14 because of the missing data for R&D expenditure during that explicit period in the majority of them. This reduced the total sample to 14 firms. The Greek pharmaceutical industry is characterized by the lack of homogeneity since foreign (mainly multinational affiliates import brand drugs to the Greek market), domestic firms (which produce brand generics or brand name drugs for other multinational firms or import pharmaceutical products) and packagers co-exist at the sector (Foundation for Economics and Industrial Research 2018).

The next step was to record the selected economic indices and numbers from the balance sheets. First, we focused on the innovative activities collecting data concerning the R&D expenditures in absolute numbers. Then, we recorded data concerning firm sales, net profit before taxes, leverage and total equity. Then, we constructed financial indices in order to test their impact on the model. In the present study, we used as a proxy for competitiveness profitability in line with literature.

In this model as dependent variable, it is used the profitability as a proxy for competitiveness. We measure profitability with the index of net profit margin (net profit before taxes to sales) in line with the literature. The factors taken as independent variables in our model based on theory and literature are indicated in Table 1. The expected relationship with the dependent variable is shown in the second column.

Independent variables used:

- **Size(+) or (−)**: This variable is measured by the natural log of the firm's total sales. It is regarded as an ambiguous variable. Larger firms have the competitive advantage because of economies of scale, having direct access to global capital. Therefore, they may realize superior profits. On the other side, larger firms may suffer from managerial inefficiencies and larger monitoring costs (Williamson 1967). Smaller firms can adjust easier to market changes and are significant drivers

Table 1 Independent variables and expected sign

Independent variables	Expected sign
Firm experience	(+)
Size of the firm	(+)/(−)
Leverage	(+)/(−)
R/D expenditures	(+)
Capital intensity	(+)
Return on equity	(+)

of innovation. Nevertheless are more risky with high cost of production (Voulgaris and Lemonakis 2014)

- **Firm Experience** (+): According to the existing literature, older firms are more profitable and efficiency due to their reputation and experience.
- **Leverage (+) or (−)**: Dependence on debt can affect positively the profitability until a certain point. High reliance on debt has a negative effect.
- **R/D intensity** (+): Innovative firms are expected to have higher profitability than non-innovative firms. So it is expected a positive relationship with profitability.
- **Capital intensity** (+): The intensive use of capitals is expected to increase the market share of the firm and consequently the profits.
- **Return on equity** (+): This variable is considered a measure of how effectively management is using a company's assets to create profits. It is expected to have a positive impact.

We used the linear regression model to determine the critical factors of profitability measured as net profit before taxes. For examining the factors that affect profitability of the pharmaceutical sector, the following model has been developed:

$$\begin{aligned} Y_{i,t} &= b_0 I, t + b_1 X_1 + b_2 X_{2i,t} + b_3 X_{3i,t} \\ &\quad + b_4 X_{4i,t} + b_5 X_{5i,t} + b_6 X_{6i,t} + \varepsilon_{i,t} \end{aligned} \tag{1}$$

where:

i refers to an individual firm; t: refers to year;
$Y_{i,t}$ the dependent variable that refers to net profit before taxes of firm i in time t;
$X_{1i,t}$ the independent variable that refers to Research and Development expenditure of firm i in time t;
$X_{2i,t}$ the independent variable that refers to return on equity of firm i in time t;
$X_{3i,t}$ is the capital intensity for firm i in time t;
$X_{4i,t}$ is the leverage of firm i in time t;
$X_{5i,t}$ is the size of firm i in time t;
$X_{6i,t}$ is the age of firm i in time t;
$E_{i,t}$ is the error term.

4 Empirical Results

We run a linear regression model on panel data for the pharmaceutical sector transforming all the variables into log in order to normalize the distribution of data.

The results of the estimation procedure are presented in Table 1. The F-statistic proves the validity of model. We could summarize the results in Tables 2 and 3.

The results from the regression indicate a positive and statistically significant at 5% level relationship between return on equity and net profits. This finding supports the view that the effective management of firm's assets can affect positively the profitability. Profitable firms can create more profits through the efficient use of its assets.

Capital intensity has a positive and significant impact on profitability. This finding is in line with the existing literature. The more intensive the use of capital, the higher the profitability of the firm would be expected. Pharmaceutical sector is characterized by capital intensity as in the developed countries abroad.

The independent variable of size has been found positive and statistically significant. The positive effect on profitability is supported by the existing empirical work.

Table 2 Regression results—pharmaceuticals

Dependent variable	Log net profit before taxes	
Variables	Coefficient	Prob
C	−5.147.128	0.064
Log rd	0.0305	0.659
Log ROE	0.58323	0.000
Log intensity	0.8997605	0.000
Log lever	0.00922	0.945
Log size	1.2223	0.000
Log age	−0.5451	0.755
R-squared	0.6854	
Adj R-squared	0.6621	
F-statistic	29.42	
Prob (F-statistic)	0.000	

Table 3 Significant determinants of profitability

Significant determinants	Pharmaceuticals
ROE	+
Capital intensity	+
Size	+

Large firms, increasing their sales, are less risky and use economies of scale and therefore they may realize superior profits.

Research and Development (R&D) leverage has been found positive but not statistically significant in contrast with other empirical studies conducted in Greece (Voulgarakis and Lemonakis 2014; Notta et al. 2010). Concerning the variable of R&D, due to the lack of domestic production of new molecular drugs, the value-added of the Greek pharmaceutical industry is regarded as low. Therefore, the expenditures on R&D cannot affect considerably the profitability.

5 Conclusions

The scope of this paper was to determine the factors affecting competitiveness using as proxy profitability in the Greek pharmaceutical industry with their own in-house Research and Development department, for the period 2004–2015. This study contributes to the limited literature for this sector in Greece on the basis of the link between the profitability and R&D.

Profitability has been used as dependent variable. Using the linear regression and based on financial data, we found that return on equity (ROE), capital intensity and firm size are significant determinants of profitability. Regarding R&D variable, there is no statistical significance on the profitability. A further analysis should be conducted in order to be tested the impact of R&D on profits. The findings in this paper do not suggest any relation of profitability with age and leverage since are not statistical significant. The use of capital, the effective management of firm's assets and the size are important factors for the profitability.

This study contributes to investigation of the factors which affect competitiveness and profitability in Greece. Since R&D variable has no statistical significance on profitability, the value-added of Research & Development in Greek pharmaceutical industry is considered as significant low. Specific actions could be undertaken by policy makers in order to give incentives to the industry for investing more in R&D. Increasing public financing for R&D and applying more equitable cost-containment methods for pharmaceutical expenditure is expected to be essential interventions for boosting innovation activity in Greek pharmaceutical industry.

The results of our study refer only to Greek pharmaceutical industry with in-house R&D activity. If replicated, results of the same study may be different in other industries. Future studies can also be conducted for different industries in Greece and to be investigated the determinants for profitability and competitiveness. Research can also be done on how R&D affects different high-technology industries, for example the pharmaceutical industry versus the information technology industry in Greece.

References

Donelson DC, Resutek J (2012) The effect of R&D on future returns and earnings forecasts. Springer science and business media
Erickson G, Jacobson R (1992) Gaining comparative advantage through discretionary expenditures: the returns to R&D and advertising. Manag Sci 38(9):1264–1279
European Federation of Pharmaceutical Industries and Associations (EFPIA) (2018) The pharmaceutical industry in Figures, www.efpia.org (accessed January 2019)
Fischer C, Schornberg S (2007) Assessing the competitiveness situation of EU food and drink manufacturing industries: an index–based approach. Agribusiness 23(4):473–495
Foundation for Economics and Industrial Research (2018) The pharmaceutical market in Greece: facts and figures in 2018, https://iobe.gr/
Ghaffar A, Khan WA (2014) Impact of research and development on firm performance. Int J Account Finan Rep 4(1):357–367
Goto A, Suzuki K (1989) R&D capital, rate of return on R&D investment and spillover of R&D in Japanese manufacturing industries. Rev Econ Stat 71(4):555–564
Griliches Z (1986) Productivity, R&D, and the basic research at the firm level in the 1970s. Am Econ Rev 76(1):141–154
Hashi I, Stojcic N (2010) The impact of innovation activities on firm performance using a multi-stage model: evidence from the community innovation survey 4. CASE network studies and analyses, No. 410
Hayes RH, Abernathy WJ (1980) Economic scene results now: pay later? The New York Times
Jefferson G, Huamao B, Xiaojing G, Xiaoyun Y (2006) R&D performance in Chinese industry. Econ Innov New Technol 15:345–366
Kafouros M (2005) R&D and productivity growth: evidence from the UK. Econ Innov New Technol 14(6):479–497
Koellinger P (2008) The relationship between technology, innovation, and firm performance-empirical evidence from e-business in Europe. Res Policy 37:1317–1328
Makris I (2008) The factors affecting firms' growth: investment in tangible versus intangible assets in the Greek pharmaceutical industry. Int J Behav Healthc Res 1(1):91–104
Makris I (2016) The effect of innovative activity in firm performanceand development: Analysing data from eurozone. Int J Bus Econ Sci Appl Res (IJBESAR) 9(2):87–92
Notta O, Vlachvei A, Samathrakis V (2010) Competitiveness-the case of Greek food manufacturing firms. Int J Arts Sci 3:211–225
OECD (2013) Science. Technology and Industry Scoreboard, OECD Publishing. https://doi.org/10.1787/sti_scoreboard-2013-en
OECD (2018) Science, technology and industry outlook. OECD Publishing, https://www.oecd.org/innovation/oecd-science-technology-and-innovation-outlook-25186167.htm
Porter ME (1990) The competitive advantage of nations. The Free Press, New York
Porter M (1980) Competitive strategy. The Free Press, New York
Voulgaris F, Lemonakis C (2014) Competitiveness and profitability: the case of chemicals, pharmaceuticals and plastics. J Econ Asymmetr 11:46–57
Vurur NS, Ilarslan K (2016) Analysis of the relationship between R & D expenditure and profitability: a sample application from BIST. J Multidisc Dev 1(1):103–112
Wakelin K (1998) Innovation and expert behavior at the firm level. Res Policy 26(7–8):829–841
Wang CH (2011) Clarifying the effects of R&D on performance: evidence from the high technology industries. Asia Pac Manag Rev 16(1):51–64

Evolution of Airline Business Models: The Case of Pegasus Airlines

Leyla Adiloğlu-Yalçınkaya and Senem Besler

Abstract Pegasus Airlines has been an unique airline, as it changed its business model from a charter airline business model to a low-cost airline business model and is currently positioned itself with low-cost network carrier business model. The aim of this study is to examine the change of business model of Pegasus Airlines, which has been operating in airline industry in Turkey since 1990. For this purpose, a single case study approach was designed to allow in-depth analysis of the airline business model. Semi-structured interviews were conducted in 2019, supported by data gathered from multiple sources. The results confirm that the change of regulations and perspectives, geographical advantages of the airports and the state support could serve as catalysts to the ability to change the airline business model. This study makes a contribution to airline business model literature by revealing the factors influencing the evolution of a business model of Pegasus Airlines.

Keywords Pegasus Airlines · Airline business model · Business model evolution

1 Introduction

In recent years, the business model has been the focus of substantial attention in the management research. Even though there is debate about the business model in the literature and there is no consensus on what the business model exactly is (Morris et al. 2005; Zott et al. 2011), the researchers combine the components of the business model to define it. Generally, a business model is the firm's core logic behind creating and capturing value (Foss and Saebi 2015) and contains value propositions, market segments, the structure of the value chain and the mechanisms of value capture (Casadesus-Masanell and Ricart 2010; Foss and Saebi 2015; Teece 2010).

L. Adiloğlu-Yalçınkaya (✉)
Faculty of Aviation and Aeronautical Sciences, Özyeğin University, Istanbul, Turkey
e-mail: leyla.adiloglu@ozyegin.edu.tr

S. Besler
Faculty of Business Administration, Anadolu University, Eskişehir, Turkey

A. Horobet et al. (eds.), *Business Performance and Financial Institutions in Europe*, Contributions to Economics, https://doi.org/10.1007/978-3-030-57517-5_4

The concept of business model is used for many different purposes in the relevant literature. These include classification of enterprise (Foss and Saebi 2017; Lambert and Davidson 2013) analysis of performance differences among companies (Zott and Amit 2007) and evaluation of technology and innovation management (Baden-Fuller and Haefliger 2013; Teece 2010). Although there are many studies focusing on the business model and summarizing business model studies (Massa et al. 2017), few studies examine the factors affecting the evolution of business models. This study aims to fill this gap in the literature by examining the external factors contributing to business model evolution.

2 Business Model

The term "business model" is defined in different ways by various researchers. Amit and Zott (2001) define the term "business model" as the design of transaction content, structure and governance aiming to create value through the exploitation of business opportunities. According to Magretta (2002), it is the story that explains the way the business works. Teece (2010) describes the business model as the way the business creates and delivers value to the customers and then converts payments received into profit. According to Casadesus-Masanell and Ricart (2010), business model is the logic that explains how the business operates and creates value for its stakeholders.

The term "business model" does not have a commonly agreed-upon definition and is interpreted differently by many researchers (DaSilva and Trkman 2014; Foss and Saebi 2017; Morris et al. 2005; Osterwalder and Pigneur 2004; Zott et al. 2011).

The business model is defined by utilizing the dimensions constituting the model. The business model is generally associated with the value proposition offered by the business, its market segment, the value chain structure and the value-capture mechanism offered by the business, and how these elements are related to each other (Casadesus-Masanell and Ricart 2010; Foss and Saebi 2015; Magretta 2002; Morris et al. 2005; Teece 2010). According to the definitions in the literature, the airline business model consists of four dimensions: the products and services provided while conducting activities in the organizational field, the relationships airlines establish with their customers, the infrastructure required for the products/services and the revenue structure. Likewise, the airline business model can be defined as "the manner and logic of realizing the passenger, freight and cargo transportation activities" based on these business model definitions (Adiloğlu-Yalçınkaya 2019).

Review of the relevant literature reveals that generally accepted classification of airline business models includes the traditional/network airline business model, low-cost business model, regional business model and charter business model (Bieger and Agosti 2017; Bieger and Wittmer 2011; Kuyucak Şengür and Şengür 2012; Sarılgan 2011; Taşçı and Yalçınkaya 2015). However, the research indicates that these business models have changed and developed over time (Lohmann and Koo 2013; Wensveen and Leick 2009), evolved and converged in terms of their characteristics (Corbo 2017; Daft and Albers 2013, 2015), and with evolving business models, the aforementioned classification of airline business models has also changed over time and that business models can now be classified in different ways according to their renewed characteristics (Urban et al. 2018).

This study will analyze the evolution of the business model of Pegasus Airlines which brought "low-cost model" to Turkey after starting scheduled flight.

3 Method

The aim of this study is to analyze, by employing the qualitative methodology, the business model evolution of Pegasus Airlines since its establishment. For this purpose, a single case study approach was designed by following the guidelines of Yin (2016) to allow in-depth analysis of business model evolution of Pegasus Airlines. Regarding the research question aiming to investigate the historical evolution of business models, representing the low-cost airlines, Pegasus Airlines business model was selected because the company has a long history and is the only airline traded in the Istanbul Stock Exchange that adopts the low-cost business model. Thus, the data needed to analyze this airline company were expected to be more accessible than other airlines. Pegasus also ranks as the third in Turkey's 500 largest service exporters in the aviation sector after Turkish Airlines and SunExpress, a subsidiary of Turkish Airlines (TIM 2018).

The primary data were obtained from the semi-structured interviews with nine senior executives. By conducting semi-structured interviews, it was aimed to explain how high-level decision makers in the organization interpret the business model changes during the period, and think about what factors play a role in the change of business model. The data obtained from the interviews were also supported by data obtained from multiple sources (e.g., Pegasus Airline's official Web site, annual reports, industry reports, press releases, announcements, academic studies on Turkish aviation industry and newspaper archives). The list of the interviewees is given in Table 1. They are listed on the basis of their interview dates and coded in order.

These interviews yielded a 484-min long interview. As the two of the interviewees did not allow voice recording, the researchers took notes during their interviews. The data obtained from the research were analyzed by using the NVivo qualitative research program. The qualitative data were coded independently by the researchers, and then categories and themes were formed through consensus codes. The research findings are presented below.

Table 1 Interview list

No	Alias	Position	Interview date	Duration of recording and method of interview
1	PGS-01	Board Member	16.01.2019	1 h 20 mins, face-to-face
2	PGS-02	Vice President	21.01.2019	50 min, face-to-face
3	PGS-03	Vice President	21.01.2019	1 h face-to-face
4	PGS-04	Board Member	24.01.2019	34 min, face-to-face
5	PGS-05	Board Member	30.01.2019	30 min, face-to-face
6	PGS-06	Director	31.01.2019	1 h, face-to-face
7	PGS-07	Vice President	31.01.2019	1 h, face-to-face
8	PGS-08	Vice President	04.02.2019	– Face-to-face
9	PGS-09	Executive	04.02.2019	– Face-to-face

4 Findings

4.1 Pegasus Airlines: 1990–2005

The Turkish civil aviation industry began to change with the Turkish Civil Aviation Act that went into effect in 1983, which allowed private airline companies' entry into the aviation market. Until then, with the exception of Bursa Airlines and Hürkuş Airlines, Turkish Airlines (THY) had monopoly as a "flag carrier" in the Turkish civil aviation industry (Gerede 2011; Yalçınkaya 2019). National newspaper Milliyet mentions this law as "*the law ending the monopoly of Turkish Airlines in the civil aviation transportation*" (Gürses 1992).

After 1983, many airlines were established in the sector but most went bankrupt. Pegasus Airlines (Pegasus Hava Taşımacılığı A.Ş.) was founded in 1990, with the partnership of Aer Lingus, Silkar Yatırım ve İnşaat Organizasyonu A.Ş (Silkar), Net Holding AS, Ö. Alper Eliçin, Conor P. McGrath (Pegasus 2019e), and has maintained its sustainability until today.

PGS-01, one of our interviewees, explains the story of the establishment:

> In 1988… An Irish gentleman came to me… He said that he came from Aer Lingus, from a small country in a corner of Europe, and their airline was very successful. He wanted to set up an airline here on the other end of Europe to cover both ends of it.

Likewise, PGS-05 says that "*The Irish wanted to do tourism-related business in Turkey … I was referred to them. They gave me a partnership for free. Together we established the Pegasus company.*"

In the interview, PGS-01 explains the reasons behind Pegasus Airlines' adoption of charter business model as:

> The legislation at the time did not allow setting up a scheduled airline, but only allowed setting up a charter airline company… When Aer Lingus came here, they came with the idea of establishing a charter airline, they did not plan to start a scheduled airline.

Interviewee PGS-05 said the following: "*Pegasus flew only charter… You could not fly on domestic flights back then. Only THY but no one else could fly on domestic lines. It was not allowed to have domestic scheduled flights anyway.*"

Actually, it was revealed that there was no legislative constraints regarding this issue mentioned by the interviewees, but that the Turkish state's practices toward the protection of THY constituted cognitive constraints on the entry into the sector (Yalçınkaya 2018). This supports the conclusion that cognitive barriers may lead to ignoring the opportunities that may be needed for business model innovation and prevent such innovation (Chesbrough and Rosenbloom 2002; Lange et al. 2015).

Pegasus Airlines was founded in 1990 with 49% partnership of Aer Lingus (Kangis and O'Reilly 2003). Established in 1936, Aer Lingus is the national airline of Ireland (Factsheet 2018).

PGS-01 talks about this 49% partnership with Aer Lingus as follows:

> They saw us in the Financial Times… They visited Besim Tibuk of Net Holding, Burhan Silahtaroğlu of Silkar, and ESKA. … Their proposal was having 15% partnership each, with 45% total, and let's get a small partner with another 4% share, and we will have 49% partnership. This was because they could not get over 49% partnership ratio.

Under Turkish Civil Aviation Law No. 2920/49, this case is described as "*the majority of those who are authorized to manage and represent the aircraft registered in the Turkish Trade Register, which are owned by the commercial companies, cooperatives and their unions, must be Turkish citizens and the majority of the voting rights must belong to Turkish partners*" (Turkish Civil Aviation Law 1983). Commercial Air Transportation Directive issued by the DGCA states that "*the majority of shares and voting rights belong to Turkish citizens, and the majority must be controlled by Turkish nationals. Majority of the board of directors members must be Turkish citizens.*" The issue of airline ownership structure and foreign partnership has always been debated as an important constraint, which is subject to change and varies from country to country (Walulik 2016).

As stated by PGS-01, "*21% of the shares held by Ö. Alper Eliçin… 15% by Silkar and Net, and the remaining 49% held by Aer Lingus,*" Pegasus Airlines began its activities as a charter airline. However, as a major partner, Aer Lingus has become a group that is involved in many businesses over time (Whiteside 2012). Then, Aer Lingus applied for state aid due to the financial downturn in 1992. The requested state aid was evaluated by the European Community (Application of Articles 92 and 93 of the EC Treaty and Article 61 of the EEA Agreement to State Aid in the Aviation Sector 1994; State Aid 1993). In 1993, the European Commission established a committee of experts called Comite des Sages to analyze the situation of civil aviation in the European Community (Application of Articles 92 and 93 of the EC Treaty and Article 61 of the EEA Agreement to State Aid in the Aviation Sector 1994). Doganis (2005) states that this was also influenced by the lobbying activities of the competitors of Aer Lingus against the Irish government's proposal to grant state support for Aer Lingus in 1993. Changing its attitude on state aids, the European Commission made new decisions on state aids based on the recommendations of the established committee ("Application of Articles 92 and 93 of the EC Treaty and

Article 61 of the EEA Agreement to State Aid in the Aviation Sector" 1994). This forced Aer Lingus as a business group to focus on air transport in Ireland, which was its main business focus, and dispose the non-core assets ("State Aid," Official Journal of the European Communities 1993). On the official Web site, Aer Lingus explained that a *"restructuring program was launched to address the commercial challenges of the airline"* for the year of 1993 (Aer Lingus 2019). While Aer Lingus has a traditional business model, its transformation into a hybrid airline business model after adopting a low-cost airlines business model is also analyzed in the relevant literature (O'Connell and Connolly 2017).

PGS-01 explains how Aer Lingus withdrew from its 49% of Pegasus partnership:

> There are two main reasons behind this Pegasus partnership being unable to continue, one of which was the financial problems of Aer Lingus in 1993; at the time the Irish government had a currency called "fund", they are now using the Euro, Aer Lingus asked for a capital support of x million funds. The Irish government thought this out and finally agreed to do that. But at that time they had just joined the European Union and did not yet use the EURO. Brussels (EU headquarters) told them that having a public company was not prohibited in the EU, but providing financial assistance to a public company was illegal because it meant manipulating the competition with the private sector; so they said that they would transfer this money to Aer Lingus only for this time, on the condition that Aer Lingus would not do anything other than its real job... The Irish (partners) started looking for customers in Europe. They asked me to seek customers in Turkey.

Aer Lingus decided to transfer its shares as a result of these problems it experienced, and Enternasyonal Turizm, which was a 100% subsidiary of Yapı Kredi Bank, acquired 85% of the Pegasus Airlines established by Irish State Airlines Aer Lingus, Net Holding and Silkar in 1990 (Milliyet 1994). Thus, as stated by PGS-01, the shareholding structure was changed as *"15% Silkar and 85% Enternasyonal Turizm."* However, this time, due to the economic crisis in 2001 in Turkey, Yapı Kredi Bank was forced to sell Pegasus Airlines with the decision to dispose of non-financial subsidiaries (Milliyet 2003). PGS-01 refers to the change in the ownership structure as follows:

> The second change was also enforced by the 2001 crisis when the banks went bankrupt. First Pamukbank and Yapıkredi bank went under. Savings Deposit Insurance Fund (TMS) stepped in, and recommended and merged them and brought Yapı Kredi back to life, but told them to sell everything they had apart from banking-related assets, it was put up for sale and Ali Bey bought it then.

Thus, Pegasus Airlines was acquired by Esas Holding AS in 2005. Having adopted the charter business model until then, Pegasus transitioned to the low-cost airline business model and began scheduled domestic flights as the fourth scheduled airline organization operating in Turkey in 2001 (Pegasus 2019a).

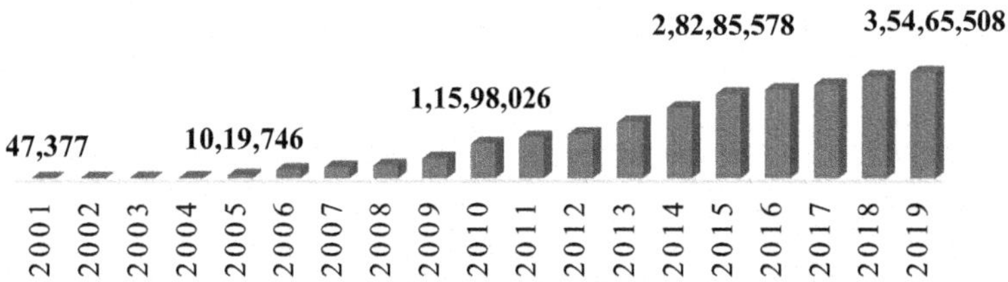

Fig. 1 Total passenger numbers at Istanbul Sabiha Gökçen International Airport (ISG 2019)

4.2 Pegasus Airlines: 2005–2019

The change in the ownership structure of Pegasus Airlines brought about a change in its business model. In 2005, the business model of Pegasus airlines was changed to low-cost business model after the acquisition by Esas Holding AS (Pegasus 2019d).

PGS-02 and PGS-07 also reported that Pegasus Airlines continued its charter flights for a while after it was acquired by Esas Holding AS. However, PGS-08 explained the reason of this change as "*this was because a period of transition was needed to prepare the necessary infrastructure.*" PGS-07 expressed that time as follows:

> During the charter period, we were questioning why we were not offering domestic scheduled flights. This was because there was a problem with taxation. Thanks to the efforts of the Ministry of Transport at the time, a new taxation regulation was introduced on the tickets and it then became feasible to fly domestic for the private sector. At that time I personally asked the Irish managers about this a lot, and they said that in a sector monopolized by Turkish Airlines (THY), you can only grow as much as THY wants you to grow, you will not grow where it does not want you to grow. They did not want to take this risk. I think Mr. Ali Sabancı also saw this risk and set up an entirely different model and picked Sabiha Gökçen Airport, which was an inactive airport.

Istanbul Sabiha Gökçen International Airport which is secondary airport in Istanbul is the main hub for Pegasus Airlines (CAPA 2018). Figure 1 shows its air passenger traffic growth after the flight operations of Pegasus Airlines.

In this process, PGS-07 noted that some meetings were held to discuss the characteristics of the airlines with low-cost airline business model and what needed to be done to achieve them. PGS-07 recalled:

> ...Well, we had defined ourselves as a low cost airline, but we asked ourselves the characteristics of the airlines flying by following the low cost model, we wondered what services they offered and how they manage these...For example low cost airlines sell the snacks, they don't give them for free, but we were not selling them, so we asked whose task that was... How long does it take for you to plan this? What does a low cost company do? It keeps the turnaround time low, but how many minutes should it be? A very big example (would be) how long does the turnaround take for the low cost airlines? 30 min. How long does it take us? One hour. The difference is 30 min. Who is responsible for this? ... How long would it take us to analyze this, and get it ready? We got all these figured out first. Step by step, we took an inventory of our status first....

As it is mentioned above, Turkish Airlines and other private airlines were not allowed to set their prices freely for their domestic flights but amendments to the price determination rules were enacted in 2001 and it gave the right to the airlines to determine the prices for the domestic flights (Gerede 2011). Majority of respondents emphasized that when the approach followed by government was dramatically changed in the 2000s, civil aviation in Turkey started to improve. In 2003, the Minister of Transport allowed competition in the domestic flights. Also, the majority of air services agreements were changed in order to provide for a multiple designation of airlines. For instance, the external factors influencing the evolution of a business model were succinctly summed up by PGS-04:

> liberalization…changes of the regulations.. the development of trade… visa abolition agreements with the countries, these are important factors…THY and Pegasus have benefited from these opportunities.

The shares of Esas Holding AS, one of the current partners of Pegasus Airlines, began to be publicly traded on the Istanbul Stock Exchange (ISE) in 2013. According to the final structure of partnership after the Initial Public Offering, 34.5% of shares are floating in Borsa Istanbul and 65.5% belongs to Esas Holding AS, whereas the rest is owned by Şevket Sabancı and his family (Pegasus 2019b). After this date, Pegasus Airlines introduced a unique business model named "*low-cost network carrier model.*" The differences of this model were explained by PGS-06:

> In 2010 we were actually providing transit routes…it was like hub-and-spoke network because we were carrying transit passengers…so we named our model as a "low-cost network carrier model".

Additionally, PGS-02 noted that:

> Yes, we use the low-cost-network business model, since we provide transit routes; we created it especially when Pegasus shares were traded on Borsa Istanbul, because, just like you do now, they were asking…We announced that we had developed a new model named "low-cost-network.

The reasons behind the changes were explained by PGS-03 as follows:

> We transfer the passenger from Europe to Istanbul during the day and we transfer them to East countries by night flights. Turkey has a geographical advantage. We couldn't say that it was "point-to-point" in the LCC definition, and turn down such an opportunity.

As this quote illustrates, country conditions can allow airline companies to attract new customers and fly to new destinations. Furthermore, all the interviewees highlight the importance of the geographical advantage of Istanbul for connecting flights. Due to its geographical location, Pegasus Airlines has been able to expand its network. Today, with its fleet composed of 83 aircraft, Pegasus Airlines flies to 109 destinations. Pegasus Airlines also owns two subsidiaries named Air Manas Company LLC and Pegasus Havacılık Teknolojileri ve Ticaret A.Ş. and two joint ventures named Pegasus Uçuş Eğitim Merkezi A.Ş. and Hitit Bilgisayar Hizmetleri A.Ş (Pegasus 2019b; c).

5 Concluding Remarks

From its date of establishment to 2005, Pegasus Airlines adopted a charter airline business model. However, the economic crises and regulations forced the company to change its business model. In 2005, the acquisition of Pegasus by Esas Holding AS and the government's support of private airlines in the Turkish civil aviation sector motivated Pegasus to enter the market with a new business model. The shares of Esas Holding AS, one of the current partners of Pegasus Airlines, began to be publicly traded on the Istanbul Stock Exchange, after which Pegasus Airlines decided that "low-cost-network business model" would be more appropriate to adopt due to the differences in their business models. The interviewees all agree that regulations, country conditions and state support are among the most important factors that affect the evolution of airline business model.

References

Adiloğlu-Yalçınkaya L (2019) Kurumsal Unsurların ve Kaynak Bağımlılıklarının Havayolu İş Modeli Değişimi Üzerindeki Etkileri: Türk Hava Yolları A.Ş. ve Pegasus Hava Taşımacılığı A. Ş. Örnekleri. Unpublished Ph.D. Thesis, Anadolu University

AerLingus (2019) About Aer Lingus. Retrieved from https://mediacentre.aerlingus.com/factsheet/about-aer-lingus

Amit R, Zott C (2001) Value creation in e-business. Strateg Manag J 22(6–7):493–520. https://doi.org/10.1002/smj.187

Application of Articles 92 and 93 of the EC Treaty and Article 61 of the EEA Agreement to State Aid in the Aviation Sector (1994).

Baden-Fuller C, Haefliger S (2013) Business models and technological innovation. Long Range Plan 46(6):419–426. https://doi.org/10.1016/j.lrp.2013.08.023

Bieger T, Agosti S (2017) Business models in the airline sector–evolution and perspectives. In: Albers S, Baum H, Auerbach S, Delfmann W (ed) Strategic management in the aviation industry. Routledge, pp 41–64

Bieger T, Wittmer A (2011) Airline strategy: from network management to business models. In: Bieger T, Müller R (eds) Aviation systems. Springer, pp 77–102

CAPA (2018) Sabiha Gökçen: growth to continue. Retrieved from https://centreforaviation.com/analysis/airline-leader/sabiha-gokcen-growth-to-continue-449781

Casadesus-Masanell R, Ricart JE (2010) From strategy to business models and onto tactics. Long Range Plan 43(2–3):195–215. https://doi.org/10.1016/j.lrp.2010.01.004

Chesbrough H, Rosenbloom RS (2002) The role of the business model in capturing value from innovation: evidence from Xerox Corporation's technology spin-off companies. Indus Corp Change 11(3):529–555. https://doi.org/10.1093/icc/11.3.529

Corbo L (2017) In search of business model configurations that work: Lessons from the hybridization of Air Berlin and JetBlue. J Air Transp Manag 64:139–150. https://doi.org/10.1016/j.jairtraman.2016.09.010

Daft J, Albers SJJoATM (2013) A conceptual framework for measuring airline business model convergence, 28, 47–54. https://doi.org/10.1016/j.jairtraman.2012.12.010

Daft J, Albers SJJoATM (2015) An empirical analysis of airline business model convergence, 46, 3–11. https://doi.org/10.1016/j.jairtraman.2015.03.008

DaSilva CM, Trkman PJLrp (2014) Business model: what it is and what it is not, 47(6):379–389. https://doi.org/10.1016/j.lrp.2013.08.004

Doganis R (2005) Airline business in the 21st century. Routledge
Factsheet (2018) Aer Lingus factsheet. Retrieved from https://mediacentre.aerlingus.com/factsheet/aer-lingus-milestones
Foss NJ, Saebi T (2015) Business models and business model innovation: bringing organization into the discussion. In: Foss NJ, Saebi TA (eds) Business model innovation the organizational dimension. Oxford University Press, UK
Foss NJ, Saebi T (2017) Fifteen years of research on business model innovation: how far have we come, and where should we go? J Manag 43(1):200–227. https://doi.org/10.1177/0149206316675927
Gerede E (2011) Türkiye'deki Havayolu Taşımacılığına İlişkin Ekonomik Düzenlemelerin Havayolu İşletmelerine Etkisinin Değerlendirilmesi. Celal Bayar Üniversitesi Sosyal Bilimler Dergisi 9(2):505–537
Gürses L (1992) Özel Sektör Havada İstikbal Bulamadı. Milliyet Newspaper, p 5
ISG (2019) ISG airport traffic report. Retrieved from https://www.sabihagokcen.aero/kurumsal-bilgiler/havalimani/havalimani-trafik-raporu
Kangis P, O'Reilly MD (2003) Strategies in a dynamic marketplace: a case study in the airline industry. J Bus Res 56(2):105–111. https://doi.org/10.1016/S0148-2963(01)00282-X
Kuyucak Şengür F, Şengür Y (2012) Havayolu İş Modelleri: Kavramsal Bir Analiz. Paper presented at the 20. Ulusal Yönetim ve Organizasyon Kongresi, İzmir
Lambert SC, Davidson RA (2013) Applications of the business model in studies of enterprise success, innovation and classification: an analysis of empirical research from 1996 to 2010. Eur Manag J 31(6):668–681. https://doi.org/10.1016/j.emj.2012.07.007
Lange K, Geppert M, Saka-Helmhout A, Becker-Ritterspach FJBJoM (2015) Changing business models and employee representation in the airline industry: a comparison of British Airways and Deutsche Lufthansa, 26(3):388–407. https://doi.org/10.1111/1467-8551.12096
Lohmann G, Koo TT (2013) The airline business model spectrum. J Air Transp Manag 31:7–9. https://doi.org/10.1016/j.jairtraman.2012.10.005
Magretta J (2002) Why business models matter. In: Harvard Business School, Boston
Massa L, Tucci CL, Afuah AJAoMA (2017) A critical assessment of business model research, 11(1), 73–104. https://doi.org/10.5465/annals.2014.0072
Milliyet (1994) Pegasus Havayolları Satıldı. Milliyet Newspaper, p 9
Milliyet (2003) Yapı Kredi'de Delux Satış. Milliyet Newspaper
Morris M, Schindehutte M, Allen J (2005) The entrepreneur's business model: toward a unified perspective. J Bus Res 58(6):726–735. https://doi.org/10.1016/j.jbusres.2003.11.001
O'Connell JF, Connolly DJTE (2017) The strategic evolution of Aer Lingus from a full-service airline to a low-cost carrier and finally positioning itself into a value hybrid airline, 23(6):1296–1320. 10.1177/1354816616683492
Osterwalder A, Pigneur Y (2004) An ontology for e-business models. In: Currie W (ed) Value creation from e-business models, vol 1. Butterworth-Heinemann, pp 65–97
Pegasus (2019a) Dünden Bugüne Pegasus. Retrieved from https://www.pegasusyatirimciiliskileri.com/tr/hakkimizda/dunden-bugune-pegasus
Pegasus (2019b) History of Pegasus. Retrieved from https://www.pegasusinvestorrelations.com/en/about-pegasus/about-pegasus
Pegasus (2019c) Pegasus airlines group companies. Retrieved from https://www.pegasusinvestorrelations.com/en/corporate-governance/group-companies
Pegasus (2019d) Pegasus business model. Retrieved from https://www.pegasusyatirimciiliskileri.com/tr/hakkimizda/urun-is-modeli
Pegasus (2019e) Pegasus primary agreement. Retrieved from https://www.pegasusyatirimciiliskileri.com/medium/image/pegasus-hava-tasimaciligi-as-ana-sozlesmesi_537/view.aspx
Sarılgan AE (2011) Türkiye'de bölgesel hava yolu taşımacılığının geliştirilmesi için yapılması gerekenler. Anadolu Üniversitesi Sosyal Bilimler Dergisi 11(1):69–88
"State Aid" (1993) Off J Eur Commun

Taşçı D, Yalçınkaya A (2015) Havayolu Sektöründe Yeni Bir İş Modeli: Bağlı Düşük Maliyetli Havayolu (Airline Within Airline) Modeli Ve Anadolujet Örneği Bağlamında Bir Karşılaştırma. Eskişehir Osmangazi Üniversitesi İİBF Dergisi 10(2):177–201

Teece DJ (2010) Business models, business strategy and innovation. Long Range Plan 43(2–3):172–194

TIM (2018) Retrieved from https://www.tim.org.tr/tr/basin-odasi-gundem-500-buyuk-hizmet-ihracatcisi-odulleri-sahiplerini-buldu.html

Turkish Civil Aviation Law (1983)

Urban M, Klemm M, Ploetner KO, Hornung M (2018) Airline categorisation by applying the business model canvas and clustering algorithms. J Air Transp Manag 71:175–192. https://doi.org/10.1016/j.jairtraman.2018.04.005

Walulik J (2016) At the core of airline foreign investment restrictions: a study of 121 countries. Transp Policy 49:234–251. https://doi.org/10.1016/j.tranpol.2016.05.006

Wensveen JG, Leick RJJoATM (2009) The long-haul low-cost carrier: a unique business model, 15(3), 127–133. https://doi.org/10.1016/j.jairtraman.2008.11.012

Whiteside R (2012) Major financial Institutions of Europe 1994. Graham and Trotman, UK

Yalçınkaya A (2018) Devlet, aktör ve değişim: 1983–2013 yılları arası Türk havayolu taşımacılığı alanında kurumsal değişim. Unpublished Ph.D. Thesis, Anadolu University

Yalçınkaya A (2019) Türk Havayolu Taşımacılığı Sektörünün Tarihsel Gelişimi ve Devlet Müdahaleleri (1933–2006). Cumhuriyet Tarihi Araştırmaları Dergisi 15(29):405–442

Yin R (2016) Qualitative research from start to finish, 2nd ed. The Guılford Press, New York

Zott C, Amit R, Massa L (2011) The business model: recent developments and future research. J Manag 37(4):1019–1042. https://doi.org/10.1177/0149206311406265

Zott C, Amit RJOs (2007) Business model design and the performance of entrepreneurial firms, 18(2):181–199. https://doi.org/10.1287/orsc.1060.0232

Decision-Making Approaches in Financial Institutions: The Case of European Banks

MCDM Approach for Assessment of Financial Performance of Serbian Banks

Ivana Marjanović and Žarko Popović

Abstract The significance and role of the banking sector for the development of national economy define the need for continuous monitoring of the performance of banks. The banking sector in the Republic of Serbia has undergone considerable changes in recent decades. The contemporaneous trend of liberalization enabled the entry of foreign capital which led to an increase in competition, and the issue of the financial performance of banks got significant attention. Adequate evaluation of banks' financial performance may provide useful guidelines to bank managers during decision-making. The problem of banks' financial performance assessment can be defined as a multi-criteria decision-making (MCDM) problem since the bank needs to check and oversee an extensive set of performance indicators. Therefore, MCDM techniques can be a useful tool for the evaluation of the financial performance of banks. In this paper, the financial performance of all banks that operated in the Republic of Serbia during the period from 2012 until 2017 was assessed using an integrated model combining the CRITIC method and the TOPSIS method. The analysis consists of two steps: in the first step, criteria weights are obtained by the CRITIC method while in the second step the ranking is performed using the TOPSIS method.

Keywords CRITIC method · TOPSIS method · Financial performance · Banks

---

I. Marjanović (✉) · Ž. Popović
Faculty of Economics, University of Niš, Trg Kralja Aleksandra Ujedinitelja, Nis, Serbia
e-mail: ivana.veselinovic@eknfak.ni.ac.rs

Ž. Popović
e-mail: zarko.popovic@eknfak.ni.ac.rs

A. Horobet et al. (eds.), *Business Performance and Financial Institutions in Europe*, Contributions to Economics, https://doi.org/10.1007/978-3-030-57517-5_5

1 Introduction

The banking sector is of vital importance to the national economy. Banks represent intermediaries whose primal role are a collection of funds and their further investment into profitable projects to achieve sustainable economic growth and development. Difficulties in the financial sector can cause disturbances in the economy, which can cause difficulties for non-financial companies to acquire resources and subsequently bound their possibilities for intended investment and enlargement. A proper examination of the bank's operations in contemporary conditions turns out to be indispensable, principally due to the severe competition caused by the modern tendencies reflected in globalization and liberalization. Since there is a mutual interdependence among performances of the banking sector and national economy, the constant evaluation and monitoring of a bank's performance concern various society sections. Evaluation of a bank's performance provides an important outcome for different stakeholders (such as investors and creditors) because it provides information about the banks' competitiveness in the sector and points out to the weaknesses but also opportunities for improvement.

Various financial ratios can be used for the evaluation of the bank's performance. However, they measure only one segment of business performance (profitability, liquidity, financial soundness, etc.). Therefore, to assess the overall financial performance of the bank, it is appropriate to integrate different ratios into unique measure using selected multiple criteria decision-making methods.

For that reason, the principal objective of this paper is to offer a comprehensive framework which can be used for evaluation of banks' financial performance. To achieve the stated objective, the key indicators of banks' financial performance will be analysed. The subject of the analysis will encompass all banks in the Republic of Serbia, which have operated constantly during the period from 2012 until 2017. The analysis will be constructed as a two-stage procedure. In the first stage, weight coefficients of the criteria will be determined by using the CRITIC method. In the second stage, an examination of the bank's financial performance and its ranking will be conducted using the TOPSIS method.

The paper contributes to the empirical literature in the field of the bank's financial performance evaluation by proposing a new approach for the financial performance assessment of banks on the example of banks operating in the Republic of Serbia.

The rest of the paper is structured so that, in addition to the introduction and conclusion, it contains the following components: (1) literature review; (2) characteristics of the banking sector in the Republic of Serbia; (3) methodology and data; and (4) results and discussion.

2 Literature Review

Numerous methods were applied to assess the bank's performance and ranking of banks.

One of the most used methods is ratio analysis. Kumbirai and Webb (2010) examined the performance of the five largest South Africa's commercial banks during the period from 2005 to 2009. As the measurements of liquidity, profitability and credit quality, they have used financial ratios. Their findings reveal that generally bank performance increased considerably in the first two years of the analysis, reached the peak during 2008–2009 followed by a fall in profitability, liquidity and credit quality in the South African banking sector. Alkhatib and Harasheh (2012) investigated the financial performance of five Palestinian commercial banks using several financial indicators (ROA, price/book value of equity and economic value added). They have also conducted correlation and multiple regression analysis of annual time series data from 2005 to 2010 to capture the impact of bank size, credit risk, operational efficiency and asset management on financial performance measured by the three indicators, and to create a good-fit regression model to predict the future financial performance of these banks. Uwuigbe and Fakile (2012) wanted to investigate the bond between corporate governance and financial performance of banks in a developing economy such as Nigeria. Results of the analysis show banks with a lower board size (less than 13) are more workable than the banks with board size beyond 13. Additionally, banks with larger boards obtained lower profits compared to the banks with smaller boards. Consequently, they have concluded that there is a significant negative relation between board size and bank financial performance. Aebi et al. (2012) inspected whether risk management-related corporate governance mechanisms are linked with an enhanced bank performance during the financial crisis of 2007/2008 using financial ratios. The findings reveal that in banks such mechanisms show significantly higher stock returns and ROE during the crisis. In contrast, standard corporate governance variables are mostly insignificantly or even negatively related to the banks' performance during the crisis.

Bank's performance can also be assessed using the CAMELS rating. CAMELS rating system encompasses six elements: capital adequacy, asset quality, management, earnings, liquidity and sensitive to market list. Wanke et al. (2016) evaluated the performance of 128 OECD banks over the period from 2004 to 2013 using various financial criteria that match the CAMELS rating system. The analysis consisted of three steps. In the first step, they have identified the key elements within each CAMELS criterion. In the second step, the TOPSIS method was applied to the identified elements to obtain a measure of bank performance. In the third step, censored quantile regressions are used to evaluate determinants of bank's performance. Dincer et al. (2011) evaluated the financial performance of state, private and foreign banks using CAMELS ratios during the 2008 global crisis and showed that CAMELS ratios encompass significant factors which reflect results of banking sector performance. Sangmi and Nazir (2010) estimated the financial performance of the two major banks operating in northern India using CAMEL ratings and discovered that the position of the analysed banks was sound and satisfactory concerning the stated ratios. Dash and Das (2009) investigated whether public sector banks outperform private/foreign banks using the CAMELS framework on a sample of Indian banks during five financial years. The findings indicate that private/foreign banks have far better performance than public sector banks on most of the CAMELS factors during the observed period.

Data envelopment analysis (DEA) is also one of the most commonly used methods to measure bank performance. Memić and Škaljić-Memić (2013) wanted to assess the bank's efficiency during the period from 2008 until 2010 using a modified DEA model to combine several financial indicators in a single efficiency measure. The obtained results reveal that the efficiency of banks was fluctuating during the stated period. Furthermore, they showed that there is no substantial difference among performances of banks in different entities of Bosnia and Herzegovina and smaller and larger banks. Jemric and Vujcic (2002) investigated bank efficiency on a sample of Croatian banks over the period 1995–2000 by using the DEA. Their findings indicate that foreign-owned banks are on average most efficient, that new banks are more efficient than old and that smaller banks are globally efficient, but large banks are efficient in the models with variable-returns-to-scale. Staub et al. (2010) examined cost, technical and allocative efficiencies for Brazilian banks in the period from 2000 to 2007 by using DEA. Brazilian banks were found to have low levels of cost-efficiency compared to banks in Europe and the USA. Evidence also indicates that state-owned banks are considerably more cost-efficient than private/foreign banks. There is no indication of dissimilarities in cost-efficiency due to the type of activity and bank size. Aggelopoulos and Georgopoulos (2017) examined efficiency change of bank branches under external environment deterioration by using bootstrap input-oriented profit DEA covering the period from January 2006 to July 2016. Their results indicate that early and deep recession reduces on average branch network efficiency and that branch size and location influence efficiency scores.

Also, various multi-criteria methods can be applied in performance evaluation of banks. Rezaei and Ketabi (2016) have evaluated the financial performance of private banks using fuzzy AHP method and TOPSIS method based on the set of indicators including equity, portfolio, sources, liquid asset, cash, net interest income and core business income. Kosmidou and Zopounidis (2008) assessed the performance of the commercial and cooperative banks in Greece during the period 2003–2004 based on the wide set of indicators. Based on evaluated performances, they created a ranking list which could be used to analyse the strengths and weaknesses of a bank compared to its competitors. Kosmidou et al. (2006) used the PAIRCLAS methodology to investigate the performance of UK small and large banks over multiple criteria, such as asset quality, capital adequacy, liquidity and efficiency/profitability in a multivariate environment during the period 1998–2002. Kosmidou et al. (2004) examined the performance of the UK banking sector to test the hypothesis of the higher performance of the domestic banks in a developed market. They have applied the UTilities Additives DIScriminantes (UTADIS) methodology to compare domestic and foreign banks' performance based on multiple criteria, such as profitability, liquidity, risk and efficiency, on a data sample covering 26 domestic and 32 foreign banks operating in the UK over the period 1998 to 2001. The outcomes of the analysis reveal that in the case of UK domestic banks achieve higher performance compared to foreign banks. Seçme et al. (2009) applied a fuzzy multi-criteria decision model to evaluate the performances of Turkish banks. They have examined the five largest commercial banks and evaluated their performance using several financial and non-financial indicators. Integrated fuzzy AHP and TOPSIS method was applied. Criteria weights were obtained using FAHP, while assessment of bank performance and ranking was attained using the TOPSIS method. Their findings suggest that both financial and non-financial performances should be taken into account in the process of evaluation of bank performance. Doumpos and Zopounidis (2010) have implemented the methodology based on the PROMETHEE II method and evaluated bank performance. Stankevičienė and Mencaitė (2012) applied the AHP model to assess the performance of banks. They have created a wide set of indicators and evaluated their relative significance afterwards which they have assessed the performance of banks, obtained their ranking and recognized the banks taking leading positions in the market. Akkoç and Vatansever (2013) have assessed the financial performance of twelve commercial banks in Turkey using seventeen financial performance indicators grouped into several categories: capital ratios, asset quality, liquidity, profitability, branch ratios and activity ratios. They have applied fuzzy AHP and fuzzy TOPSİS methods, and the results reveal that the applied two methods provide a similar ranking of banks. Wu et al. (2009) used a fuzzy MCDM (FMCDM) approach for evaluation of banking performance based on the 23 criteria identified using the BSC framework. The criteria weights were obtained by FAHP. Furthermore, three MCDM analytical tools (SAW, TOPSIS and VIKOR) were applied to obtain the bank performance. Cuong et al. (2018) have developed a multi-criteria decision-making model which integrated fuzzy AHP (FAHP) and fuzzy TOPSIS (FTOPSIS). Based on the proposed model, they have assessed and ranked five Vietnamese commercial banks. Gavurova et al. (2017) used a comprehensive set of methods to evaluate bank performance. They have evaluated and compared the performance of selected Czech and Slovak banks. Their results revealed that all of the applied methods have approximately the same results.

Regarding the analysis of banks' financial performance in the Republic of Serbia, several authors have researched this area. Mandić et al. (2014) evaluated banks' financial performance by using integrated fuzzy AHP and TOPSIS method on the sample which comprises entire banking sector in the Republic of Serbia over the period from 2005 until 2010. Stanujkić et al. (2013) investigated outcomes of several MCDM methods to give an overview of various MCDM methods which could be applied in the analysis of the financial performance of banks. Marinković and Radović (2014) examined bank-specific, industry-specific and macroeconomic factors of the net interest margin in the Serbian banking industry. Findings of the analysis indicate that among bank-specific factors equity-to-asset ratio and proxy for loan default risk have a statistically significant influence on NIM value. Regarding industry-specific determinants, only the proxy for concentration has significant influence on NIM.

3 Characteristics of the Banking Sector in the Republic of Serbia

The banking sector in the Republic of Serbia has experienced notable modifications in the last two decades, principally characterized by the formation of the developed banking system, reduction of the number of state banks and restoration of the population trust (Marjanović 2018). Preceding the reforms undertaken starting from 2001, Serbia banking sector was dealing with serious problems. Leading characteristics of the banking sector in that period were low profitability, high level of insolvency of the largest banks and the extraordinary amount of non-performing loans. The reform process marked the beginning of the banking sector improvement. Insolvent banks were liquidated, and foreign capital was permitted to enter the market. This has caused the reduction of the number of banks and enabled the creation of a competitive banking sector.

At present, 28 banks with work permit operate in the Republic of Serbia, with an organizational network of 1610 business units and 23,067 of employees (Banking Sector in Serbia: Report for the 3rd quarter of 2018). During the third quarter of 2018, the overall banking sector has operated profitably, wherein profit was recorded by 24 banks.

Regarding the structure of banking sector, it can be observed that ten banks control almost 80% of the market, measured in by the total balance sheet asset value, while twenty banks control almost 98% of the market (Table 1).

It can be concluded that the banking sector in the Republic of Serbia is highly consolidated. Additionally, reduction and consolidation of banking sector endorsed the enlargement of the banking sector profitability.

The trend of banking sector profitability growth can be observed after 2013 through analysis of ROA and ROE indicators (Fig. 1).

It can be observed that lowest values of ROA and ROE indicators were recorded in 2013 and since then their values have an upward trend (value of ROA was −0.07 in 2013 and 2.08 in 2017, while the value of ROE was −0.36 in 2013 and 10.57 in 2017), showing that presently banking sector has acceptable profitability rates. Regarding the attained level of capital adequacy indicators and the regulatory capital structure, the banking sector of Serbia has been satisfactorily capitalized. Serbian banking sector recorded an average value of capital adequacy indicators above 20% which is considerably beyond the prescribed minimum by the National Bank of Serbia (8%). In terms of liquidity, the Serbian banking sector has a significant surplus of liquid funds during a longer period.

The observed volatility of profitability indicator movement was primarily influenced by the macroeconomic environment. The indirect impact of the spillover of the global economic crisis on Serbia in 2009 resulted in a 3% drop in the gross domestic product (National Bank of Serbia 2010). During the crisis years, the Balkan region has been affected by financial instability in the euro area, whose adverse effects have particularly affected trade and foreign investment. Given that about 55 per cent of Serbia's foreign trade is performed with the European Union, the negative

Table 1 Balance sheet assets (in RSD), share in total balance sheet assets (%) and cumulative share (%) of banks in the Republic of Serbia

Bank	Total assets	Share (%)	Cumulative (%)
Banca Intesa	574,218,511.00	16.11	16.11
UniCredit Bank	417,137,136.00	11.71	27.82
Komercijalna banka	389,695,845.00	10.94	38.76
Société Générale Bank	300,960,522.00	8.45	47.20
Raiffeisen banka	284,249,317.00	7.98	55.18
AIK Bank	192,579,014.00	5.40	60.58
Erste Bank	192,538,987.00	5.40	65.99
Eurobank	163,028,297.00	4.58	70.56
Bank Poštanska štedionica	162,545,265.00	4.56	75.12
Vojvođanska banka	125,353,489.00	3.52	78.64
Sberbank	113,284,786.00	3.18	81.82
ProCredit Bank	108,864,954.00	3.06	84.88
Addiko	94,473,183.00	2.65	87.53
Crédit Agricole Bank	94,403,883.00	2.65	90.18
OTP Bank	78,401,522.00	2.20	92.38
Halkbank	52,826,539.00	1.48	93.86
NLB Bank	52,106,665.00	1.46	95.32
Piraeus Bank	37,071,864.00	1.04	96.36
Direktna Bank	28,250,838.00	0.79	97.16
Expobank	16,826,093.00	0.47	97.63
Opportunity Bank	16,442,236.00	0.46	98.09
Telenor Bank	15,344,846.00	0.43	98.52
JUBMES Bank	14,954,729.00	0.42	98.94
VTB Bank	11,030,248.00	0.31	99.25
MTS Bank	9,239,383.00	0.26	99.51
Srpska Bank	9,215,660.00	0.26	99.77
MIRA Bank	5,709,310.00	0.16	99.93
Bank of China	2,581,827.00	0.07	100.00

(continued)

Table 1 (continued)

Bank	Total assets	Share (%)	Cumulative (%)
Total	3,563,334,949.00	100.00	

Source Balance sheets and income statements

Fig. 1 ROA and ROE values for the banking sector. *Source* National Bank of Serbia

impact of the eurozone crisis has not bypassed Serbia, putting additional pressure on existing domestic economic problems. The instability of the macroeconomic environment, characteristic of Serbia's economy during the crisis, was reflected in negative economic growth, high and volatile inflation and high fiscal and external imbalances. Unemployment has increased, domestic demand has decreased, and the liquidity of the real economy has seen a significant decline. In these circumstances, the capacity of the business sector to borrow and repay loans has become largely limited. The level of non-performing loans has increased significantly, forcing banks to become extremely cautious about risk management and resort to conservative lending policy. To resolve these issues, several steps have been taken. The Government of the Republic of Serbia and the National Bank of Serbia have adopted in 2012, the Memorandum on the Dinarization Strategy of the Serbian Financial System, which aimed at increasing the degree of dinarization of the domestic financial system and reducing foreign exchange risk in the financial system. The Memorandum aimed to strengthen the confidence in the national currency and its greater use in the financial system. Also, in 2015, a strategy for resolution of non-performing loans was adopted. Due to the successful implementation of the strategy, as well as the growth of lending activity, the share of non-performing loans in total loans continues to show a declining trend. From the beginning of 2016 to September 2018, the level of non-performing loans decreased by more than 67%, which resulted in an improvement in the quality of banks' portfolios and the banking sector has recorded the lowest share of non-performing loans to total loans (Annual Report 2018a). In the monetary policy lessening cycle, launched in May 2013, the central bank repeatedly lowered its reference interest rate, and now the reference interest rate is at 3.0%, historically the lowest level. In the context of low inflation, the easing of monetary conditions made it possible to further lower interest rates on loans in dinars, which stimulated the revival of lending activity of banks. With low interest rates in the international market, strong competition among banks and strong economic growth, this trend fuelled overall lending activity, which increased by 6.1% during the first nine months of 2018 (Annual Report 2018a). During 2018, indicators of systemic stress and financial health indicate a period of extremely low risk, with a low and stable system component. Low inflationary pressures, favourable fiscal developments, capital inflows into Serbia, prudent monetary policy and a stable banking system have all contributed to maintaining and strengthening the resilience of the domestic financial system and the country's macroeconomic stability (National Bank of Serbia 2018).

4 Methodology and Data

A two-step analysis will be conducted to assess the financial performance of each of the banks during the observed period. The objective criteria weights will be determined during the first step. In the second step, the ranking of banks based on the financial performance will be constructed using the TOPSIS method.

4.1 Critic Method

CRiteria Importance Through Inter-criteria Correlation (CRITIC) is one of the possible ways to determine the objective values of the criteria weight coefficients which includes the intensity of the contrast and the conflict between the criteria inherent in the problems of multi-criteria decision-making (Milićević and Župac 2012). By analytical analysis of the decision-making matrix, CRITIC method determines the information content of each of the criteria. The process of determining the contrast within the criteria requires the use of a standard deviation of the normalized criteria values, as well as the correlation coefficients of all pairs of criteria (Milićević and Župac 2012).

The CRITIC method consists of six steps (Diakoulaki et al. 1995):

Step 1. Determination of standardized values r_{ij} using a relation for linear normalization:

$$r_{ij} = \frac{x_{ij} - x_{ij}^{\min}}{x_{ij}^{\max} - x_{ij}^{\min}} \tag{1}$$

where $x_{ij}^{\max} = \max\limits_{i} x_{ij}$ and $x_{ij}^{\min} = \min\limits_{i} x_{ij}$, $i = 1, 2, \ldots, m$, $j = 1, 2, \ldots, n$.

Step 2. Determination of the standard deviation σ_j of each vector r_j in a normalized decision matrix. Standard deviation represents the measure of the intensity of contrast for the observed criterion.

Step 3. Construction of a symmetric matrix of dimensions $n \times n$ with elements R_{ij} representing the correlation coefficients between each pair of normalized criteria in the model. Therefore, a greater difference between the criteria values leads to a lower value of the coefficient of correlation R_{ij} and vice versa.

Step 4. Determining the extent of the conflict between the criteria by applying the relation:

$$\sum_{j=1}^{n}(1 - R_{ij}) \tag{2}$$

Step 5. Determination of the amount of information C_j emitted by the jth criteria:

$$C_j = \sigma_j \sum_{j=1}^{n}(1 - R_{ij}) \tag{3}$$

The higher value of C_j points to a greater amount of information contained in the given criterion and, consequently, to its greater relative significance.

Step 6. Determination of the criteria weight coefficients by applying the relation:

$$w_j = \frac{C_j}{\sum_{j=1}^{n} C_j} \tag{4}$$

4.2 *TOPSIS Method*

The name TOPSIS represents the acronym of the Technique for Order of Preference by Similarity to Ideal Solution. It is a method of multi-criteria analysis developed by Hwang and Yoon in 1981 (Yoon and Hwang 1981).

The essence of this method is that the optimal solution should be closest to the positive-ideal solution, and furthest from the negative-ideal solution in the geometric sense (Todorović and Stanković 2011). In doing so, the ideal solution is the point where the utility for the decision-maker is greatest, that is, the point where the value of the revenue criteria is highest, while at the same time the value of the cost criteria is the lowest. The ideal solution is usually not feasible, but all methods of multi-criteria analysis tend to make the optimal solution as close as possible to the ideal one. Therefore, the optimal solution is the solution that meets most of the criteria.

The TOPSIS procedure can be represented by the following algorithm (Yoon and Hwang 1995):

Step 1. Determination of a normalized decision matrix with coefficients r_{ij}, where the coefficients are determined using the following relation:

$$r_{ij} = \frac{x_{ij}}{\sqrt{\sum_{i=1}^{m} x_{ij}^2}}, \quad i = 1, 2 \ldots m, \quad j = 1, 2 \ldots n \tag{5}$$

Step 2. Calculation of the coefficients v_{ij} which form a preferentially normalized matrix. The coefficients v_{ij} can be calculated as:

$$v_{ij} = r_{ij} \cdot w_j \tag{6}$$

Different methods can be applied in determining the weight coefficients, whereby the obtained preferences can be subjective or objective, depending on the applied method for determining the preferences of the decision-makers.

Step 3. The third step of the TOPSIS procedure includes determining a positive-ideal and negative-ideal solution. The elements of the positive-ideal solution $v_j{}^*$ and the negative-ideal solution $v_j{}^-$ are determined by relations:

$$\begin{aligned} A^* &= \left\{v_1^*, v_2^* \ldots v_j^* \ldots v_n^*\right\} \\ &= \left\{\left(\max_i v_{ij} | j \in J_1\right)\left(\min_i v_{ij} | j \in J_2\right), \quad i = 1, 2 \ldots m\right\} \end{aligned} \tag{7a}$$

$$\begin{aligned} A^- &= \left\{v_1^-, v_2^- \ldots v_j^- \ldots v_n^-\right\} \\ &= \left\{\left(\min_i v_{ij} | j \in J_1\right)\left(\max_i v_{ij} | j \in J_2\right), \quad i = 1, 2 \ldots m\right\} \end{aligned} \tag{7b}$$

where J_1 represents a set of revenue criteria and J_2 represents a set of cost criteria.

Step 4. The main step of TOPSIS procedure involves determination of the distance between the alternative and the positive-ideal solution on the one hand, and alternative and negative-ideal solution, on the other hand. The relation for determination of the distance of the alternative from the positive-ideal solution is given by the expression:

$$S_i^* = \sqrt{\sum_{j=1}^{n}\left(v_{ij} - v_j^*\right)^2}, \quad i = 1, 2 \ldots m \tag{8}$$

Conversely, the relation for determining the distance of the alternative from the negative-ideal solution is given by the expression:

$$S_i^- = \sqrt{\sum_{j=1}^{n} \left(v_{ij} - v_j^-\right)^2}, i = 1, 2 \ldots m \tag{9}$$

Step 5. The determination of the proximity index (C_i^*). The proximity index represents the relative proximity of the considered alternative to the positive-ideal solution and is defined as:

$$C_i^* = \frac{S_i^-}{S_i^* + S_i^-}, \quad i = 1, 2, \ldots m \tag{10}$$

where $0 \le C_i^* \le 1$. If the value of the proximity index is equal to zero, the alternative A_i coincides with the negative-ideal solution, while if it is equal to one the alternative A_i coincides with the positive-ideal solution.

Step 6. In the final step of the TOPSIS procedure, the ranking of alternatives is conducted based on the relative proximity index, where the best-ranked alternative is the one with the highest value of the relative proximity index.

4.3 Data

To conduct an analysis, the data from balance sheets and income statements of the specified 25 banks, which operated in Serbia during the period from 2012 to 2017, were used to analyse financial performance. After an examination of the relevant literature, six indicators were selected:

- Return on assets (ROA) represents one of the basic indicators of the bank's profitability. Based on this indicator, bank's management can assess its earning capacity. It is determined as the ratio of net profit and total assets.
- Capital adequacy ratio (CAR) denotes an indicator of a bank's financial stability. Its primal role is the protection of depositors and the promotion of financial efficiency and stability. The higher levels of CAR indicate enhanced safety of depositor's assets.
- Loan loss reserves to loans (LLRL) demonstrates the bank's capability to deal with losses caused by non-performing loans. It represents an indicator of loans' quality. The higher value of LLRL indicates a better ability of the bank to cover possible losses.
- Loans-to-deposits (LTD) ratio specifies the financial liquidity of the bank and shows the magnitude of sustainable credit activity growth. Higher levels of LTD could indicate the bank's greater risk exposure in the short term due to potential liquidity difficulties caused by unexpected deposit withdrawal. On the other hand, higher values of LTD may yield greater profitability; therefore, banks tend to increase this indicator.

- Net interest margin (NIM) denotes indicator of the bank's profitability. It is an especially important indicator for banks since it represents its earning capacity. The net interest margin quantifies the difference between the sum of interest paid to depositors and the amount of interest earned through the loaning of these funds.
- Cash and cash equivalent to deposits (CCED) represent an indicator of liquidity risk. It is expected that banks with a higher level of CCED have better ability to cope with a sudden deposit withdrawal.

5 Results and Discussion

In the first part of the financial performance index construction, CRITIC method has been used to determine the weights of the criteria in each of the observed years and the results are shown in Table 2.

According to the obtained results, the importance of all indicators through the years is changeable. However, some general conclusions can be drawn. It can be observed that the importance of profitability indicators and credit risk indicators for the assessment of overall bank performance dropped. On the other hand, liquidity indicators and indicators of financial soundness are now more important in the assessment of a bank's performance than they were five years ago.

The next stage in the analysis is the determination of a single measurement of bank's financial performances, based on the integration of the stated indicators, and ranking of banks consistent with the attained results (Table 3).

Obtained results indicate that through the years there have been a lot of fluctuations in achieved values of financial performance, so it cannot be concluded that there is a bank with superior financial performance in the analysed sample. Aggregation of the proximity index obtained using the TOPSIS method for each bank and all analysed years can provide a better insight into the overall ranking of banks in the Republic of Serbia (Table 4).

Based on the aggregated results, Raiffeisen banka had the best financial performance in the observed period based on the analysed financial performance indicators, followed by NLB Bank and UniCredit Bank. Further examination of Raiffeisen banka's business supports the results obtained using multi-criteria analysis. With a

Table 2 Criteria weights obtained by CRITIC method

Year	ROA	CAR	LLRL	LTD	NIM	CCED
2012	0.12685	0.12837	0.20939	0.18768	0.18629	0.16141
2013	0.17082	0.15600	0.14525	0.16990	0.16661	0.19143
2014	0.17818	0.14733	0.17414	0.16228	0.17127	0.16680
2015	0.15557	0.15218	0.13475	0.23778	0.13683	0.18289
2016	0.15006	0.14716	0.14173	0.19988	0.13556	0.22561
2017	0.13979	0.16692	0.17556	0.19048	0.13028	0.19698

Table 3 Financial performance and ranking of banks

Banks	2012		2013		2014		2015		2016		2017	
	Proximity index	Rank	Proximity index	Rank	Proximity index	Rank	Proximity index	Rank	Proximity index	Rank	Proximity index	Rank
Addiko bank	0.654602	9	0.618103	14	0.497142	8	0.468071	6	0.49647	11	0.46048	17
AIK	0.640077	12	0.622631	12	0.489368	12	0.270386	23	0.51776	8	0.47328	14
Credit Agricole	0.634176	14	0.585303	22	0.487948	14	0.403254	17	0.41252	18	0.48287	11
Direktna Bank	0.532609	18	0.592604	20	0.439207	24	0.346983	20	0.39438	20	0.48661	10
Erste Bank	0.312974	24	0.631193	10	0.479584	21	0.455904	8	0.55343	3	0.64594	2
Eurobank	0.558692	17	0.614153	16	0.509755	1	0.504700	2	0.55055	4	0.57743	3
Expobank	0.477860	21	0.613070	17	0.507494	2	0.469207	5	0.48452	14	0.50164	8
Halkbank	0.654625	8	0.567073	23	0.484678	17	0.426581	13	0.39521	19	0.49646	9
Banca Intesa	0.640532	11	0.618752	13	0.504874	3	0.481252	3	0.49137	13	0.40903	22
JUBMES Bank	0.734496	5	0.661747	9	0.502947	4	0.470875	4	0.51068	9	0.52911	5
Komercijalna banka	0.634768	13	0.612883	18	0.487370	15	0.426343	14	0.45200	17	0.42199	21
MTS Bank	0.615092	15	0.623353	11	0.488769	13	0.454503	9	0.49789	10	0.4619	16
NLB Bank	0.678288	6	0.616140	15	0.483655	18	0.617647	1	0.61555	2	0.47203	15
Opportunity Bank	0.415083	23	0.346826	25	0.453726	23	0.276609	22	0.22418	25	0.27584	25
OTP Bank	0.582949	16	0.589869	21	0.494674	10	0.463554	7	0.49238	12	0.45418	19
Bank Poštanska štedionica	0.503039	19	0.595221	19	0.486864	16	0.435085	12	0.45892	16	0.45555	18
ProCredit Bank	0.477457	22	0.542687	24	0.482493	20	0.436048	11	0.28888	24	0.34492	24

(continued)

Table 3 (continued)

Banks	2012		2013		2014		2015		2016		2017	
	Proximity index	Rank	Proximity index	Rank	Proximity index	Rank	Proximity index	Rank	Proximity index	Rank	Proximity index	Rank
Raiffeisen banka	0.853739	1	0.767696	2	0.498879	5	0.425507	15	0.52198	6	0.44119	20
Sberbank	0.786331	4	0.750016	5	0.474025	22	0.106954	25	0.52105	7	0.40533	23
Société Générale Bank	0.797889	2	0.742309	6	0.498503	6	0.339056	21	0.38054	21	0.51046	7
Srpska Bank	0.658449	7	0.758415	4	0.389102	25	0.212581	24	0.29012	23	0.47584	13
Telenor Bank	0.151507	25	0.808407	1	0.483169	19	0.416170	16	0.64318	1	0.78808	1
UniCredit Bank	0.646117	10	0.739830	7	0.498094	7	0.439046	10	0.54409	5	0.56728	4
Vojvođanska banka	0.491498	20	0.765645	3	0.495722	9	0.390675	18	0.46012	15	0.47817	12
VTB Bank	0.787309	3	0.726398	8	0.493370	11	0.382846	19	0.37257	22	0.51390	6

Table 4 Overall ranking of banks

Banks	Aggregate value of proximity index	Rank
Raiffeisen banka	0.585020063	1
NLB Bank	0.580555009	2
UniCredit Bank	0.572707560	3
JUBMES Bank	0.568368653	4
Eurobank	0.552657624	5
Telenor Bank	0.548526910	6
VTB Bank	0.546221289	7
Société Générale Bank	0.544933299	8
Addiko bank	0.532558585	9
Banca Intesa	0.524416106	10
MTS Bank	0.523665184	11
Vojvođanska banka	0.513825864	12
Erste Bank	0.513206921	13
OTP Bank	0.513055357	14
Expobank	0.509037382	15
Sberbank	0.507369589	16
Komercijalna banka	0.505961548	17
Halkbank	0.504164622	18
AIK Bank	0.502286847	19
Credit Agricole	0.501058131	20
Bank Poštanska štedionica	0.489164463	21
Direktna Bank	0.465479641	22
Srpska Bank	0.464257112	23
ProCredit Bank	0.428836897	24
Opportunity Bank	0.332069906	25

market share of around 8.7% in the cash loan segment, Raiffeisen banka occupies one of the leading positions in the market (Annual Report 2018b). During 2018, growth in new placements was over 20% compared to the previous year. The corporate segment managed to significantly increase both the portfolio assets and the volume of liabilities, maintaining a rigorous approach to risk from previous years, resulting in a significant improvement in portfolio quality and a large decrease of non-performing loans. In the segment of micro-enterprises and entrepreneurs, in 2018, a significant increase of the most important business parameters compared to the previous year was achieved: the number of new clients increased by 17%, credit portfolio by 39% and customer deposits by 25% (Annual Report 2018b). All this resulted in a 29% increase in total micro-segment revenue compared to the previous year. Profit before tax in 2018 amounted to EUR 64.6 million, which is 4% more than in the previous year. This proves that Raiffeisen banka has successfully responded to all the challenges and changes in the market.

Regarding the proposed method based on the application of multi-criteria analysis for the evaluation of banks' financial performance, it defers from other usually applied methods in practice. Among the vast number of performance measures for banks used by academics and practitioners alike, a distinction can be made among traditional, economic and market-based measures of performance (ECB 2010). Nevertheless, most of these measures mainly relate to only one aspect of the business and involve the analysis and evaluation of only one indicator. Gavurova et al. (2017) state that existing methodologies of credit rating agencies along with present methodologies applied by the European Central Bank are currently unadjusted to measure the performance of banks in modern conditions.

In today's market conditions, the use of multi-criteria analysis methods enables prompt assessments, allowing the management of a bank or controller to provide rapid response to the situation (Ginevičius and Podviezko 2013). The advantage of applying multi-criteria analysis methods over ordinary ratio analysis is that several criteria can be taken into account during the evaluation, whereby the banks subject to the assessment are compared with each other in terms of each criterion (Gavurova et al. 2017). It is often the case that a bank that has been identified as the best based on a single criterion by ratio analysis is not the best when all criteria are taken into account. Also, the advantage of multi-criteria methods is that there is no limit on the number of criteria that can be evaluated.

An evaluation based on the methodology presented can be very useful to different stakeholders. On the one hand, presenting business performance with a single metrics can facilitate the interpretation of the bank's general position to both, the bank's management and its clients. On the other hand, the results obtained can also be used for regulatory purposes since they indicate banks that may face difficulties in operating shortly. Also, the proposed methodology indicates the areas of business that require particular attention. According to the identified criteria weights, liquidity indicators and indicators of financial soundness are becoming increasingly important for the assessment of financial performance. Therefore, the results of this study can provide useful guidelines to bank managers as well as government authorities. Bank managers may improve the bank's financial performance by adequate risk management, particularly by controlling liquidity and solvency risks. Furthermore, government authorities should continue efforts to create and maintain a stable macroeconomic environment in which banks will operate profitably and sustainably and thus help further stabilization of the economy.

The proposed approach for assessing bank performance can be broadly implemented and involve several economic variables, at the micro- or macroeconomic level. Consequently, evaluation of financial performance may be focused on the bank's branches, on certain financial services within the bank as well as the performance of the entire banking sector.

6 Conclusion

The banking sector in the Republic of Serbia has undergone extensive changes in recent decades. Due to increased competition caused by liberalization and the entry of foreign capital, the issue of the bank's financial performance gained notable attention. Proper evaluation of banks' financial performance could offer valuable information to bank managers. The usage of multiple criteria decision-making tools could provide them with useful guidelines during decision-making.

Therefore, a comprehensive analysis of the financial performance of banks in the Republic of Serbia was conducted using integrated CRITIC-TOPSIS method. Obtained results could be used by bank managers to evaluate the performance of a specific bank through a single measure. The main advantage of this approach is reflected in the fact that usage of a single financial ratio, or group of ratios analysed separately, could lead to misleading conclusions. The proposed approach gives a unique measure of financial performance obtained through the integration of several financial ratios.

However, the results should be interpreted carefully since they depend on the selected set of indicators and used multiple criteria methods. Usage of different indicators and methods could produce different results. The proposed methodology aims to point out at the possibilities and benefits of applying methods of multi-criteria analysis, where further research is needed to find the best set of indicators and methods to be used for assessment of bank's financial performance.

The research is faced with the usual limitations related to the nature of the data from financial statements since their reliability depends on the respect of basic principles of financial reporting.

The study could be extended in a variety of directions. One of the possible further research directions could be to analyse the influence of different methods and different sets of indicators on the ranking of the banks. The second possible direction could be focused on the extension of the sample with the data from the years before 2012 and examining relevant determinants that can affect the financial performance of banks using multiple regression analysis.

Acknowledgements The paper is a part of the research done within the projects 179066 and 179013 funded by the Ministry of Education, Science and Technology of the Republic of Serbia.

References

Aebi V et al (2012) Risk management, corporate governance, and bank performance in the financial crisis. J Bank Finance 36(12):3213–3226

Annual Report (2018a) Banca Intesa—Annual Report for 2018. https://www.bancaintesa.rs/upload/Godi_nji_izve_taj_2018.pdf. (28.11.2019)

Annual Report (2018b) Raiffeisen bank—Annual Report (2018) https://www.raiffeisenbank.rs/wp-content/uploads/2018/07/AR-2018-WEB.pdf (29.11.2019)

Aggelopoulos E, Georgopoulos A (2017) Bank branch efficiency under environmental change: a bootstrap DEA on monthly profit and loss accounting statements of Greek retail branches. Eur J Oper Res 261(3):1170–1188

Akkoç S, Vatansever K (2013) Fuzzy performance evaluation with AHP and Topsis methods: evidence from Turkish banking sector after the global financial crisis. Eurasian J Bus Econ 6(11):53–74

Alkhatib A, Harasheh M (2012) Financial performance of Palestinian commercial banks. Int J Bus Soc Sci 3(3):175–184

Balance Sheets and Income Statements, https://www.nbs.rs/internet/latinica/50/50_5.html, (10.03.2019)

Banking sector in Serbia: Report for the 3rd quarter of 2018, https://www.nbs.rs/internet/latinica/55/55_4/kvartalni_izvestaj_III_18.pdf, (19.03.2019)

Cuong DX et al (2018) Multi-criteria Decision-making model evaluating the performance of Vietnamese commercial banks. Int J Finan Res 9(1):132–141

Dash M, Das A (2009) A CAMELS analysis of the Indian banking industry. Available at SSRN 1666900, pp 1–10

Diakoulaki D et al (1995) Determining objective weights in multiple criteria problems: the CRITIC method. Comput Oper Res 22(7):763–770

Dincer H et al (2011) A performance evaluation of the Turkish banking sector after the global crisis via CAMELS ratios. Procedia-Soc Behav Sci 24:1530–1545

Doumpos M, Zopounidis C (2010) A multicriteria decision support system for bank rating. Decis Support Syst 50(1):55–63

ECB (2010) Beyond ROE—how to measure bank performance. Appendix to the report on EU banking structures, European Central Bank, https://www.ecb.europa.eu/pub/pdf/other/beyondroe howtomeasurebankperformance201009en.pdf

Gavurova B et al (2017) Comparison of selected methods for performance evaluation of Czech and Slovak commercial banks. J Bus Econ Manag 18(5):852–876

Ginevičius R, Podviezko A (2013) The evaluation of financial stability and soundness of Lithuanian banks. Econ Res-Ekonomska Istraživanja 26(2):191–208

Jemric I, Vujcic B (2002) Efficiency of banks in Croatia: a DEA approach. Comp Econ Stud 44(2–3):169–193

Kosmidou K et al (2004) Foreign versus domestic banks' performance in the UK: a multicriteria approach. CMS 1(3–4):329–343

Kosmidou K et al (2006) Assessing performance factors in the UK banking sector: a multicriteria methodology. CEJOR 14(1):25–44

Kosmidou K, Zopounidis C (2008) Measurement of bank performance in Greece. South-Eastern Europe J Econ 1(1):79–95

Kumbirai M, Webb R (2010) A financial ratio analysis of commercial bank performance in South Africa. Afr Rev Econ Finan 2(1):30–53

Mandic K et al (2014) Analysis of the financial parameters of Serbian banks through the application of the fuzzy AHP and TOPSIS methods. Econ Model 43:30–37

Marinković S, Radović O (2014) Bank net interest margin related to risk, ownership and size: an exploratory study of the Serbian banking industry. Econ Res-Ekonomska Istraživanja 27(1):134–154

Marjanović I (2018) The evaluation of bank's financial performance and its determinants: a case study on Serbia. In: Karabašević D, Vukotić S, Maksimović M (eds) Innovation as an initiator of the development inovations—basic for development. Faculty of Applied Management, Economy and Finance Belgrade, pp 367–391

Memić D, Škaljić-Memić S (2013) Performance analysis and benchmarking of commercial banks operating in Bosnia and Herzegovina: a DEA approach. Bus Syst Res 4(2):17–37

Milićević MR, Župac GŽ (2012) An objective approach to determining criteria weights. Vojnotehnički Glasnik 60(1):39–56

National Bank of Serbia (2010) Report on the state of the financial system (In Serbian). https://nbs.rs/internet/latinica/90/90_2/finansijski_sistem_2010.pdf, (28.11.2019)
National Bank of Serbia (2018) Annual Report on the stability of the financial system (In Serbian). https://www.nbs.rs/internet/latinica/90/90_2/finansijska_stabilnost_2018.pdf, (28.11.2019)
Rezaei M, Ketabi S (2016) Ranking the banks through performance evaluation by integrating fuzzy AHP and TOPSIS methods: a study of Iranian private banks. Int J Acad Res Account Finan Manag Sci 6(3):19–30
Sangmi MUD, Nazir T (2010) Analyzing financial performance of commercial banks in India: application of CAMEL model. Pak J Comm Soc Sci (PJCSS) 4(1):40–55
Seçme NY et al (2009) Fuzzy performance evaluation in Turkish banking sector using analytic hierarchy process and TOPSIS. Expert Syst Appl 36(9):11699–11709
Stankevičienė J, Mencaitė E (2012) The evaluation of bank performance using a multicriteria decision making model: a case study on Lithuanian commercial banks. Technol Econ Dev Econ 18(1):189–205
Stanujkić D et al (2013) Comparative analysis of some prominent MCDM methods: a case of ranking Serbian banks. Serb J Manag 8(2):213–241
Staub RB et al (2010) Evolution of bank efficiency in Brazil: a DEA approach. Eur J Oper Res 202(1):204–213
Todorović O, Stanković J (2011) TOPSIS method as a means of optimizing decision-making in crisis conditions (in Serbian). Faculty of Economics, Nauka i svetska ekonomska kriza, Niš
Uwuigbe OR, Fakile AS (2012) The effects of board size on financial performance of banks: A study of listed banks in Nigeria. Int J Econ Finan 4(2):260–267
Yoon PK, Hwang CL (1981) Multiple attribute decision making methods and applications: A state-of-the-art survey. Lecture notes in economics and mathematical systems. Berlin: Springer-Verlag
Yoon KP, Hwang CL (1995) Multiple attribute decision making: an introduction, vol 104. Sage publications
Wanke P et al (2016) Efficiency factors in OECD banks: a ten-year analysis. Expert Syst Appl 64:208–227
Wu HY et al (2009) A fuzzy MCDM approach for evaluating banking performance based on balanced scorecard. Expert Syst Appl 36(6):10135–10147

Digital Banking in the New Era: Exploring Customers' Attitudes

Stavros Valsamidis, Lambros Tsourgiannis, Dimosthenis Pappas, and Eirini Mosxou

Abstract The digitalization of banking sector is a direct consequence of the overall digitalization of the economy. Today's demand is anytime anywhere banking. This requires innovative, robust, secure, optimized and ready to meet the expectations of empowered and tech-savvy customers. As a result of these changes, it is important to capture the new reality in relation to the banking environment, through the views of customers. This study aims to explore customers' attitudes towards the use of digital services and applications in banking sector. In particular, it aims to identify the factors that affect customers' attitudes towards those applications, to classify them into groups according to their similar behaviour patterns and to profile each group of customers according to their demographic characteristics and other factors. Principal component analysis (PCA) was conducted to identify the main factors that affect citizens' attitudes towards the use of digital services and applications in banking sector. Cluster analysis was performed to classify citizens into groups with similar behaviour whilst discriminant analysis conducted to check cluster predictability. Non-parametric tests performed to profile each group of customers according to their demographic characteristics and other factors. PCA identified three main factors that customers' attitudes towards those applications: (a) better service, (b) cautiousness and (c) timelines/directness. Cluster analysis classified customers into three groups according to their purchasing behaviour towards the use of those digital services/applications (i) those that are in favour of, (ii) opportunists and (iii)

S. Valsamidis (✉) · D. Pappas · E. Mosxou
Department of Accounting and Finance, International University of Greece, Campus of Kavala, 65404 Agios Loukas, Kavala, Greece
e-mail: svalsam@teikav.edu.gr

D. Pappas
e-mail: dpappas@teiemt.gr

E. Mosxou
e-mail: irini_m@otenet.gr

L. Tsourgiannis
Department Directorate of Public Health and Social Care of Regional District of Xanthi, Region of Eastern Macedonia and Thrace, Xanthi, Greece
e-mail: ltsourgiannis@gmail.com

A. Horobet et al. (eds.), *Business Performance and Financial Institutions in Europe*, Contributions to Economics, https://doi.org/10.1007/978-3-030-57517-5_6

sceptical. Chi-square analysis indicated that demographic characteristics such as gender, age, education, marital status, income have an impact on customers' particular behaviour. Furthermore, Friedman non-parametric test identified that some other opinion of customers regarding the use of digital applications in comparison with those of traditional banking services are also related with their behaviour towards those digital banking applications.

Keywords Digital banking · Customers · Questionnaire · Principal component analysis · Cluster analysis · Discriminant analysis

Jel Classification G21 · L86

1 Introduction

The last 10 years technology has undergone tremendous progress. The ways of communication have changed radically and everything is easier to be transferred or uploaded (Fenton 2016). Social media and applications are widely used as they provide numerous services which can make life simpler (Li et al. 2015). Traditional banking services which used to be costly have transformed to adopt this digital-era (Dery et al. 2017). Banking industry is at a border of a massive digital transformation and automatization (Hirt and Willmott 2014). Many banks tried to keep up one step ahead and launched various initiatives of different scales (Courbe and Lyons 2016). Banks are now feeling the full force of digital disruption, which made its presence known a few years ago (Martino and Schaffner 2015). The implications of such a revolution were unknown and there was no clear direction about the changes required to efficiently weather the transition into the digital world. Nevertheless, many banks tried to keep one step ahead and launched various initiatives of differing scales (McKinsey & Company et al. 2017).

Today's customers are more sophisticated and tech-savvy, and to cater to their specific needs, each customer needs a unique experience from banking (Venkateswari 2018). They want the companies to understand their unstated needs as well as their likes (Härle et al. 2016). Thus, it should come as no surprise that these customers are expecting similar kinds of response and service from banking institutions too. From researching new services, opening an account, checking balance, conducting transactions, loans, credits, wealth management, customer support, delivering experience has become a key to success in this competitive market place (Kamra 2014). As a result of this, banks are becoming more digitally oriented in order to satisfy their customers' new preferences and demands (Ortstad and Sonono 2017).

Even in the face of growing expectations and competition, financial services institutions remain in the best position to be at the centre of customers' financial lives (Hough and Chan, 2018). To fully capitalize on that opportunity, they will need to enhance and innovate products that deliver the just-in-time and just-in-case experiences customers crave (McKinsey & Company et al. 2017). Financial institutions will also need to renew their education focus in order to dispel myths, build awareness and drive adoption and they will need to market the most salient value propositions of their products to potential new users. There is little doubt that customers need and want digital banking services. The only real question is who will be the first to deliver the solutions they want most (Cuesta et al. 2015). Traditional retail banking models with costly full-service branch infrastructure and limited integrated digital channels are transforming to adapt to the digital era. This evolution has driven increased customer expectations around turnaround times, availability of customer service, a superior customer experience and ongoing competitive pricing. The banking landscape is changing rapidly and innovative models are being tested and deployed as an attempt by Financial Services companies to remain relevant in the digital era (Cuesta et al. 2015).

Digital transformation differs from every industry and company. In general terms, it is the integration of digital technology into all areas of a business. That integration leads to fundamental changes in how the business operates and delivers value to its customers (Rieker 2018).

Over the last decade, the impacts of digital technologies on business have changed significantly, rendering many business models obsolete. Accordingly, digital transformation—namely, the integration of digital technologies into business processes—has become increasingly imperative for contemporary organizations seeking to survive and attain competitive advantages in a digital economy (Bharadwaj et al. 2013).

According to Yousafzai and Yani-de-Soriano (2012) the development of the Internet and mobile technologies has influenced the transformation of many industrial branches, including particular economies. The increasing use of mobile phones and the use of the Internet have changed many industries, including banking. Digital transformation is about more than just providing online and mobile functionality (Gupta, 2013).

The implementation of e-banking projects highlights the importance of digital transformation for contemporary organizations in order to survive and achieve competitive advantage in a digital economy (Sullivan et al. 2014). For example, many banks are now implementing e-banking projects in order to pursue competitive advantage (Shah and Siddiqui 2006). Banks running on a digital core can see reduced costs and streamlined processes (Liu et al. 2011). This end-to-end integration also helps provide a more seamless, engaging customer experience. And it makes room for further business transformation with new digital technologies like blockchain and artificial intelligence (Rieker 2018).

As reported by Kolodinsky et al. (2004) both theoretical and empirical literature related to the general adoption of technology provides a framework to examine the adoption of e-banking technologies. If the promise of increased efficiency for the banking industry and increased convenience and service for the consumer is to be realized, then understanding the factors that affect the acceptance of new products will allow businesses to create a climate in which technological advances with real advantages can be embraced by the majority instead of just a few techno-savvy customers. Empirically, they examine whether and how the characteristics that describe the adoption of new innovations are related to customer adoption of e-banking technologies.

Relative advantage and compatibility jump to the top of the list of characteristics of e-banking technologies to highlight for customers. Thus trialability, simplicity, observability, risk, and safety were not significant across all the technologies they examined, including these characteristics in a marketing campaign certainly would not hurt the chances of customers adopting e-banking. Both the financial services marketplace and the available technologies are evolving quickly—and although it appears that a broad range of customers are adopting these technologies, and that a rising tide does indeed lift all boats, monitoring these changes and their implications for customers will be an ongoing challenge.

Even if digital transformation is a priority for most retail banks, reality shows there is still quite some work in the area of digitization, a condition since qua non for digital transformation, and of underlying processes that are often overlooked. McKinsey London's Tunde Olanrewaju, wrote that "*retail bank customers do not experience the same level of digital choice, freedom and empowerment as in other industries*" such as travel, to quote just one. And that is a challenge as the experiences, choice and digital expectations of consumers are shaped by those in all industries (McKinsey & Company et al. 2019). We expect the same level of service and—even more importantly, empowerment—from retail banks as we do from other industries leading the digital evolutions (Baudouin 2016). On the other hand, as they dive into digitization, many banks and credit unions are disappointed in the initial results. Implementation is often slower than expected. It's difficult to scale digital initiatives across the institution. They do not have the talent with the necessary digital and analytics skills. The organization does not want to change. And the impact on the bottom line is much smaller than they thought it would be. As a result, initial enthusiasm wanes over the course of the project. Challenges become roadblocks. Integrating digital applications with the legacy infrastructure is a particular sticking point.

When it comes to spotting fraud, banks have a unique advantage. Bankers are at the frontline, positioned to identify any unusual or suspicious behaviour early on. Older customers are far more likely to know and be known by their bankers because they still visit the bank regularly. Thanks to this trend, bank tellers often know their older customers on a first-name basis and have an opportunity to establish a rapport with them. This makes it sometimes possible for bank employees to spot changes in mood or behaviour that may signal a concern, and then address it (Lock 2016).

Conforming to Mbama et al. (2018) bank employees who frequently interact with customers are the most important link in service delivery, building trust and influencing customer behaviour (Karatepe and Aga 2016). Given that managers are responsible for implementing DB services, capturing their opinion through their reaction and interaction with customers is also critical to understanding customer experience and financial performance impact. There have been studies that capture gaps between managers' perceptions and customers' service expectations in the leisure sector (Luk and Layton 2002). Similarly, Julien and Tsoni (2013) study banking staff and customer perceptions focusing on identifying perception-based gaps and improving service quality co-production.

However, at the same time, there is an increasingly strong interest in understanding individuals' beliefs about technology and how these beliefs may influence the design requirements of technology-related products and services and, ultimately, determine the success or failure of such technologies. The most widely applied theory in this context, the technology acceptance model (TAM) (Davis et al. 1989), hypothesizes that a person's acceptance of new technology is determined by his voluntary intention to use that technology (Yousafzai and Yani-de-Soriano 2012).

One of the more prominent effects of the Internet's continuing expansion and development is that the companies and customers acquire more ways of communicating with one another, leading to profound impact on the banking industry (Ganguli and Roy 2011). Customers no longer need to abide by the bank's opening hours or spend time waiting in phone queues in order to get into contact with their bank advisors (Zook and Smith 2016). A large-scale study revealed that modern bank customers of today desire freedom in where to conduct their business, while also requiring a deeper personal relationship with their bank advisors (Accenture 2015). If the customers have a good rapport with their retailer, especially one international. The results indicate that the banks need to garner a better understanding of their customers. The respondents perceive the customers to seek simple and swift solutions who will turn to whatever actor who can best supply such a service. The respondents would indeed often reiterate that a deep and loyal relationship with the customer could only be generated through providing good service and availability. Paradoxically, however, the respondents also claimed that the banks aspired to make the customers more autonomous and independent in order to reduce their need of keeping frequent contact with the banks (Larsson and Viitaoja 2017).

In this environment, financial institutions must understand the needs of customers and remain focused on enabling the control, convenience and speed that they demand. To support these efforts, the 2014 Fiserv Consumer Trends Survey delivers insights into customer attitudes and behaviours related to digital banking and payments services and makes recommendations on how financial institutions can capitalize on the research to drive adoption, satisfaction and growth. The vast majorities of customers across demographic segments are interested in digital banking and payment options and value the role these services play in their lives (Crowe et al. 2015).

The purpose of this study is to explore the banking services provided to customers. It examines the changes in the banking services and more precisely the fact that some banking services are being replaced by the technology and the use of new models but also how the digitalization has influenced the relationship of the banks with the customers (Keskar and Pandey 2018; Rieker 2018). The study uses quantitative data from other surveys regarding the big influence of digitalization in the banking industry, the automation in the services and generally the changes in the banking industry. Extensive demographic data was collected to profile these respondents and identify key customer groups. In today's highly competitive financial services market, knowledge of key customer segments factors can help banks to enhance the customer experience. This provides valuable information that banks could use to improve online banking services and develop new products and programs. In this regard, an understanding of the service dimensions, and relative importance of the service attributes of digital banking service is of critical importance to banks. The research was conducted in the area of Eastern Macedonia and Thrace.

2 Methodology

The current study aims to explore customers' attitudes towards digital banking applications. In particular, aims to identify the factors that affect customers' attitudes towards those applications, to classify them into groups according to their similar behaviour patterns and to profile each group of customers according to their demographic characteristics and other factors.

In particular, this study examines the rejection of the following research null hypotheses:

Ho1: Banking customers cannot be classified into groups according to the factors that affect their attitudes towards digital banking applications.

Ho2: Customers' demographic characteristics are not significantly related to particular purchasing behaviour.

A primary survey was conducted with 100 banking customers to gather the necessary information. Customers were selected randomly, with the criterion that the interviewer was to solicit every sixth customer who came into the survey area (Fink 2015). Information was gathered through an interview survey with the use of a structured questionnaire as people are familiar with this kind of research and their educational level is suitable for the use of this kind of survey method (Oppenheim 2000). The survey was conducted in November 2017–March 2018 in the area of Eastern Macedonia and Thrace.

Principal Component Analysis (PCA) was used to identify the variables that accounted for the maximum amount of variance within the data in terms of the smallest number of uncorrelated variables (components). This method consists of a dimensionality-reduction method that is often used to reduce the dimensionality of large data sets, by transforming a large set of variables into a smaller one that still contains most of the information in the large set. PCA is mostly used as a tool in exploratory data analysis and for making predictive models. Hence, the basic concept of PCA is simple—reduce the number of variables of a data set, while preserving as much information as possible. This statistical analysis is mainly conducted in the following 2 steps: (a) calculating the data covariance (or correlation) matrix of the original data and performing eigenvalue decomposition on the covariance matrix. In particular, the anti-image correlation matrix, as well as the Bartlett's test of sphericity and the Measure of Sampling Adequacy (MSA) were used, in order to check the appropriateness of the data for subsequent factor analysis. The variables with a high proportion of large absolute values of anti-image correlations and MSA less than

0.5 were removed before analysis. An orthogonal rotation (varimax method) was conducted and the standard criteria of eigenvalue = 1, scree test and percentage of variance were used in order to determine the factors in the first rotation (Hair et al. 1998). Different trial rotations followed, where factor interpretability was used to compare the reduced through PCA 10 variables related to banking customers' attitudes towards digital banking applications to a smaller set of key factors. These PCA scores were then subjected to cluster analysis to group customers with similar patterns of scores into similar clusters of attitudes towards digital banking applications.

Cluster analysis is an exploratory data analysis tool for organizing observed data or cases into two or more groups. Unlike Linear Discriminant analysis, cluster analysis requires no prior knowledge of which elements belong to which clusters. The clusters are defined through an analysis of the data. Cluster analysis maximizes the similarity of cases within each cluster while maximizing the dissimilarity between groups that are initially unknown. Hierarchical cluster analysis is a statistical method for finding relatively homogeneous clusters of cases based on dissimilarities or distances between objects. It starts with each case as a separate cluster and then combines the clusters sequentially, reducing the number of clusters at each step until only one cluster is left. *K*-means clustering is a non-hierarchical method of clustering that is used when the number of clusters present in the objects or cases is known. It is an unsupervised method of centroid-based clustering. In general, the *k*-means method will produce exactly *k* different clusters. The main idea is to define *k* centroids, one for each cluster. These centroids should be placed as far away from each other as possible. The next step is to take each point belonging to a given data set and associate it with the nearest centroid. When no point is pending, the positions of the *k* centroids are recalculated. This procedure is repeated until the centroids no longer move. In this study both hierarchical and non-hierarchical methods of cluster analysis were used (Hair et al. 1998) in order to develop a typology of the customers' attitudes.

Linear Discriminant Analysis (LDA) and Quadratic Discriminant Analysis (QDA) are two classic classifiers, with, as their names suggest, a linear and a quadratic decision surface, respectively. These classifiers are attractive because they have closed-form solutions that can be easily computed, are inherently multiclass, have proven to work well in practice, and have no hyperparameters to tune. Quadratic discriminant analysis is closely related to linear discriminant analysis but in LDA it is assumed that the measurements from each class are normally distributed. Unlike LDA however, in QDA there is no assumption that the covariance of each of the classes is identical. Quadratic Discriminant Analysis (QDA) was performed in this study to assess how accurately the key identified factors that could predict and discriminate cluster membership through factor analysis. Furthermore, the chi-square analysis was performed to develop the profile of each group of customers regarding their demographic characteristics (Aliaga and Gunderson 2000).

3 Results

3.1 Factors Affecting Banking Customers Towards Digital Banking Applications

The variables and the three main key factors affecting the banking customers' attitudes towards digital banking applications along with their eigenvalues and the percentage of variance results from PCA are portrayed in Tables 1 and 2.

Hence, PCA identified three main factors that affect the attitudes of banking customers towards banking digital applications are: (a) Better services, (b) cautiousness, (c) timeless/directness.

In the next stage, hierarchical and non-hierarchical clustering methods were used to develop a typology of banking customers' attitudes towards digital banking applications (Hair et al. 1998). Cluster analysis was conducted on the 100 observations, as there were no outliers.

It identified three groups of banking customers that were named according to their attitudes towards those applications (Table 3). These are the (a) Positive, (b) Opportunists, (c) Conscious.

In particular, the Positive customers comprise 48% of the sample. They believe that digital banking applications are more efficient, safer and better supported by customers' support services. They also think that those applications are more direct, available in use by customers and with more attractive environment than traditional banking applications; whilst they do not think these applications consist of inflexible procedures and easily accessible. Moreover, they are not afraid of using those applications.

On the other hand, opportunists consist of 26% of the sample. These customers are not interested in any of the aforementioned factors.

Table 1 Variables affecting the banking customers' attitudes towards digital banking applications

Component	Eigenvalues	% of variance	Cumulative variance
1	4.076	40.759	40.759
2	1.800	17.996	58.755
3	1.056	10.564	69.318
4	0.748	7.482	76.801
5	0.611	6.108	82.909
6	0.466	4.662	87.571
7	0.420	4.201	91.772
8	0.335	3.354	95.126
9	0.291	2.907	98.033
10	0.197	1.967	100.00

Table 2 The main factors affecting banking customers' attitudes towards digital banking applications

Main factors	Factor loadings
Better services	
Digital banking services are more efficient than traditional banking services	0.858
Digital banking services are safer than traditional banking services	0.845
Digital banking services are better supported by customers' support services than the traditional banking services	0.723
Digital banking services are more friendly user than traditional banking services	0.537
Cautiousness	
Digital banking services consist of inflexible procedures	0.890
Digital banking services are not easily accessible	0.858
Customers afraid using digital banking services	0.700
Timelines/directness	
Digital banking services are more direct than traditional banking services	0.908
Digital banking services are available in use than traditional banking services	0.755
Digital banking services have more attractive environment than traditional banking services	0.600

KMO MSA = 0.768; Bartlett test of sphericity 4,053,429; $P < 0.001$

Table 3 Classification of banking customers according to their attitudes towards those applications

Key consumption dimensions	Positive	Opportunists	Conscious	P
Better services	−0.05767	−0.15395	0.23501	0.001
Cautiousness	−0.52070	0.22678	0.37404	0.001
Timelines/directness	0.49710	−0.21281	−0.36108	0.005
Number of customers ($n = 100$)	48	26	26	

Besides, the remaining 26% of the sample are the conscious customers who believe that digital banking application consist of inflexible procedures are not easily accessible and are afraid of using those applications.

Discriminant analysis was conducted to evaluate the prediction of group membership by the predictors derived from the factor analysis. The summary of the cross-validation classification derived by the quadratic discriminant analysis is shown in Table 4.

Thus, the three key factors are those describe banking customers' attitudes towards digital banking applications could accurately predict and discriminate consumers' group membership. Thus, the hypothesis *Ho1: "Banking customers cannot be classified into groups according to the factors that affect their attitudes towards digital banking applications"* can be rejected.

Table 4 Summary of classification with cross-validation

Actual classification	Predicted classification		
	Positive	Opportunists	Conscious
Positive	46	1	0
Opportunists	1	24	1
Conscious	0	1	25
Total *N*	48	26	26
N correct	47	24	25
Proportion (%)	97.9	92.3	96.0
$N = 100$	N correct = 96	Proportion correct	96%

3.2 *Profiling Each Group of Banking Customers Regarding Their Demographic Characteristics*

A chi-square analysis was performed to profile each group of banking customers regarding their demographic characteristics. As Table 5 indicates that most of the customers of the positive group are between 26 and 35 years old, hold a university degree, are married and their family income is between 10,000 and 20,000 Euro annually. On the other hand, the majority of the opportunist customers are between 36 and 45 years old, divorced, with family income between 10,000 and 20,000 Euro annually. Moreover, the conscious customers are between 36 and 45 years old, finished the high school, are married and their family income is between 10,000 and 20,000 Euro annually. The bold values in Table 5 are the highest values in each group regarding their demographic characteristics.

Hence, the hypothesis *Ho2: "Consumers' demographic characteristics are not significantly related to particular purchasing behaviour"* can be rejected.

4 Discussion and Conclusions

The digitization of banking transactions as a direct consequence of the overall digitization of the economy is now a reality that, although it has not yet completed the transformation of the economy, has in any case already brought about significant changes. The most significant example of the digitization of banking transactions is the widespread use of digital banking transactions. Therefore, the research carried out in the framework of this research has as a central objective the mapping of the new reality in relation to the banking environment, through research on the views of individuals on the digitization of banking services, at least at the degree which has already happened. Thus, initially, it should be noticed that almost the entire sample is aware of digital banking services, although a significant 30% of them do not use them. Generally speaking, the majority of the sample considers digital banking

Table 5 Profiling banking customers' according to their demographic characteristics

Banking customers' demographic characteristics		Positive		Opportunists		Conscious	
Age	<25 years old	$x^2 =$ 17.149 $P < 0.05$	15%	$x^2 = 11.692$ $P < 0.001$	4%	$x^2 = 7.846$ $P < 0.05$	0%
	26–35 years old		**35%**		15%		35%
	36–45 years old		31%		**42%**		**42%**
	46–55 years old		13%		27%		12%
	>55 years old		4%		12%		12%
Education	Primary school	$x^2 =$ 19.915 $P < 0.001$	2%	n.s.	0%	$x^2 = 8.769$ $P < 0.001$	8%
	High school		23%		4%		**54%**
	Technical education after high school		10%		23%		15%
	University degree		**40%**		46%		15%
	Postgraduate degree		23%		27%		8%
Marital status	Single	$x^2 =$ 9.936 $P < 0.001$	10%	$x^2 = 9.385$ $P < 0.05$	15%	$x^2 =$ 19.385 $P < 0.001$	12%
	Married		**42%**		19%		**46%**
	Divorced		25%		**46%**		31%
	Widow		21%		19%		12%
Family annual income	<10,000 Euro	$x^2 =$ 46.702 $P < 0.001$	29%	$x^2 = 23.154$ $P < 0.001$	19%	$x^2 = 3.846$ $P < 0.05$	31%
	10,000–20,000 Euro		**63%**		**77%**		**46%**
	20,001–30,000 Euro		4%		4%		0%
	>31,000 Euro		2%		0%		0%

services to be easy to access and use, while at the same time they are considered more convenient and reliable than traditional banking. In addition, it is important to note that in general the public shows confidence in digital banking and does not consider it to be particularly expensive compared to the traditional banking service. However, emphasis should be placed on the importance that customers give to the security and quality of digital transactions. Important advantages of digital banking services are 24 h support, better time usage and simplified procedures. However, on the other hand, most respondents consider their personal contact with banking staff necessary, useful and efficient.

The above conclusions should be studied by policy makers in banking institutions in the sense that customers' concerns and expectations should be taken seriously in relation to digital banking services. For example, the fact that customers are particularly concerned about trade security, which has been identified in other surveys (Llewellyn 1999) should be a goal for those who are responsible or convincingly presenting the level of security of transactions through technology to make it possible to increase the level of consumer confidence in digital services. Moreover, the fact that many respondents consider the interpersonal relationship with bank employees something generally useful, this fact should be a starting point for those in charge of seeking a golden intersection between digital banking and traditional banking in order to prevent breach between the new banking reality and the real needs of their customers.

In addition, necessary emphasis should be placed on the identifying factors that seem to influence the views of respondents about digital banking. According to the results of the survey, as they were presented earlier, the age and education of individuals seem to play the most important role in how respondents' views are shaped in relation to other demographics data. More specifically, both younger more educated people think more positively about digital banking. It worth noting that in almost all the statistically significant differences identified in the present study, older and less educated people were those who had the views that were identical with a profile of a person who is reluctant to technology, does not understand it and he does not trust her. The results of this research are in harmony with other international surveys that are mainly geared to the age of individuals, such as the Ipsos survey (2017). Moreover, this should be an important reminder for the banking industry's designers of the different approaches to be adopted for different consumer communities. Identifying key customer segments enables banks to enhance customer experiences.

All the above conclusions offer a lot of actionability and this is the main contribution of the study for the design and the implementation of digital banking. Its originality derives from both the methods used (Principal component analysis, Cluster analysis, Discriminant analysis) and the aforementioned results. In conclusion, the digitization of banking transactions is now a reality. It is up to the banking industry to convince the consumer that this change is in his best interest.

It is hardly possible to conduct a study that does not contain weaknesses or an element of bias. Therefore, there are some limitations in this study as well. More specifically, the short time available to the author of this research did not help to gather a larger sample and, above all, a sample representing, if not customers from all parts of Greece. The sample size is relatively small (100 customers) and may not be adequate to generalize to the entire population. This research, despite its limitations, can contribute, to the existing knowledge. Moreover, it is important to repeat this study in the future to better understand the dynamics of this competitive and changing industry. In this regard, an understanding of the service dimensions and relative importance of the service attributes of digital banking service is of critical importance to banks.

References

Aliaga M, Gunderson B (2000) Introduction to quantitative research. Doing quantitative research in education with SPSS. Sage, Thousand Oaks, pp 1–11

Baudouin T (2016) Consumer/retail banking: digital transformation, optimization and digitization. https://www.i-scoop.eu/retail-banking-digital-transformation/. Accessed 5 Dec 2019

Bharadwaj A, El Sawy OA, Pavlou PA, Venkatraman N (2013) Digital business strategy: toward a next generation of insights. MIS Q 471–482

Courbe J, Lyons J (2016) Financial services technology 2020 and beyond: embracing disruption. In: PWC, p 48

Crowe M, Tavilla E, McGuire B (2015) Mobile banking and mobile payment practices of US financial institutions: results from 2014 survey of FIs in five federal reserve districts. Federal Reserve Bank of Boston, p 17

Cuesta C, Ruesta M, Tuesta D, Urbiola P (2015) The digital transformation of the banking industry. BBVA Research. https://www.bbvaresearch.com/wp-content/uploads/2015/08/EN_Observatorio_Banca_Digital_vf3.pdf. Accessed 18 Sept 2019

Davis FD (1989) Perceived usefulness, perceived ease of use, and user acceptance of information technology. MIS quarterly 319–340

Dery K, Sebastian IM, Van der Meulen N (2017) The digital workplace is key to digital innovation. MIS Q Exec 16(2)

Fenton N (2016) Left out? Digital media, radical politics and social change. Inf Commun Soc 19(3):346–361

Fink A (2015) How to conduct surveys: a step-by-step guide. Sage

Ganguli S, Roy SK (2011) Generic technology-based service quality dimensions in banking: impact on customer satisfaction and loyalty. Int J Bank Mark 29(2):168–189

Gupta S (2013) The mobile banking and payment revolution. Eur Financ Rev 2(36):215254

Harle P, Havas A, Kremer A, Rona D, Samandari H (2015) The future of bank risk management. McKinsey Working Papers on Risk; McKinsey & Company.

Hair JF, Anderson RE, Tatham RL, Black WC (1998) Multivariate data analysis. Prentice Hall Inc., New Jersey

Hirt M, Willmott P (2014) Strategic principles for competing in the digital age. McKinsey Q 5(1):1–13

Hough J, Chan K (2018) Factors influencing the acceptance of digital banking international association for management of technology

Ipsos (2017) Global trends survey 2017. https://www.ipsos.com/sv-se/global-trends-survey-2017. Accessed 12 Dec 2019

Julien A, Tsoni C (2013) Front-line employee versus customer perceptions of quality attributes. Qual Manag J 20(2):48–59

Kamra S (2014) Digital transformation in banking—the future of banking. Happiest Minds Technologies, sl: sn. https://www.happiestminds.com/whitepapers/digital-transformation-in-banking.pdf. Accessed 1 Dec 2019

Karatepe OM, Aga M (2016) The effects of organization mission fulfilment and perceived organizational support on job performance: the mediating role of work engagement. Int J Bank Mark 34(3):368–387

Keskar MY, Pandey N (2018) Internet banking: a review (2002–2016). J Internet Commer 17(3):310–323

Khan I, Rahman Z, Fatma M (2016) The role of customer brand engagement and brand experience in online banking. Int J Bank Mark 34(7):1025–1041

Kolodinsky JM, Hogarth JM, Hilgert MA (2004) The adoption of electronic banking technologies by US consumers. Int J Bank Mark

Larsson A, Viitaoja Y (2017) Building customer loyalty in digital banking: a study of bank staff's perspectives on the challenges of digital CRM and loyalty. Int J Bank Mark

Li C (2010) Groundswell. Winning in a world transformed by social technologies. Strateg Dir 26(8)

Li S, Da Xu L, Zhao S (2015) The internet of things: a survey. Inf Syst Front 17(2):243–259

Liu DY, Chen SW, Chou TC (2011) Resource fit in digital transformation: lessons learned from the CBC bank global e-banking project. Manag Decis 49(10):1728–1742

Llewellyn DT (1999) The new economics of banking, no. 5. In: SUERF studies

Lock SL (2016) Age-friendly banking: how we can help get it right before things go wrong. Public Policy & Aging Report 26(1):18–22

Luk ST, Layton R (2002) Perception gaps in customer expectations: managers versus service providers and customers. Serv Ind J 22(2):109–128

Martino P, Schaffner J (2015) Impact of digital transformation on banking operating models

Mbama CI, Ezepue P, Alboul L, Beer M (2018) Digital banking, customer experience and financial performance: UK bank managers' perceptions. J Res Interact Mark 12(4):432–451

McKinsey & Company, Brodsky L, Oakes L (2017) Data sharing and open banking. McKinsey on payments, Sept 2017. https://www.mckinsey.com/industries/financial-services/our-insights/data-sharing-and-open-banking. Accessed 24 Sept 2019

McKinsey & Company, Gujral V, Malik N, Taraporevala Z (2019) Rewriting the rules: succeeding in the new retail banking landscape. Global Banking, Feb 2019. https://www.mckinsey.com/~/media/mckinsey/industries/financial%20services/our%20insights/rewriting%20the%20rules%20in%20retail%20banking/rewriting-the-rules-succeeding-in-the-new-retail-banking-landscape.ashx. Accessed 11 Sept 2019

Oppenheim AN (2000) Questionnaire design, interviewing and attitude measurement. Continuum, New York

Ortstad R, Sonono B (2017) The effects of the digital transformation process on banks' relationship with customers: case study of a large Swedish bank. Published master's thesis, Department of Business Studies, Uppsala University

Rieker F (2018) Embracing digital transformation: the future of banking, customer experience. Digitalist Magazine, Feb 2018. https://www.digitalistmag.com/customer-experience/2018/02/21/embracing-digital-transformation-future-of-banking-05880240. Accessed 11 Sept 2019

Shah MH, Siddiqui FA (2006) Organisational critical success factors in adoption of e-banking at the Woolwich bank. Int J Inf Manage 26(6):442–456

Sidel R (2013) After years of growth, banks are pruning their branches. The Wall Street Journal A1

Skan J, Dickerson J, Masood S (2015) The future of Fintech and banking: digitally disrupted or reimagined. Accenture, London

Sullivan B, Garvey J, Alcocer J, Eldridge A (2014) Retail banking 2020: evolution or revolution. Accessed 24 Aug 2019

Venkateswari V (2018) Technology innovation in banks—need for omnichannel services. Int J Res—GRANTHAALAYAH 6(1):150–155

Yousafzai S, Yani-de-Soriano M (2012) Understanding customer-specific factors underpinning internet banking adoption. Int J Bank Mark

Zook Z, Smith PR (2016) Marketing communications: offline and online integration, engagement and analytics. Kogan Page Publishers

Assessing Artificial Neural Networks (ANNS) Adequacy Against Econometric Models for Decision Making Approaches in Banking Industry

Sotirios J. Trigkas and Konstantinos J. Liapis

Abstract The purpose of this paper is to test the effect of non-parametric methodology of ANNs on enhancing decision-making procedures compared to classic multivariate Regression models. We implement the two methods on decision-making for loan allowances and on a valuation of collaterals using data from a Small Medium Greek Bank. Using sensitivity analysis, we also find the key points where decision-making results change. We provide all the estimations and a comparable matrix is produced in order to point out the similarities and differences between the two methodologies. Also, the key points in decision-making approach are presented. The practical implication is that crucial for decision-making approach in the banking industry and affects bank's risk management. From the presentation of comparison between the two methodologies, we also provide the relationship between independent variables along with decision-making options. The debate in academic society for theoretical and non-theoretical approaches in decision-making procedure is crucial the last decades. Our paper contributes also to this academic debate, by presenting advantages and disadvantages per methodology. This study demonstrates a practical tool for decision roles and units who are trying to define the best practice for decision-making procedures.

Keywords Banking · Artificial neural networks · Regression analysis · Decision making

Jel Classification G21 · C44 · C45

S. J. Trigkas (✉) · K. J. Liapis
Department of Economic and Regional Development, Faculty of Sciences of Economy and Public Administration, Panteion University of Social and Political Sciences, 136, Syngrou Ave., 17671 Athens, Greece
e-mail: s.trigas@panteion.gr

K. J. Liapis
e-mail: konstantinos.liapis@panteion.gr

A. Horobet et al. (eds.), *Business Performance and Financial Institutions in Europe*, Contributions to Economics, https://doi.org/10.1007/978-3-030-57517-5_7

1 Introduction

The efficiency of Banking Institutions has been a constant research field for many years. The effect of financial risk (credit risk) on efficiency and profitability appears to vary from study to study. In most studies, the financial risk is measured by the subprime estimate ratio to all loans. The course of this factor alters efficiency and profitability in future time. Especially, the last decade due to the financial crises of 2008 the volatility of banking efficiency has increased substantially, leading also to an increase of the interest of the scientific research regarding the modelling and forecasting of Key Performance Indicators. Efficiency and profitability are the primary goal of any business formation. The long-term progress of a business cannot be achieved without a substantial level of efficiency and profitability. Therefore, the measurement (quantification) of current, past, and future efficiency and profitability is considered imperative and to a significant extent ensures the survival of the business formation. Essentially by using these terms we refer to the ability of the company to generate profits through its activity at the lowest cost and risk.

The credit rating process is very important for credit institutions as it is used to separate borrowers from "good" and "bad" in terms of their creditworthiness. The process of assessing borrowers is a classic example of asymmetric information where a bank tries to reveal hidden information about its client, which is crucial for the smooth service of the requested loan. Credit scoring in its automated form is often the only way to assess credit ratings as banks do not have enough resources to individually investigate the specific characteristics of each borrower separately. The methods generally used for credit rating are primarily based on statistical techniques for the recognition of standards. These sophisticated methods negate the perception that often refers to credit scoring, as it is a simple process of data creation. Statistical model recognition is a growing area of research.

2 Literature Review

The basic statistical techniques that have been widely applied for the construction of credit scoring models are Linear Discriminant Analysis, Multivariate Discriminant Analysis (Altman et al. 1994; Altman and Saunders 1997; Beaver 1966; Karels and Prakash 1987; Reichert et al. 1983), Logistic regression analysis—Logit and Probit models (Thomas 2000; Baesens et al 2003; Lee et al. 2002; West 2000), Multivariate Adaptive Regression Splines (Friedman 1991). Among these, the logarithmic regression model is the most commonly used model in the banking industry due to its desirable features (eg robustness and transparency—Hand and Henley 1997; Louzada et al. 2012).

In recent years, many studies have shown that Artificial Intelligence techniques such as Artificial Neural Networks (West 2000), Decision Trees (Jiang et al. 2009) Case-Based Reasoning (Shin and Han 2001) and Vector Machines (Schebesch and

Stecking 2005) can be used as alternative methods for credit rating and show higher prediction accuracy. According to Vojtek and Koèenda (2006) discriminant analysis was first used by Fisher (1936), who explored the best way to separate two groups using a linear combination of variables. Eisenbeis (1977), Hand and Henley (1997) where also contributed to the research of Linear Discriminant Analysis in credit rating. Altman (1968), who was the first to apply discretionary analysis, constructed the so-called *z*-score, which is a linear combination of the various interpretive variables in the case of the problem of lending to business. He found that the model was extremely expensive to properly predict bankruptcy.

The advantages of the LDA method are that it is simple, can be appreciated very easily and works well. It is often used by banks to create credit-scoring systems. The downside is that the LDA requires normally distributed data, but the available data is often non-regular. One way to overcome problems with data irregularity is to use an extension of the LDA model that allows for some parametric distribution. In this case, a suitable extension is a generalized linear model known as a logistic regression model. One of the advantages of logarithmic regression analysis with respect to LDA is the use of the maximum probability method for estimating the wi parameters. Another advantage is that one can provide the chances of being in a particular group. The Log Regression method can also deal with categorized data through usage of dummy variables for each category of such data. Several studies have found that the logarithmic regression model outperforms the distinctive analysis (LDA).

Lawrence and Arshadi (1995) used the logit model to analyze the management of problem loans and the determinants of the analysis options using a series of variables between the borrower and the bank. In the field of mortgage lending Campbell and Dietrich (1983), used a logit model to show that the age of a mortgage, the mortgage-to-mortgage ratio, interest rates and unemployment rates are important for explaining early repayments, delays and bad debts. Gardner and Mills (1989), recognizing that negligent borrowers do not have to end in a definitive delay, use a logit regression model to assess the probability of terminating loans that are not serviced smoothly. They point out that bankers use this method to determine the seriousness of the problem and thus form an appropriate response to the improper servicing of the loans.

The most recent and increasingly used method in assessing creditworthiness according to Vojtek and Koèenda (2006) is so-called neural networks. A neural network (NNW) is a mathematical representation inspired by the human brain and its ability to adapt based on the influx of new information. Mathematically, neural networks are a nonlinear optimization tool. Numerous different types of neural networks are identified in the literature. Neural networks were described in the 1960s, but their first appearance in credit scoring is found only in the early 1990s. Altman et al. (1994) uses LDA and a neural network to diagnose corporate financial risk for 1000 Italian companies and concluded that neural networks are not purely the dominant mathematical technique compared to traditional statistical techniques such as the distinctive analysis and that the LDA compares quite well with the neural network in the accuracy of the decision. On the other hand, with different results Tam and Kiang

(1992) studied the application of the neural network model to predict banking failure in Texas for the period 1985–1987. They compared the accuracy of the neural network prediction with that of LDA, logarithmic regression, k-NN and decision tree. Their results show that neural networks are the most accurate, followed by linear discriminant analysis (LDA), logarithmic regression, decision trees, and finally k-NN. In an aggregate accounting level studies regarding the analysis of financial statements have been conducted during the financial crises by Chatzi et al. (2015) and Liapis et al. (2018) who follow a data panel statistical and econometric approach by using the financial data for the four Systemic Banking Groups in Greece. Also, an aggregate accounting level approach, but with the use of Additional Fund Needed AFN methodology, research has been conducted by Spanos et al. (2019) which use Monte Carlo simulation and mathematical programming and find that the AFN formula is an appropriate methodology to calculate the capital requirements under uncertainty and thus apply any optimization techniques in cooperations. Turning the research with AFN methodology to banking Liapis and Trigkas (2019) follow a prototype economic modelling approach for Small Medium Banks (SMBs) business plans according to structure of Additional Funds Needed (AFN) models, and find it has a strong fundamental use in strategic financial planning for SMBs, although in an aggregate accounting level.

In direct relation to credit scoring in retail banking, Desai et al. (1996) investigates a neural network of multi-layered perception, a mix of an expert's neural networks, a linear distinct analysis, and logarithmic regression for the rating of potential borrowers of credit institutions. Their results show that custom neural networks offer a very promising direction if the measure of return is the percentage of bad loans correctly classified. However, if the measure of return is the percentage of good and bad loans correctly classified, logarithmic regression produces comparable results with the approach of neural networks.

In the literature, in most cases of comparative analysis of credit scoring models, neural networks are more expensive than linear resolution and logarithmic regression analysis models (Lee et al. 2002; Piramuthu 1999; West 2000).

3 Data and Methodology

Taking our data from a retail car loan portfolio, we have 500 cases of car loans with independent variables the client characteristics for: (a) Age, (b) Home Ownership, (c) Salary, and (d) Amount of Loan. We use Palisade statistic suite to run Neural Networks methodology for the assessment of every clients' Creditworthiness. We also use Regression Analysis, in order to construct a model with the same independent variables and the result of estimated y (dependent variable) as an indicator of creditworthiness. Then we compare the results of the two methodologies, to access the predictive power of each. In Table 1 we exhibit the Descriptive statistic of a sample Car Loan Portfolio.

Table 1 Descriptive statistic of a sample car loan portfolio

Age		Home → 0 = Owned 1 = Rented	Salary	Loan
Mean	38,832	0.466	56,254	19,694.2
Standard error	0.520720512	0.022331264	1064.912694	388.4093928
Median	38	0	57,500	19,300
Mode	38	0	92,000	8100
Standard deviation	11.64366462	0.499342253	23,812.17174	8685.098055
Sample variance	135.5749259	0.249342685	567,019,523	75,430,928.22
Kurtosis	−1.215705058	−1.989279201	−1.262610066	−1.227654802
Skewness	0.080155143	0.136726047	−0.010697151	0.051371451
Range	40	1	80,000	29,900
Minimum	20	0	15,000	5000
Maximum	60	1	95,000	34,900
Sum	19,416	233	28,127,000	9,847,100
Count	500	500	500	500
Confidence level (95.0%)	1.023074895	0.043874892	2092.265269	763.1193498

Source Authors work

3.1 *The Neural Network Approach*

Based on the above data we proceed with the steps as explained below:

As we observe in Table 2 Net information of ANNs approach, we follow the configuration of PNN Category Predictor with total cases of 500. We have one Dependent Category Variable (Result) and four Independent Variables which are:

- The Age of the Client,
- The Ownership or Rent of Home (represented by 0 and 1 respectively),
- The amount of Salary or Income,
- The amount of Loan.

Table 2 Net information of ANNs approach

Net information
Number of total cases: 500
Name: net trained on CAR LOAN
Configuration: PNN category predictor
Independent numeric variables: 4 (age, home ownership/rent, salary, amount of loan)
Dependent variable: category var. (result)

Source Authors work

We first divide the process into main subprocesses of training, testing, and prediction.

We used 400 cases to run 73 trials for our training session of ANNs. Then we used another 100 cases for our testing session of ANNs. Finally, we proceed to a prediction with 2 cases and used all 502 cases to conduct a Variable impact Analysis. During the ANNs procedures, the Dependent Variable Result was divided into Creditworthy, Not Creditworthy and Insolvent. For the purpose comparison with the implementation of Regression Analysis, we treat Result as a Var which takes the values 1 = Creditworthy and 0 = Not Creditworthy.

3.2 The Regression Analysis Approach

By using the same sample of the above data, we proceed with the steps as explained below:

We run a Regression Analysis where Dependent Variable (Result) and four Independent Variables which are:

- The Age of the Client,
- The Ownership or Rent of Home (represented by 0 and 1 respectively),
- The amount of Salary or Income,
- The amount of Loan.

In this approach, we set the constant to zero, which mean that there is no coefficient for constant.

4 Findings

4.1 The Neural Network Approach

As we can observe from Table 3 The Training session of ANNs, we used 400 cases to run 73 trials. The training session resulted in a 3% of Bad Predictors, with a mean Incorrect Probability of 7.3527% and a Std. Deviation of Incorrect Probability of 14.05%.

Moving to Table 4. The Testing session of ANNs we utilize of the remaining 100 cases. The testing session resulted in a 7% of Bad Predictors, with a mean Incorrect Probability of 10.445% and a Std. Deviation of Incorrect Probability of 20.0745%.

Finally, we proceed with the Prediction session with the results being constant to our previous process findings (Tables 5 and 6).

The resulting report of Variable Impact Analysis is illustrated in Table 7. As we can observe Salary is the variable with the highest impact with a 53.8851%, followed

Table 3 The training session of ANNs

Training session of NNs
Number of cases: 400
Training time: 00:00:00
Number of trials: 73
Reason stopped: auto-stopped
% bad predictions: 3.0000%
Mean incorrect probability: 7.3527%
Std. deviation of incorrect prob.: 14.0500%

Source Authors work

Table 4 The testing session of ANNs

Testing session of ANNs
Number of cases: 100
% bad predictions: 7.0000%
Mean incorrect probability: 10.4450%
Std. deviation of incorrect prob.: 20.0745%

Source Authors work

Table 5 The prediction session of ANNs

Prediction
Number of cases: 2
Live prediction enabled: YES
Data set
Name: CAR LOAN
Number of rows: 502
Manual case tags: NO

Source Authors work

by Amount of Loan with a 25.5697%, Home Ownership or Rent with a 13.8291% and Age with a 6.7161%.

4.2 The Regression Analysis Approach

As we already mentioned, for the purpose of applying the Regression Analysis, we treat Result as a Var which takes the values 1 = Creditworthy and 0 = Not Creditworthy. The purpose is to construct a model were the estimates can result in a estimates Result = y for every case and that way we can compare with the historical data and results from ANNs in order to access the efficiency. The results of the

Table 6 Train-test-predict report of ANNs

Train-test-predict report for net trained on car loan										
State of client	Age	Home ownership/rent	Own_0 Rent_1	Salary	Amount of loan	Tag used	Prediction	Prediction (%)	Incorrect (%)	Good/bad (%)
New client	40	Rent	1	30,000.00	10,000.00	Predict	Creditworthy	99.85	0.15	Good
New client	25	Rent	1	20,000.00	15,000.00	Predict	Not creditworthy	59.14	40.86	Good

Source Authors work

Table 7 Variable impact analysis in ANNs

Variable impact analysis
Salary: 53.8851%
Amount of loan: 25.5697%
Home ownership/rent: 13.8291%
Age: 6.7161%

Source Authors work

Table 8 Results of the regression analysis with no constant

	Coefficients	Standard error	*t* stat	*P*-value	Signif.
Intercept	0	#N/A	#N/A	#N/A	
Age	0.00875666	0.000833259	10.50893122	1.85556E−23	***
Own_0 Rent_1	−0.175324349	0.026530991	−6.608284928	1.00535E−10	***
Salary	1.25495E−05	4.93158E−07	25.44726137	5.10206E−92	***
Amount of loan	−1.06333E−05	1.37253E−06	−7.747239296	5.33993E−14	***
Signif. codes: 0 '***' 0.001 '**' 0.01 '*' 0.05 '.' 0.1 ' '					
Regression statistics					
Multiple *R*			0.939824507		
R square			0.883270104		
Adjusted *R* square			0.880547947		
Standard error			0.30179059		
Observations			500		

Source Authors work

Regression Analysis are illustrated in Table 8 Results of the Regression Analysis with no constant.

As we observe our model has a very strong Adjusted *R* Square and all coefficients of independent variables are significant.

Age and salary have a positive relation to the dependent variable, result of creditworthiness. On the other hand, ownership Own_0 Rent_1 and Amount of Loan have a negative relation.

The equation then is expressed as

$$y = 0.00876 * \text{Age} - 0.17532 * \text{Own\_0 Rent\_1} + 1.25495\text{E} - 05 * \text{Salary} - 1.06333\text{E} - 05 * \text{Amount of Loan}. \quad (1)$$

By applying the data from our sample, we get Table 9 Descriptive statistics for the resulted estimated y.

Taking the mean as the threshold for accessing where or not the Client is creditworthy or not, we continue to the below comparison.

Table 9 Descriptive statistics for the resulted estimated *y*

Predicted *y*	
Mean	0.754883448
Standard error	0.015101662
Median	0.76391883
Mode	#N/A
Standard deviation	0.337683432
Sample variance	0.1140301
Kurtosis	−0.683927423
Skewness	−0.096898348
Range	1.627488664
Minimum	−0.069297943
Maximum	1.558190721
Sum	377.4417241
Count	500
Confidence level (95.0%)	0.02967068

Source Authors work

4.3 Comparison of the Two Estimation Results

Because we examine 500 cases, we have constructed Table 10 Comparison of ANNs and Regression Analysis Results, in order to summarize and compare the results from the two methodologies.

As we observe from Table 10. Comparison of ANNs and Regression Analysis results the two methodologies are not very close regarding their outcomes. Although

Table 10 Comparison of ANNs and regression analysis results

Methodology	Number of bad outcome (other than historic data)	Number of test cases	Percentage of bad outcome to test cases (%)
Initial NNs estimate with Category variable Creditworthy = 1, Not Creditworthy = 0 and Insolvent = -1	7	100	7.00
Modified NNs estimate with Numeric variable Creditworthy = 1, Not Creditworthy = 0	3	100	3.00
Regression analysis	132	500	26.40

Source Authors work

initial ANNs estimate has a 7.00% Bad Outcome Rate, we must point out that variations between Not Creditworthy = 0 and Insolvent = −1, are being merged in the other two estimations and therefore are not accounted for. The 23.4% is a significant difference making ANNs methodology preferable. We can observe a more conservative trend as far as the Regression Analysis methodology since all 132 bad outcomes where resulting in a not creditworthy Client while the historic data where presenting the opposite.

5 Conclusions

In this simplified test model of a car loan retail portfolio, we have used historic data as variables to test the prediction outcomes of two main Credit Scoring approaches, the one of Neural Networks and the one of Regression Analysis. From the findings, we conclude that both methods have a strong predictive power, wet not a similar rate of bad prediction. ANNs have a significant lower bad prediction rate compared to Regression Analysis, making them more efficient. In future research, we can explore similarly the predicting power using other regression technics as well as Classification and Regression Trees (CART).

References

Altman EI (1968) Financial ratios, discriminant analysis and the prediction of corporate bankruptcy. J Finance 23(4):589–609
Altman EI, Saunders A (1997) Credit risk measurement: developments over the last 20 years. J Bank Finance 21(11–12):1721–1742
Altman EI, Marco G, Varetto F (1994) Corporate distress diagnosis: comparisons using linear discriminant analysis and neural networks (the Italian experience). J Bank Finance 18(3):505–529
Baesens B, Setiono R, Mues C, Vanthienen J (2003) Using neural network rule extraction and decision tables for credit-risk evaluation. Manage Sci 49(3):312–329
Beaver WH (1966) Financial ratios as predictors of failure. J Account Res 71–111
Campbell TS, Dietrich JK (1983) The determinants of default on insured conventional residential mortgage loans. J Finance 38(5):1569–1581
Chatzi IG, Diakomihalis MN, Chytis E (2015) Performance of the Greek banking sector pre and throughout the financial crisis. J Risk Control 2(1):45–69
Desai VS, Crook JN, Overstreet GA Jr (1996) A comparison of neural networks and linear scoring models in the credit union environment. Eur J Oper Res 95(1):24–37
Eisenbeis RA (1977) Pitfalls in the application of discriminant analysis in business, finance, and economics. J Finance 32(3):875–900
Fisher RA (1936) The use of multiple measurements in taxonomic problems. Ann Eugen 7(2):179–188
Friedman JH (1991) Multivariate adaptive regression splines. Ann Stat 1–67
Gardner MJ, Mills DL (1989) Evaluating the likelihood of default on delinquent loans. Financ Manag 55–63
Hand DJ, Henley WE (1997) Statistical classification methods in consumer credit scoring: a review. J R Stat Soc Ser A (Stat Soc) 160(3):523–541

Jiang L, Li C, Cai Z (2009) Learning decision tree for ranking. Knowl Inf Syst 20(1):123–135
Karels GV, Prakash AJ (1987) Multivariate normality and forecasting of business bankruptcy. J Bus Finance Account 14(4):573–593
Lawrence EC, Arshadi N (1995) A multinomial logit analysis of problem loan resolution choices in banking. J Money Credit Bank 27(1):202–216
Lee TS, Chiu CC, Lu CJ, Chen IF (2002) Credit scoring using the hybrid neural discriminant technique. Expert Syst Appl 23(3):245–254
Liapis KJ, Trigkas SJ (2019) The control of small medium banks profitability using financial modeling approach under certainty and uncertainty. Financial Studies 24(4):53–84
Liapis KJ, Trigas SJ, Patsis PA (2018) Financial and spatial analysis of the Greek systemic banks before and during the financial crisis. In: The political economy of development in Southeastern Europe. Springer, Cham, pp 109–126
Louzada F, Ferreira-Silva PH, Diniz CA (2012) On the impact of disproportional samples in credit scoring models: an application to a Brazilian bank data. Expert Syst Appl 39(9):8071–8078
Piramuthu S (1999) Financial credit-risk evaluation with neural and neurofuzzy systems. Eur J Oper Res 112(2):310–321
Reichert AK, Cho CC, Wagner GM (1983) An examination of the conceptual issues involved in developing credit-scoring models. J Bus Econ Stat 1(2):101–114
Schebesch KB, Stecking R (2005) Support vector machines for classifying and describing credit applicants: detecting typical and critical regions. J Oper Res Soc 56(9):1082–1088
Shin KS, Han I (2001) A case-based approach using inductive indexing for corporate bond rating. Decis Support Syst 32(1):41–52
Spanos PM, Galanos CL, Liapis KJ (2019) Corporate financial modeling using quantitative methods. In: Economic and financial challenges for Eastern Europe. Springer, Cham, pp 161–183
Tam KY, Kiang MY (1992) Managerial applications of neural networks: the case of bank failure predictions. Manage Sci 38(7):926–947
Thomas LC (2000) A survey of credit and behavioural scoring: forecasting financial risk of lending to consumers. Int J Forecast 16(2):149–172
Vojtek M, Koèenda E (2006) Credit-scoring methods. Czech J Econ Finance 56(3–4):152–167
West D (2000) Neural network credit scoring models. Comput Oper Res 27(11–12):1131–1152

Economy-Wide Risks and Opportunities for Business Development: Lessons from Europe and Abroad

Tendencies of Trade in Business Services in Visegrad Countries

Tatiana Corejova, Roman Chinoracky, Birgit Franken, and Maria Rostasova

Abstract Rapid changes in technology, integration and specialization of individual economies reinforce trade motives and the consequences of integration into the world trade system. The Visegrad countries (Czech Republic, Hungary, Poland and Slovakia) have undergone fundamental structural changes in recent years, characterized at the turn of the century mainly by the opening of the economy and the influx of foreign direct investment into the industry. They are currently classified as high-income countries. Developments in the trade in services in these countries indicate changes in the business environment, firms and the challenge of improving their position on the international market. Visegrad countries belong to highly open economies, because of its heavy dependence on foreign trade and considerable sensitivity to the global economic environment. Each of these countries represents a small internal market, which is unable to cover the raw material requirements and is substantially dependent on the export of domestic production to foreign markets. The discussion of the assessment of the development of foreign trade in business services of Visegrad countries and identification of the presence of their comparative advantages is the object of the contribution. International trade in services in the V4 countries increased by 7% on the export side in 2013–2016, on the import side it decreased by 0.85%, of which trade in business and management consulting and public relations services increased by 76% on the side export and 53% in import. Trade in services, in spite of the V4 membership of the EU28 and the single market, is under constant pressure from a variety of factors, including pressures of associations, interest associations or

T. Corejova (✉) · R. Chinoracky · M. Rostasova
University of Zilina, Zilina, Slovakia
e-mail: tatiana.corejova@fpedas.uniza.sk

R. Chinoracky
e-mail: roman.chinoracky@fpedas.uniza.sk

M. Rostasova
e-mail: maria.rostasova@fpedas.uniza.sk

B. Franken
DHBW, Fakultät Wirtschaft Erzbergerstraße 121, Karlsruhe, Germany
e-mail: birgit.franken@dhbw-karlsruhe.de

A. Horobet et al. (eds.), *Business Performance and Financial Institutions in Europe*, Contributions to Economics, https://doi.org/10.1007/978-3-030-57517-5_8

groups. Three of the V4 countries are not members of the Euro area, and the use of national currencies and their own monetary policy also affects international trade in the trade in services.

Keywords Business services · Trade · Visegrad countries · Import · Export

1 Introduction

Significant changes in technology, innovation, removing barriers, opening up markets are strengthening trade motives and the consequences of integrating individual economies into the world trade system (Franken 2009). The differences between sectors are no longer as clear as the boundary between production and service activities. On the contrary, the integration of manufacturing and service activities becomes the rule (Lay 2002). Schmidt (2000) described this phenomenon as the "internal tertiarization" of the industry. The structure of the economy is changing in terms of industry's share of GDP or in the volume of import and export, especially in the area of high value-added services (Corejova and Al Kassiri 2015).

The provision of business services in individual countries suggests changes in the business environment, companies and the challenge to improve their position on the international market (Madlenak and Madlenakova 2015). Both manufacturers and customers are also rethinking their strategies. Many of them are not only interested in the product itself, but require a comprehensive product, comprising the substance of the product and the added services that satisfy their needs comprehensively as the product itself. A closer look at services activities should be distinguished according to their relation to the product produced. Services that could hardly be provided without production knowledge are gaining importance (Lay 2002). Customer's decision to purchase is increasingly determined by the supplier's ability to provide customers with comprehensive solutions throughout the product lifecycle (Schuh and Speth 2000). In fact, it is almost impossible to offer a number of basic products without corresponding services. Business services can no longer be perceived as exclusive and in isolation as secondary services, but as an integral part of the ideal solution of customer requirements also in the international dimension.

The countries of Central Europe, which form a regional group called Visegrad group or V4, have undergone a major economic transformation in the past thirty years and since 2004 are all members of the EU. The period of transformation is also characterized by the inflow of foreign direct investment into the region, especially in the automotive industry. These investments create extensive job opportunities in individual countries. On the other hand, the automotive industry nowadays also includes many services. This raises questions about the share of these countries in the import and export of business services and what trend can be seen in this area.

2 Theoretical Background

When assessing and identifying trends in trade in services, export and import, it is necessary to define two key areas, namely the definition of services and processes related to foreign trade. Unlike physical goods, services are essentially classified as intangible goods. However, the degree of intangibility is not sufficient to distinguish between two types of goods (Grönroos 1998; Homburg and Garbe 1996). As there are no separate categories, it is more appropriate to consider the difference between them as gradual and linked to a smooth transition to the tangible or intangible continuum (Fisk et al. 2004). Existing approaches to service definition can be divided into three categories (Meffert and Bruhn 2006):

- enumerative approaches that define services by giving concrete examples (Langeard 1981)
- approaches that describe services as opposed to physical goods (Altenburger 1981)
- approaches that explicitly define services using their essential characteristics (Scheuch 2002).

The last group of approaches is best suited to derive a more operational perspective. The basic characteristic is an attribute that describes the essence of the service (Nüttgens et al. 1998). When structuring service elements, three different basic characteristics are appropriate. Meffert and Bruhn (2006) identify three types of classic definitions:

- potentially oriented definitions
- process-oriented definitions
- result-oriented definitions.

However, none of the above-mentioned approaches is suitable to cover all kinds of services. In order to gain real mutual understanding, it is necessary to combine potential, process and result-oriented approaches. The classification of services refers to demand at the level of differentiation. These services are not provided to individuals or groups of individuals, but to companies or organizations. They are therefore called business services. As regards supply at the level of differentiation, a distinction can be made between service companies offering services as their core business and producers offering services as ancillary to their core business.

Growing importance of services in creation of GDP and added value is related to their changes in terms of international trade (Corejova and Al Kassiri 2016). Import and export belong to the basic foreign trade activities. They reflect the advantages and disadvantages of individual economies, or they reflect government policies (Kastakova and Ruzekova 2014; Drienikova and Zubalova 2013). From the time of mercantilism, the efforts of governments promoting export and import restrictions have been observed. Smith and Ricardo pointed to the need for a free market with the invisible hand of the market and without restrictions. It was their approach that emphasized that countries and their economies are differentiated according to their ability to efficiently produce the goods.

A significant shift was the Heckscher–Ohlin theory of international trade and comparative advantages, which points to a connection with various national subsidies. Subsidies or restrictions affect the efficiency of production, as well as the intensive use of own resources in exports and the acquisition of what is rare in import (Hill 1998). Porter's theory of national competitive advantage (Porter 1985) includes the impact of factors of production, domestic demand conditions, support industries and corporate strategies, market structure and competition. New trade theories point to other characteristics in the economy, industries and sectors (Chapsa et al. 2015; Gill 2004; Fraunhofer IPT, Droege & Comp. 2006). Most theories deal with trade with goods, less with services.

3 Data and Methodology

The aim of this paper is to point out the state and basic tendencies in trade in business services in relation to trade in services based on international statistics.

Research questions are aimed at assessing the level of imports and exports in business services. We are interested in what kind of business services dominate in the Visegrad countries? Are there differences in the scope of services in the V4 countries? Is there any specialization between these countries? Have there been changes in trade between countries in 2013 and 2016? Which business services dominate in which country?

The Visegrad group (also V4) includes four countries: Czech Republic (CR), Hungary (H), Poland (PL) and Slovakia (SR). They are located in Central Europe and joined the EU in 2004. Between 1990 and 2004, they were included together as transition economies. The economies of these countries are closely linked (Corejova and Rostasova 2015). The social and cultural environment has similar features (Corejova and Al Kassiri 2016). Historically, they are connected by many ties and business relationships. Table 1 contains initial data on the V4 countries, which show

Table 1 Main indicators for Visegrad countries in 2013 and 2016 (OECD 2013–2016)

Country	Indicators	2013	2016
Czech Republic (CZ)	Population (mil.)	11.0	10.5
	GDP per capita (USD)	27,164.8	31,549.5
Hungary (H)	Population (mil.)	10.4	9.9
	GDP per capita (USD)	19,754.0	26,222.0
Poland (PL)	Population (mil.)	39.7	38.6
	GDP per capita (USD)	20,976.1	26,455.3
Slovak Republic (SK)	Population (mil.)	5.6	5.4
	GDP per capita (USD)	24,283.6	29,720.1

Table 2 Heat map of GII for Visegrad economies in comparison with regional averages in 2016

Index	CZ	H	PL	SK	Europe—Region
Global innovation index	**49.40**	44.71	40.22	41.70	**48.0**
Innovation output sub-index	**44.53**	40.47	31.73	35.43	**42.5**
Innovation input sub-index	**54.82**	48.94	48.71	47.96	**53.5**
Ratio innovation efficiency index	**0.82**	**0.83**	0.65	0.74	**0.8**

Source OECD (2016)
The marked values of indicators in bold are in cases where they are higher than the value in Europe-Region

the value of GDP per capita in USD and now rank V4 countries as high-income countries. The Visegrad supine represented 64.4 million EU citizens in 2016.

Based on the levels of the Global Innovation Index, including its input and output side sub-indices compared to the average level in Europe, a heat map was created (see Table 2). Analysis of the heat map shows that the Czech Republic is the leading country in this region. The Czech Republic ranked 24th in GII in 2016 (OECD 2016). Between 2013 and 2016, improving the country in the GII assessment was constantly.

Individual data on competitiveness, innovation and trade in services in countries are based on OECD statistics. Trade in services includes, according to OECD statistics, the value of services exchanged between residents and non-residents of the economy, including services provided through foreign affiliates resident abroad. This indicator is measured in millions of USD and the percentage of GDP in exports, imports and net trade. Services include transport, travel, communication, construction, insurance and financial services, computer and information services, royalties and royalties, other business services, cultural and recreational services, and government services not included in another service group. Trade in services leads to exchanges of ideas, know-how and technology, although it is often constrained by barriers such as national regulations (OECD 2018a).

In identifying the state and basic tendencies in trade in business services and their components, we used OECD (2018b) statistical data, which contain data used for trade, export and import analysis.

In the analysis of trade in services, we used a modification of the Balassa RCA index (Hinloopen and Marrewijk 2000; Kastakova 2015). The existence of comparative advantages of a country in exports in a given commodity group is indicated by an RCA indicator value greater than 1. If the index of the given commodity group is less than 1, this is a comparative disadvantage (Vokorokosova 2004). Indicates that in a given commodity, a country exports less than the average for the reference group.

4 Comparison of Business Services Trade

The level of trade in business services in the Visegrad four countries on both the export and import sides in 2013–2016 was stable. However, developments varied from country to country. There was a slight increase in trade services imports in Slovakia and Poland, the Czech Republic and Hungary (Table 3). On the export side, the increase was only 2.4% in Hungary, while in other countries the decrease was between 0.1% in Poland and 3% in Slovakia.

Taking a closer look at the structure of trade in business services, trade in R&D services (further R&D) increased by 1.72% and imports by 2.63%. A positive trend may indicate the strengthening of the importance of own R&D services in the V4 economy and their dependence on imports, as well as progress on elements related to the knowledge economy. If we look at individual Visegrad countries in 2013–2016, two of them (CR and PL) recorded an increase in imports and exports, two (SR and H) reduced imports and exports of Research and Development services (see Fig. 1).

Based on the data in Table 3, we can say that business and management consulting and public relations services account for the largest share of total imports with other business services. Export of these services and their share in trade with other business services also increased significantly in Slovakia. For the Visegrad countries, from 2013 to 2016, imports of these services accounted for more than half of imports of business services and about a third of exports. The development of service trade indicators suggests a deepening of interdependence on the common market and at the same time the need to link services with the development of industrial production focused on international markets, not only national or local markets.

Accounting, auditing, accounting and tax consultancy, as well as advertising, market research and opinion polling also show a relatively high share of trade in other business services in terms of export volume in the V4 countries (see Fig. 2).

When we assess exports and the potential comparative advantage of the Visegrad countries in other business services through the Balassa RCA index (Kastakova 2015), it can also be stated (Table 4) that:

- Slovakia has identified a strong comparative advantage in legal services (the Balassa RCA index is more than 4), which increased even more in the period under review, and accounting, auditing, accounting and tax advisory services also had an upward trend (the index indicates only a weak comparative advantage), but the highest of the Visegrad four countries, which is mainly due to the allocation of shared service centres in Slovakia. In other countries, only a comparative advantage (Balassa RCA index between 1 and 2) was recorded in the Czech Republic and Hungary in R&D services, in Poland in advertising, market research and opinion polling.

Table 3 Share of other business services in trade in services and their structure in Visegrad countries in 2013–2016 in %

Services	Trade	SR		CR		H		PL		V4	
		2013	2016	2013	2016	2013	2016	2013	2016	2013	2016
Business services	Export	20.94	17.91	21.42	19.97	19.43	21.89	21.98	21.81	21.18	21.08
	Import	20.28	21.32	24.35	23.87	36.59	34.39	24.01	24.91	26.42	26.23
Research and Development services (R&D)	Export	4.26	3.75	6.58	11.50	12.91	11.43	8.16	9.82	8.40	10.12
	Import	7.35	6.14	9.89	12.90	26.36	16.25	3.32	3.67	12.08	9.45
Legal services	Export	20.51	14.27	1.81	2.13	2.12	1.53	2.65	2.21	3.96	2.91
	Import	12.61	8.99	1.17	1.12	0.65	0.91	1.62	1.41	2.13	1.92
Accounting, auditing, bookkeeping and tax consulting services	Export	16.46	18.08	8.56	9.71	12.91	12.46	10.67	14.04	11.15	13.03
	Import	4.58	5.84	4.01	4.73	1.20	1.53	2.81	3.19	2.75	3.33
Advertising, market research and public opinion polling services	Export	11.58	7.44	11.95	11.40	7.64	5.71	20.56	18.79	15.00	13.30
	Import	6.95	7.44	12.26	9.92	4.88	5.45	9.99	12.62	8.73	9.54
Architectural services	Export	0.16	0.12	0.25	0.33	0.27	0.13	0.51	0.30	0.37	0.26
	Import	0.17	0.10	0.12	0.04	0.11	0.15	0.48	0.34	0.26	0.20
Business and management consulting and public relations services	Export	5.09	19.35	28.94	25.51	17.18	22.86	17.73	40.56	19.18	31.63
	Import	21.20	19.58	35.40	34.78	24.56	25.88	41.32	86.31	33.26	51.71

Source OECD (2016)

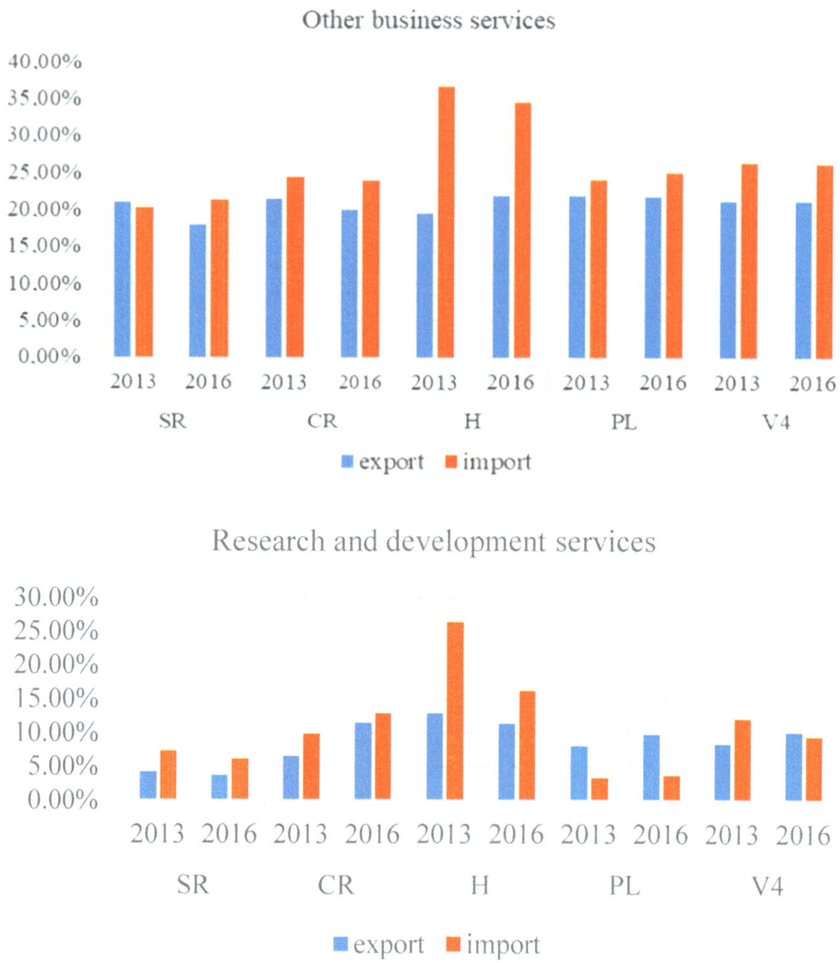

Fig. 1 Comparison of the import and export rates of the business services and R&D services in Visegrad countries in the 2013 and 2016 years

5 Conclusion

Based on an analysis of data on trade in business services of the Visegrad countries, it can be concluded that:

- Trade in business services is an important part of both import and export services in all V4 countries and has the potential to further develop. We can unequivocally agree and conclude that other business services are becoming increasingly important, as evidenced by both import growth and export growth over the period.
- Significant market dynamics in three service groups are foreseen—accounting, auditing, accounting and tax consultancy; advertising, market research and

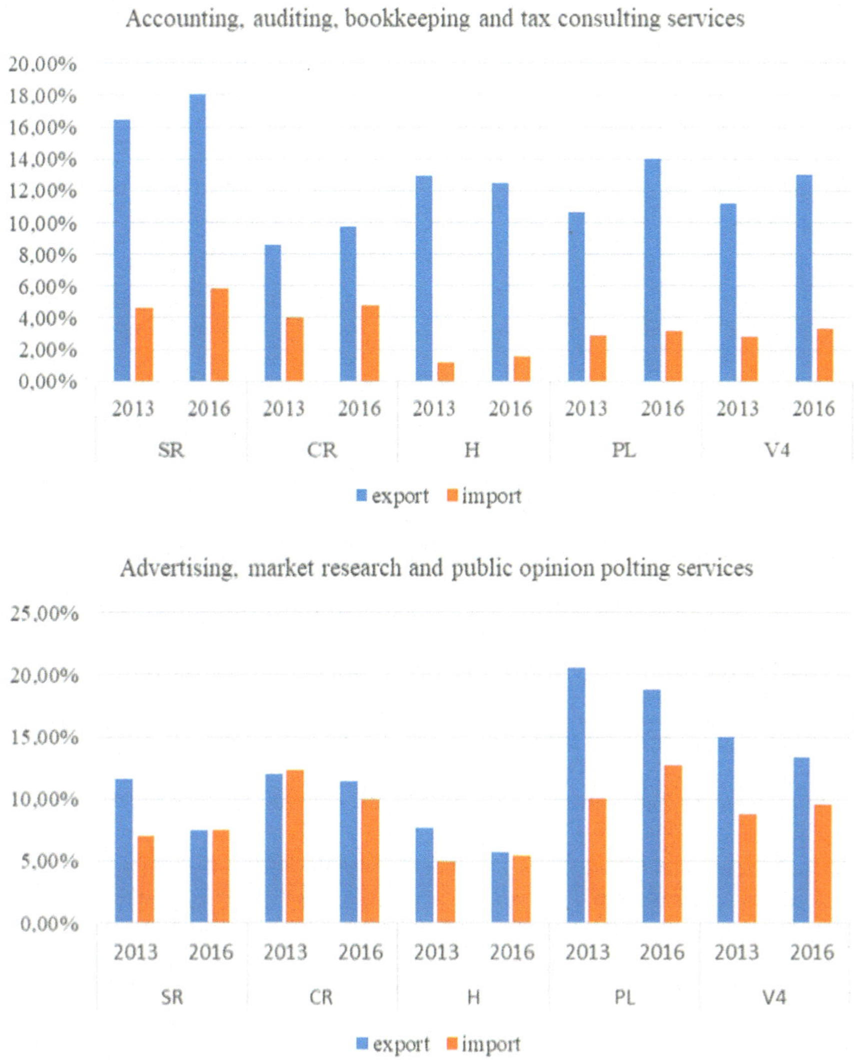

Fig. 2 Comparison of the import and export rates of the two groups of the business services in Visegrad countries in the 2013 and 2016 years

opinion polling; and business and management consultancy and public relations consultancy. They indicate the allocation of shared services centres, data processing centres, etc. in the Visegrad countries.

- The growth of R&D in trade in services in the Czech Republic and Poland and the opposite development in the Slovak Republic and the H are associated with different levels of support for Research and Development at the national level and subsequently manifested at the level of the global innovation index.

Table 4 Balassa index RCA for the export of other business services in Visegrad countries in 2013 and 2016

Services	SR		CR		H		PL	
	2013	2016	2013	2016	2013	2016	2013	2016
Research and Development services (R&D)	0.51	0.44	0.77	**1.20**	**1.68**	**1.09**	0.94	0.94
Legal services	**5.24**	**5.77**	0.45	0.77	0.58	0.51	0.65	0.73
Accounting, auditing, bookkeeping and tax consulting services	**1.49**	**1.63**	0.76	0.79	**1.26**	0.92	0.92	**1.04**
Advertising, market research and public opinion polling services	0.78	0.66	0.79	0.90	0.56	0.41	**1.32**	**1.37**
Architectural services	0.43	0.56	0.68	**1.36**	0.81	0.49	**1.34**	**1.15**
Business and management consulting and public relations services	0.27	0.72	**1.49**	0.85	0.98	0.70	0.89	**1.24**

The marked values of the Balassa index RCA index in bold acquire a value higher than 1, which indicates a certain level of comparative advantages

- The key to business growth is the strategic location of the business service portfolio in each country and the specialization or exploitation of the comparative advantages of the V4 countries in terms of their location and available labour resources.

International trade in services in the V4 countries increased overall by 7% in 2013–2016, on the import side it decreased by 0.85%, of which trade in business and management consulting and public relations services increased by 76.9% on the export side and 53% on the import side.

Trade in services despite the V4 membership in the EU28 and in the single market is under constant pressure from various factors, such as those of associations, interest groups or other groups (Corejova and Al Kassiri 2015; Majercakova 2014). Three of the V4 countries are not members of the Euro area, and the use of national currencies and their own monetary policy also affects international trade in the trade in services. However, new technological solutions create new opportunities in the trade in services and need to be constantly addressed. Technological changes in different industries and markets lead to changes in the trade in services, which are inevitably linked to international trade and the use of the comparative advantages of individual countries in the international environment (Jankalova 2013).

Acknowledgements This contribution was undertaken as a part of the research projects 1/0152/18 VEGA Business models and platforms in the digital space and 1/0087/18 VEGA Enhancing competitiveness of the Zilina region by increasing influence of the University of Zilina in the region and in Zilina town.

References

Altenburger OA (1981) Ansätze zu einer Produktions- und Kostentheorie der Dienstleistungen. Berlin, München

Chapsa X, Tsanana E, Katrakilidis C (2015) Growth and convergence in the EU-15: more evidence from the cohesion countries. In: 7th international conference, the economies of Balkan and Eastern Europe countries in the changed world, EBEEC 2015, 8–10 May 2015. Procedia Econ Finance 33:55–63

Corejova T, Al Kassiri M (2015) The power of knowledge-intensive services. In: 4th international conference on social sciences and society (ICSSS 2015), Paris. Advances in education research, vol 70, pp 354–357

Corejova T, Al Kassiri M (2016) Knowledge as the key to the global cooperation and its important role among nations. In: Lee G (ed) 3rd international conference on PES 2016. Lecture notes in earth sciences-LNES, vol 4. Bangkok, pp 181–183

Corejova T, Rostasova M (2015) Regional development, innovation and creativity. In: Proceedings from IX international conference on applied business research (ICABR2014), Talca, 06–10 Oct 2014. Mendel University, Brno, pp 114–127

Drienikova K, Zubalova L (2013) Zahraničnoobchodná politika EÚ v meniacich sa podmienkach globálneho hospodárskeho prostredia. Vydavateľstvo EKONÓM, Bratislava

Fisk RP, St. Grove J, Joby J (2004) Interactive services marketing, 2nd edn. Boston

Franken B (2009) The relevance of industrial services in business-to-business relationships. An empirical study in the machine and plant construction industry and the chemical industry. Dissertation, University of Zilina, Zilina

Fraunhofer IPT, Droege & Comp. (2006) Internationale Servicestrategien im Maschinenbau 2006. Düsseldorf, Aachen

Gill C (2004) Architektur für das Service-Engineering zur Entwicklung von technischen Dienstleistungen, Schriftenreihe Rationalisierung und Humanisierung. Aachen

Grönroos C (1998) Marketing services, the case of a missing product. J Bus Ind Mark 13(4/5):322–328

Hill CWL (1998) International business: competing in the global marketplace. Irwin/McGraw-Hill. ISBN 0-256-27053-8

Hinloopen J, Marrewijk C (2000) On the empirical distribution of the Balassa index. Retrieved 19 June 2015 from https://www2.econ.uu.nl/users/marrewijk/eta/pdf%20files/ballassa%20wwa.pdf

Homburg C, Garbe B (1996) Towards an improved understanding of industrial services, quality dimensions and their impact on buyer-seller relationships. J Bus Bus Mark 6(2):39–71

Jankalova M (2013) Conception based on definition of business factors of successfulness for the support of reaching the excellence of enterprise subjects. Procedia Soc Behav Sci 81:531–535. ISSN 1877-0228

Kastakova E (2015) Odhalené komparatívne výhody Slovenska pri prenikaní na zahraničné trhy. Stud commer Bratisl, 31 8:384–392

Kastakova E, Ruzekova V (2014) Operácie v zahraničnom obchode—teória a prax. Vydavateľstvo EKONÓM, Bratislava

Langeard E (1981) Grundfragen des Dienstleistungsmarketing. ZFP 3(4):233–240

Lay G (2002) Service provider industry, industrial migration from manufacturing to selling products and services. Fraunhofer Institute Systems and Innovation Research, Karlsruhe

Madlenak R, Madlenakova L (2015) The differences in online advertising acceptance in China and Slovakia. In: International conference on management engineering and management innovation, Changsha, pp 45–49

Majercakova M (2014) Vplyv regulácie na vývoj roamingových cien operátorov v Slovenskej a Českej republike. In: IPoCC—international postal and e-communications conference, proceedings, Pardubice, 18–19 Sept 2014, pp 132–137. ISBN 978-80-86530-94-9. CD-ROM

Meffert H, Bruhn M (2006) Dienstleistungsmarketing, Grundlagen, Konzepte, Methoden, 5th edn. Wiesbaden

Nüttgens M, Heckmann M, Luzius MJ (1998) Service Engineering Rahmenkonzept. In: IM—Fachzeitschrift für Information, Management und Consulting, Sonderausgabe Service Engineering, Aug 1998, pp 14–19

OECD (2016) The global innovation index 2011–2016. www.oecd.org

OECD (2018a) https://data.oecd.org/trade/trade-in-services.htm

OECD (2018b) Statistics on international trade in services, vol 2017, issue 2. Detailed tables by partner country. https://doi.org/10.1787/sits-v2017-2-en

Porter ME (1985) Competitive advantage. New York

Scheuch F (2002) Dienstleistungsmarketing. München

Schmidt N (2000) Tertiarisierung—Ende der Industriegewerkschaften? Zum Verhältnis von Industriesektor und industriellen Dienstleistungen. In: Peters J (ed) Dienstleistungsarbeit in der Industrie. Hamburg, pp 20–49

Schuh G, Speth C (2000) Gestaltung von industriellen Dienstleistungen, Arbeitspapier des Instituts fur Technologiemanagement. St. Gallen

Vokorokosova R (2004) Komparatívne a konkurenčné výhody v období globalizácie. Vydavateľstvo EKONÓM, Bratislava

Measuring States of Inefficiency and Decoupling in the European Union

Tania Muñoz-Ramos, Edgar J. Saucedo-Acosta, and Jesús Díaz-Pedroza

Abstract The climate change is a global externality that requires international efforts. The European Union has subscribed international agreements and internally has launched the European Union 2020 Strategy, with specific environmental targets. In this context, it is important to measure the environmental damage and economic growth relationship in the European Union. The paper aims to evaluate the decoupling of the gross domestic product and greenhouse gas emissions and to analyse the effects of population growth and gross domestic product on increase of greenhouse gas emissions and energy inefficiency in the members of the European Union. To do that, we use Data Envelopment Analysis models, which were applied to analyse the inefficiency levels and the population growth and gross domestic product decoupling of the 28 member countries of the European Union using data from the years 1995, 2000, 2005, 2010 and 2014. It was found that Luxembourg, Austria, Denmark, Malta, UK and Italy are the economies that turn out to be the most decoupled, and there is a reduction of inefficiency rates from 2010 to 2014 that could be affected by the great recession of 2009.

Keywords European Union · Decoupling · Inefficiency · Population growth

Jel Classification Q56

T. Muñoz-Ramos · E. J. Saucedo-Acosta (✉)
IIESES-University of Veracruz, Xalapa, Mexico
e-mail: esaucedo@uv.mx

T. Muñoz-Ramos
e-mail: taniamr16@gmail.com

J. Díaz-Pedroza
Autonomous Metropolitan University-Iztapalapa, Mexico City, Mexico
e-mail: jdp@xanum.uam.mx

A. Horobet et al. (eds.), *Business Performance and Financial Institutions in Europe*, Contributions to Economics, https://doi.org/10.1007/978-3-030-57517-5_9

1 Introduction

The global crisis we face today is a combination of several worrisome changes, among which we can include the crisis for food security (Christiaensen 2009), high levels of environmental degradation, loss of biodiversity (UNEP 2012) and climate change (Richardson et al. 2009). In order to address some of these issues, the European Union (EU) and its member states launched a sustainable growth strategy in 2010, the so-called Europe 2020 Strategy (Saucedo-Acosta 2013), in which five objectives have been set in terms of employment, innovation, education, social integration, climate change and energy. The latter is one of the most challenging objectives and in which the participation of the EU members is important. Therefore, such economies have committed themselves to reducing greenhouse gas (GHG) emissions by 20%, increasing the use of renewable energies by 20% and increasing energy efficiency by 20% (European Commission 2011).

To achieve the previous environmental goals set, the EU has proposed a series of long-term political plans in the fields of energy, transport, industry, communication and technologies to combat climate change, converting the economies of the EU member states into low-carbon economies. However, the EU is in the process of achieving the goals mentioned above, with the energy sector being one of the biggest challenges in which no significant progress has been made. Therefore, it is necessary to make greater efforts and focus on structuring policies and actions that improve energy issues (European Commission 2011).

The assessment of the main driving forces in the increase of the GHG emissions and a decoupling evaluation can act as a tool to help decision-makers to formulate and evaluate public policies on environmental matters. The term decoupling describes the relationship between economic growth and environmental damage, and in this paper, we use this term to characterise the relationship between the increase in gross domestic product (GDP) and GHG emissions.

This paper proposes the application of nonparametric models of enveloping data to analyse population growth and economic growth (measured in GDP) as two of the main pollution factors in the 28 member countries of the EU, using data from 1995, 2000, 2005, 2010 and 2014. This approach can also be used to analyse the decoupling situation between GDP and GHG emissions.

The decoupling GDP-GHG has been studied under various parametric methodologies that have used processes of decomposition of identities, elastic change measures and the evaluation of the existing correlation using diverse panel data methodologies. However, the Data Envelopment Analysis (DEA) can be used as a nonparametric alternative to calculate the decoupling of economic growth and GHG emissions. This approach is based on the productivity theory to measure the efficiency of a cluster of observations.

The DEA models proposed in this paper attempt to measure inefficiency indexes using data series of population and GDP as inputs and GHG emissions and energy efficiency as outputs of environmental damage. We use GDP as an input, unlike standard studies (Färe et al. 1989; Lozano and Gutiérrez 2008; Zhou et al. 2006), because one of the objectives of the paper is to measure the decoupling of GDP and GHG emissions. Therefore, it was required to use the GDP as input of the GHG emissions in the first model.

Findings show Luxembourg, Austria, Denmark, Malta, UK and Italy are the countries that could be considered the most decoupled of the EU in 2014. There was a reduction of inefficiency rates from 2010 to 2014, which coincides with the great recession 2009, and affected the entire period (1995–2014).

2 Literature Review

The term decoupling has been used in environmental studies to characterise the relationship between economic activity and the degradation of the environment. This has not been the first concept proposed to describe the effort that economies have made to achieve economic growth causing the least damage to the environment.

However, controversy arises regarding the real possibility of achieving the decoupling of economic growth with respect to the level of ecological degradation, but several studies have reported the possibility of total or partial decoupling of the economy from CO_2 emissions and other studies from GHG emissions. To characterise this relationship, different tools have been used, one of which is the IPAT approach, in which different environmental impacts can be analysed at different levels, since according to Ehrlich and Holdren (1970) and Commoner (1971) the main driving forces of the GHG increase are: the population, affluence and technology development.

In 1989, another approach emerged called the Kaya Identity (Eq. 1), which offers an explanatory analysis of different factors that influence the amount of emissions and their variation over periods of time (Yamaji et al. 1991).

$$CO_2 = P \cdot \frac{GDP}{P} \cdot \frac{Energy}{GHG} \cdot \frac{CO_2}{Energy} \qquad (1)$$

The Kaya Identity has also been used in several studies (Ang and Zhang 1999; Mielnik and Goldemberg 1999; Sun 2005). Additionally, Zhang (2000) used the decomposed form of the Kaya Identity, as shown in Formula (2), where CO_2 is equal to CO_2 emissions, (CO_2/TPES) expresses the amount of CO_2 emissions per unit of the total primary energy supply (TPES) which depends on the emission factors and the fuel combination, (TPES/TFC) is the total supply of primary energy by total energy consumption (TFC) which depends on the efficient conversion of energy and the combination of fuels, (TFC/GDP) is the amount of final energy consumed per unit of GDP, which depends on the final use of energy intensity, (GDP/P) is GDP divided by population (P) and depends on the activity and the structure of the economy.

$$KI_d = CO_2 \cdot \frac{CO_2}{TPES} \cdot \frac{TPES}{TFC} \cdot \frac{CO_2}{GDP} \cdot \frac{GDP}{P} \cdot P \qquad (2)$$

The Kaya Identity decomposition form was also used to analyse Ireland's primary emission factors from 1990 to 2010 (O'Mahony 2013). Ren et al. (2014) analysed the impacts of CO_2 emissions from China's manufacturing industry during the 1996–2010 period through the logarithmic average currency index (LMDI) based on the modification of the Kaya Identity. Robalino-López et al. (2015) analysed the possible changes of the main primary CO_2 emission factors in Venezuela for the period 1980–2025, using an extended methodology of the Kaya Identity and hypothetical Kuznets curve. The decoupling status of CO_2 emissions and GDP was studied alongside the main factors of the increase of CO_2 emissions in South Africa from 1990 to 2012 and were evaluated using the decomposition of the Kaya Identity (Lin et al. 2015).

Another of the methodologies used to measure the decoupling of economic growth and environmental damage is the so-called decoupling elasticity. Vehmas et al. (2003) built a frame of reference for the different linking states, which can occur in sectors, countries or groups of countries. Tapio (2005) studied the relationship between GDP, traffic volume and CO_2 emissions from transport in 15 EU countries; he also analysed the special case of road traffic in Finland between 1970 and 2001 and proposed a new framework for reference which proposes eight visible decoupling states. Enevoldsen et al. (2007) followed a decoupling elasticity methodology to study the impact of energy prices and taxes on energy efficiency and carbon emissions of 10 industrial sectors in three Scandinavian countries. Lu et al. (2015) investigated the state of decoupling by elasticity and the influential factors in energy consumption and CO_2 emissions of the industrial sector of the Jiangsu province in China from 2005 to 2012.

However, these tools (IPAT, KAYA, decoupling elasticity) are approaches that have limitations because they are multiplicative identities, so certain proportions are assumed between the different variables (Lozano and Gutierrez 2008).

In this way, various panel data analysis methodologies were proposed as tools that can measure decoupling. Niu et al. (2011) evaluated the relationship between energy consumption, GDP and CO_2 emissions for eight countries in Asia and the Pacific using a panel regression model to estimate the parameters of the variables. Hatzigeorgiou et al. (2011) studied the causal relationship between GDP, energy intensity and CO_2 emissions of Greece from 1977 to 2007, using Johansen co-integration tests and Granger causality tests, based on a multivariate correction vector model. Farhani et al. (2013) investigated the causal relationship between energy consumption, CO_2 emissions, economic growth, trade opening and urbanisation of 11 countries in the Middle East and North Africa from 1980 to 2009 using co-integration and causality tests and concluded that with higher energy consumption there is greater economic growth and greater economic opening; therefore, there is an increase in the amount of CO_2 emissions. Kasman and Duman (2015) investigated the causal relationship between energy consumption, CO_2 emissions, economic growth, commercial openness and urbanisation of members and candidates to the EU, using unit root tests, co-integration panel and causality tests.

The analysis through panel data has also been used to evaluate the hypothesis known as the environmental Kuznets curve (EKC), where according to Grossman and Krueger (1993), there is an empirical relationship between per capita income and certain environmental measures, and the environmental quality tends to improve as economic development reaches a certain high level, producing a relationship where environmental quality could be represented graphically in the form of an inverted U.

Nasir and Rehman (2011) used panel data to evaluate the EKC to investigate the relationship between CO_2 emissions, income, energy consumption and commercial openness in Pakistan from 1997 to 2008, finding that there is no evidence in that country of the presence of the EKC in the short term. Hamit-Haggar (2012) estimated the long-term relationship and the causal relationship between greenhouse gas emissions, energy consumption and economic growth for Canadian industrial sectors from 1990 to 2007 using a panel data methodology based on the hypothesis of the EKC finding that there is a long-term equilibrium between energy consumption as a significantly positive impact on greenhouse gas emissions, while there is a nonlinear relationship between emissions and economic growth consistent with that established in the hypothesis of the EKC. Lapinskienė et al. (2014) used various panel data tests to confirm the presence of the EKC in 27 countries of the EU from 1995 to 2010, using the cubic equation to validate the hypothesis. However, these methodologies have the disadvantage do not measure the degrees of inefficiency and the decoupling.

The DEA models emerge as a nonparametric alternative that serves to calculate the decoupling of economic growth and GHG emissions. This approach was formally introduced by Charnes, Cooper and Rhodes in 1978, but was based on Farrell's productivity efficiency theory (1957), which proposed to visualise efficiency from a non-ideal real perspective, where production will be evaluated under the relative behaviour of different units in which the presence of multiple inputs and outputs makes it difficult to compare their performance (Lopez et al. 2007). Therefore, the efficiency measures will be relative and not absolute, and the value reached by a certain productive unit will correspond to an expression of the observed deviation with respect to those considered more efficient, given the information available (Schuschny 2007).

The DEA method consists of a mathematical programming technique that, given a set of decision making units (DMU), could work with different contexts of inputs and outputs to be able to identify another set of units that serve to build a base production boundary with which we can compare the original DMU.

To analyse how different DMUs evolve in terms of efficiency during different periods of time, the Malmquist indexes (1953) are used, which represent different relationships in multi-output and multi-input spaces based on distance calculation, existing between one period and the other.

Schuschny (2007) applied DEA models and Malmquist indexes to study the efficiency of energy consumption and the substitution of non-renewable energies for renewable energy sources in Latin America and the Caribbean. Zhou et al. (2008) used DEA models to measure the environmental performance of eight regions of the world to demonstrate the advantages to use DEA models with non-increasing returns on DEA models with constant returns. Zhou and Ang (2008) proposed a decomposition methodology based on enveloping data to solve seven variables that act as factors that affect the change of emissions over time by the use of technologies. Lozano and Gutierrez (2008) studied the environmental performance of most countries of Annex B of the Kyoto Protocol, using DEA models under different specifications of inputs and outputs to characterise the relationship between the different factors, which according to the Identity of Kaya, increase the amount of CO_2 emissions from the countries under study. Zhou et al. (2010) use Malmquist indexes to measure the performance in the total change of CO_2 emissions, considering the technological innovations of 18 of the countries with the highest amount of emissions from 1997 to 2004.

3 Methods and Data

A nonparametric DEA methodology was used to analyse the inefficiency levels, decoupling and to evaluate the amount of population, as a factor of environmental degradation of the 28 EU member countries: Germany, Austria, Belgium, Bulgaria, Cyprus, Croatia, Denmark, Slovakia, Slovenia, Spain, Estonia, Finland, France, Greece, Hungary, Ireland, Italy, Latvia, Lithuania, Luxembourg, Malta, the Netherlands, Poland, Portugal, the UK, Czech Republic, Romania and Sweden, for years 1995, 2000, 2005, 2010 and 2014.

We use the following variables: GDP from the World Bank database (2017) referred in dollars at constant prices to 2010, population growth (P) from the Eurostat database (2017), primary energy production (PE) in thousands of tonnes of oil equivalent (TOE) from the Eurostat database (2017) and greenhouse gas (GHG) emission data in millions of tonnes (Mt) from the Eurostat database (2017) which includes CO_2 emissions, N_2O in CO_2 equivalent, CH_4 in CO_2 equivalent, HFC in CO_2 equivalent, PFC in CO_2 equivalent, SF_6 in CO_2 equivalent and NF_3 in CO_2 equivalent.

The methodological process consisted in modelling the existing relationships between, GDP, P, PE and GHG through the formulation of two models to analyse two of the main pollution factors that according to Kaya (1990) and Yamani et al. (1991) are: GDP and P. The following approach differs from previous papers, as the aim is to evaluate the inefficiency levels instead of efficiency levels.

3.1 Proposed DEA Models

The first proposed model (3) considers GDP as input and GHG and PE as controlled outputs. We use GDP as an input, unlike standard studies (Färe et al. 1989; Lozano and Gutiérrez 2008; Zhou et al. 2006), because one of the objectives of the paper is to measure the decoupling of GDP and GHG emissions. Therefore, it was required to use the GDP as input of the GHG emissions in the first model. This model estimates the percentages of inefficiency obtained with the calculation of the DEA model, and indirectly the decoupling relationship between environmental damage (GHG emissions) and economic growth (GDP) of the countries under study associated with energy inefficiency values (primary energy production). This proposed approach can be can be written vectors as $g = (\text{GHG}_0\ \text{PE}_0 \mid \text{GDP}_0)$, where GHG_0 PE_0 and GDP_0 are the given values of previous variables.

$$
\begin{aligned}
&\text{Min}\beta \\
&\text{s.t} \\
&\sum_{J-1}^{N} \lambda_J \text{GDP}_J \leq \text{GDP}_0 \\
&\sum_{J-1}^{N} \lambda_J \text{PE}_J = \text{PE}_0 \cdot (1+\beta) \\
&\sum_{J-1}^{N} \lambda_J \text{GHG}_J = \text{GHG}_0 \cdot (1+\beta) \\
&\lambda_j \geq 0 \forall j \quad \beta \geq 0
\end{aligned}
\tag{3}
$$

In (3), N represents the number of observations in the sample, β is the size of the inefficiency and λ_j are non-negative multipliers that will define the linear combination of the sample observations. The values of β close to zero will denote a certain degree of efficiency in the parameters, the larger the value of β the greater the inefficiency.

The second model (4) is formulated in a way that inefficiency can be found, given the variables P, PE and GHG, where population is considered as an input and PE and GHG are the controlled outputs. We use P as an input, like standard studies (Färe et al. 1989; Lozano and Gutiérrez 2008; Zhou et al. 2006). This model estimates the percentages of inefficiency obtained with the calculation of the DEA model, using the P as input. The model described vectors remains as: $g = (\text{GHG}_0\ \text{PE}_0 \mid \text{P}_0)$, where GHG_0 PE_0 and P_0 are the given values of previous variables.

$$
\begin{aligned}
&\text{Min}\beta \\
&\text{s.t} \\
&\sum_{J-1}^{N} \lambda_J P_J \leq P_0 \\
&\sum_{J-1}^{N} \lambda_J \text{PE}_J = \text{PE}_0 \cdot (1+\beta) \\
&\sum_{J-1}^{N} \lambda_J \text{GHG}_J = \text{GHG}_0 \cdot (1+\beta)
\end{aligned}
\tag{4}
$$

$$\lambda_j \geq 0 \forall j \quad \beta \geq 0$$

4 Results

To illustrate the DEA approach proposed in the previous section, growth data of P, GDP, PE and GHG emissions have been used, coming from the 28 member countries of the EU. Table 1 shows the β of the computation of the model (3), with vector $g =$ ($GHGI_0$ PE_0 | GDP_0), using the Frontier Analysis software, where the β shows the percentages of the inefficiency values, the higher the β the greater the inefficiency.

According to the results in 2014, the countries with the lowest inefficiency rate are: Luxembourg (15.7%), Austria (17.3%), Denmark (18.5%), Malta (18.7%), UK (18.8%) and Italy (18.9%). The least efficient countries regarding GDP as input and GHG, PE as controlled outputs are: Bulgaria (100%), Estonia (100%), Poland (65.5%), Romania (61.6%) and Czech Republic (58.8%); nevertheless, it should be noted that the last three countries show a rate of decrease in their index over time.

Overall, Fig. 1 shows that there was an increase (on average) on inefficiency levels from 1995 to 2010, and then a reduction of inefficiency in 2010–2014. The above may be due to the 2009 great recession where there was a reduction of economic activity. Using the inefficiency trends of Fig. 1, it can be said that there was not a GDP-GHG emissions decoupling, on average, from 1995 to 2010, and a decoupling from 2010 to 2014. It is not clear that the decoupling in the 2010–2014 period is due to EU public policies or the effect of the great recession of 2009, or a combination of both.

Table 2 shows the results of the computation of the DEA model (4) proposed in the previous section, where the inefficiency data are shown considering P, PE and GHG emissions.

According to the results in 2014, the amount of GHG and PE generated for the amount of P, the least efficient countries are: Estonia (100%), Luxembourg (100%), Sweden (80.1%), Netherlands (78.7%), Finland (75.4%) and Czech Republic (73.1%). However, the vast majority of the member countries of the EU exceed the 40% of the inefficiency index, demonstrating the existence of a severe ineffectiveness of public policies and actions aimed at improving energy efficiency and the reduction of greenhouse gas emissions. The countries with the lowest inefficiency rates are: Malta (26%), Croatia (31.4%), Latvia (33.7%), Romania (34.4) and Hungary (34.6%).

On average, Fig. 2 shows that there was a marginal increase of inefficiency from 1995 to 2010, and then, from 2010 to 2014 a reduction of inefficiency. UK had a high reduction (33.6%) of inefficiency from 1995 to 2010, and then, from 2010 to 2014 that country showed another reduction (17.2) in its inefficiency levels. Denmark achieved an increase of inefficiency (10.9%) from 1995 to 2010, and then, a high increase of efficiency (34.8%).

Table 1 Percentages of inefficiency obtained with the calculation of the DEA model (3)

Country/Period	1995	2000	2005	2010	2014
Austria	11.9	13.5	17.6	18.5	17.3
Belgium	18.7	20.4	22.4	23.6	20.9
Bulgaria	100	100	100	100	100
Croatia	32.2	30.3	34.9	40.0	35.5
Cyprus	19.5	23.8	28.0	30.2	32.2
Czech Republic	61.4	67.7	74.1	65.0	58.8
Denmark	16.1	30.8	39.6	28.1	18.5
Estonia	90.1	75.0	79.8	100	100
Finland	22.0	23.5	28.6	29.3	28.9
France	15.8	18.3	21.8	20.0	19.6
Germany	17.1	18.8	21.6	23.6	22.9
Greece	22.8	28.5	31.3	33.8	38.2
Hungary	41.4	38.7	40.0	42.8	38.1
Ireland	24.8	23.6	22.7	24.0	22.4
Italy	12.4	15.2	18.8	20.5	18.9
Latvia	41.0	34.5	31.7	43.3	38.5
Lithuania	54.1	44.4	45.1	46.2	40.1
Luxembourg	15.0	12.9	19.5	19.5	15.7
Malta	15.7	15.8	17.7	29.4	18.7
Netherlands	28.7	26.2	32.7	33.0	27.1
Poland	100	80.2	84.2	72.1	65.6
Portugal	17.1	21.2	26.7	25.2	26.4
Romania	81.3	86.2	79.4	68.9	61.6
Slovak Republic	50.4	49.9	50.4	44.1	38.0
Slovenia	28.5	29.1	32.5	35.7	33.0
Spain	15.0	18.9	22.6	21.6	22.1
Sweden	24.1	25.2	31.1	26.4	26.0
UK	36.6	43.0	35.1	24.9	18.8

Source Own elaboration based on the data:

- GDP in dollars at constant prices to 2010 from the World Bank database (2017)
- Primary energy production (PE) in thousands of tonnes of oil equivalent (TOE) from the Eurostat database (2017)
- Greenhouse gas (GHG) emissions in millions of tonnes (Mt), from the Eurostat database (2017), which includes CO_2 emissions, N_2O in CO_2 equivalent, CH_4 in CO_2 equivalent, HFC in CO_2 equivalent, PFC in CO_2 equivalent, SF_6 in CO_2 equivalent, NF_3 in CO_2 equivalent

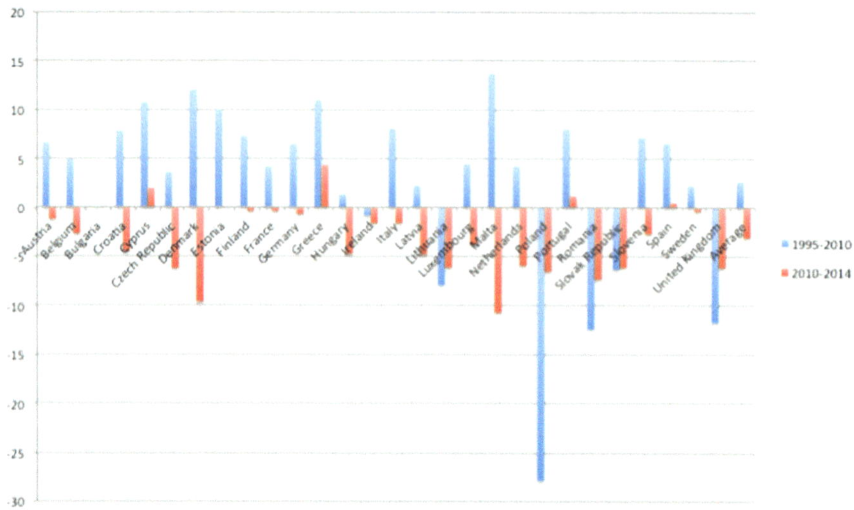

Fig. 1 Changes (%)[a] on inefficiency levels by EU member according model 1. *Source* Own elaboration from Table 1. [a]Positive levels mean an increase in inefficiency, and negative levels mean a reduction of inefficiency

5 Conclusions

In this study, we applied two nonparametric models of enveloping data to analyse growth P and growth GDP as two of the main pollution factors in the 28 member countries of the EU, using data of the following years: 1995, 2000, 2005, 2010 and 2014. The DEA models follow a different approach to previous papers, because the aim it is to characterise indexes of inefficiency instead of efficiency (Schuschny 2007; Zhou and Ang 2008; Lozano and Gutierrez 2008) subject to different inputs, translated as primary factors that influence the amount of GHG emissions and energy efficiency (translated in terms of primary energy production). Besides, we use GDP as an input, unlike standard studies (Färe et al. 1989; Lozano and Gutiérrez 2008; Zhou et al. 2006), because one of the objectives of the paper is to measure the decoupling of GDP and GHG emissions.

The results of the first model can be considered as a measure of the GDP-GHG decoupling levels. Low levels of inefficiency rates mean some degree of GDP-GHG emissions decoupling, because with low levels of pollution is possible to obtain a certain level of economic activity. Based on the results obtained with the first model in 2014, the countries with the highest levels of decoupling and efficiency were Luxembourg, Austria, Denmark, Malta, UK and Italy. It is also interesting to note a clear increase of the inefficiency rates from 1995 to 2010 and then a reduction from 2010 to 2014, and in the entire period (1995–2014) there was, on average, a reduction of inefficiency that it was affected by the last period (2010–2014). The reduction of inefficiency in 2010–2014 coincides with the great recession (2009),

Table 2 Percentages of inefficiency obtained with the calculation of the DEA model (4)

Country/Period	1995	2000	2005	2010	2014
Austria	50.2	56.5	51.1	57.1	52.9
Belgium	71.8	78.9	61.2	66.0	58.6
Bulgaria	46.2	42.5	42.3	48.6	47.7
Croatia	29.1	33.5	34.7	39.2	31.4
Cyprus	44.1	55.9	43.6	45.8	52.2
Czech Republic	90.3	91.3	83.5	89.0	73.1
Denmark	87.3	100	100	98.2	63.4
Estonia	75.1	74.4	75.3	100	100
Finland	79.6	84.9	77.9	93.6	75.4
France	56.5	58.7	52.5	55.7	46.7
Germany	71.5	72.3	58.7	64.8	65.3
Greece	50.2	62.9	52.8	53.1	53.4
Hungary	41.6	42.3	36.3	39.0	34.6
Ireland	76.5	91.0	62.8	60.4	70.5
Italy	42.6	50.2	40.1	41.5	39.6
Latvia	24.8	24.4	25.6	34.0	33.7
Lithuania	32.8	31.2	34.9	31.3	37.1
Luxembourg	100	100	100	100	100
Malta	21.7	24.9	17.7	30.6	26.0
Netherlands	100	91.8	84.6	100	78.7
Poland	69.9	63.6	57.0	63.2	59.9
Portugal	31.7	41.3	32.8	33.4	35.5
Romania	45.8	39.3	37.8	39.5	34.4
Slovak Republic	49.2	51.8	45.1	47.5	43.9
Slovenia	50.1	56.7	52.6	58.7	47.6
Spain	40.3	51.0	42.0	40.0	41.0
Sweden	81.0	65.5	66.7	82.8	80.1
UK	100	90.0	74.2	66.4	49.2

Source Own elaboration based on the data:

- Population growth (P) from the Eurostat database (2017)
- Primary energy production (PE) in thousands of tonnes of oil equivalent (TOE) from the Eurostat database (2017)
- Greenhouse gas (GHG) emissions in millions of tonnes (Mt), from the Eurostat database (2017), which includes CO_2 emissions, N_2O in CO_2 equivalent, CH_4 in CO_2 equivalent, HFC in CO_2 equivalent, PFC in CO_2 equivalent, SF_6 in CO_2 equivalent, NF_3 in CO_2 equivalent

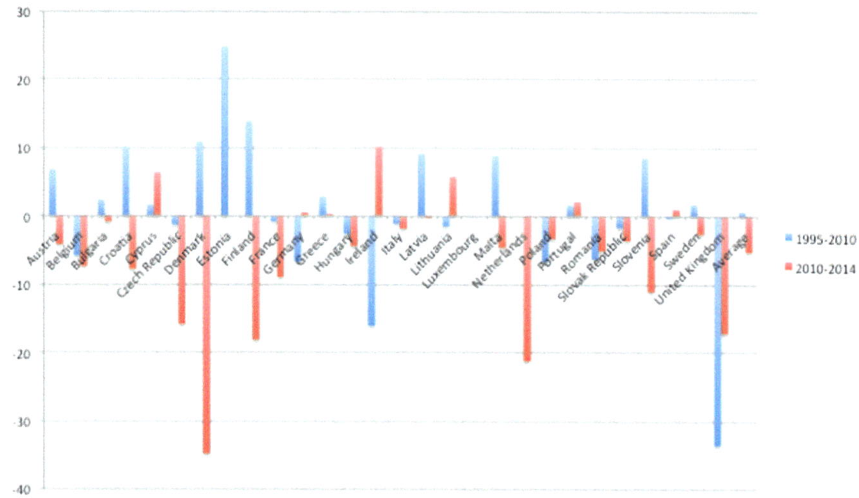

Fig. 2 Changes (%)[a] on inefficiency levels by EU member according model 2. *Source* Own elaboration from Table 2. [a]Positive levels mean an increase in inefficiency, and negative levels mean a reduction of inefficiency

where there was a generalised reduction of GDP in Europe. It is not clear that the decoupling in the 2010–2014 period is due to EU public policies or the effect of the great recession of 2009, or a combination of both.

The second model turns out to be an optimal tool to evaluate the structure and activity of the population with the purpose of not only reducing greenhouse gas emissions, but also reducing energy waste. The second model shows that there was a marginal increase of inefficiency from 1995 to 2010, and then, from 2010 to 2014 a reduction of inefficiency. UK had a high reduction (33.6%) of inefficiency from 1995 to 2010, and then, from 2010 to 2014 that country showed another reduction (17.2) in its inefficiency levels. Denmark achieved an increase of inefficiency (10.9%) from 1995 to 2010, and then, a high increase of efficiency (34.8%).

This research shows the degree of decoupling of the EU members states, which could be used by decisions makers to suggest some environments policies at national level, and this way to achieve the EU 2020 targets. From this paper, future research could be focused to analyse the implications of COVID-19 in reducing the GDP and CO_2 emissions, as well as its effect on the degree of decoupling.

References

Ang B, Zhang F (1999) Inter-regional comparisons of energy-related CO_2 emissions using the decomposition technique. Energy 24:297–305

Christiaensen L (2009) Revisiting the global food architecture. Lessons from the 2008 crisis. Rev Bus Econ 54:345–361

Commoner B (1971) The closing circle: nature, man and technology. Knopf, New York
Ehrlich P, Holdren J (1970) The people problem. Satur Rev 4:42–43
Enevoldsen MK, Ryelund AV, Andersen MS (2007) Decoupling of industrial energy consumption and CO_2-emissions in energy-intensive industries in Scandinavia. Energy Econ 29:665–692
European Commission (2011) Europe 2020. https://ec.europa.eu/europe2020/index_en.htm. Accessed 02-01-2017
Färe R, Grosskopf S, Lovell CAK, Pasurka C (1989) Multilateral productivity comparisons when some outputs are undesirable: a nonparametric approach. Rev Econ Stat 71(1):90–98
Farhani S, Shahbaz M, Arouri MEH (2013) Panel analysis of CO_2 emissions, GDP, energy consumption, trade openness and urbanization for MENA countries. MPRA paper no. 49258
Grossman GM, Krueger AB (1993) Environmental impacts of a North American free trade agreement. In: Garber PM (ed) The Mexico-US free trade agreement. MIT Press, Cambridge, pp 13–56
Hamit-Haggar M (2012) Greenhouse gas emissions, energy consumption and economic growth: a panel cointegration analysis from Canadian industrial sector perspective. Energy Econ 34:358–364
Hatzigeorgiou E, Polatidis H, Haralambopoulos D (2011) CO_2 emissions, GDP and energy intensity: a multivariate cointegration and causality analysis for Greece, 1977–2007. Appl Energy 88:1377–1385
Kasman A, Duman YS (2015) CO_2 emissions, economic growth, energy consumption, trade and urbanization in new EU member and candidate countries: a panel data analysis. Econ Model 44:97–103
Lapinskienė G, Tvaronavičienė M, Vaitkus P (2014) Greenhouse gases emissions and economic growth—evidence substantiating the presence of environmental Kuznets Curve in the EU. Technol Econ Dev Econ 20:65–78
Lin SJ, Beidari M, Lewis C (2015) Energy consumption trends and decoupling effects between carbon dioxide and gross domestic product in South Africa. Aerosol Air Qual Res 15:2676–2687
López J, Fernández S, Morales M (2007) Application of the skill DEA (data envelopment analysis) in the determination of efficiency of centers of costs of production. Sci Tech 37:395–400 ((In Spanish))
Lozano S, Gutierrez E (2008) Non-parametric frontier approach to modelling the relationships among population, GDP, energy consumption and CO_2 emissions. Ecol Econ 66:687–699
Lu Q, Yang H, Huang X, Chuai X, Wu C (2015) Multi-sectoral decomposition in decoupling industrial growth from carbon emissions in the developed Jiangsu Province, China. Energy 82:414–425
Mielnik O, Goldemberg J (1999) Communication The evolution of the "carbonization index" in developing countries. Energy Policy 27:307–308
Nasir M, Rehman FU (2011) Environmental Kuznets curve for carbon emissions in Pakistan: an empirical investigation. Energy Policy 39:1857–1864
Niu S, Ding Y, Niu Y, Li Y, Luo G (2011) Economic growth, energy conservation and emissions reduction: a comparative analysis based on panel data for 8 Asian-Pacific countries. Energy Policy 39:2121–2131
O'Mahony T (2013) Decomposition of Ireland's carbon emissions from 1990 to 2010: an extended Kaya Identity. Energy Policy 59:573–581
Ren S, Yin H, Chen X (2014) Using LMDI to analyze the decoupling of carbon dioxide emissions by China's manufacturing industry. Environ Dev 9:61–75
Richardson K, Steffen W, Schellnhuber H, Alcamo J, Barker T, Kammen D, Leemans R, Liverman D, Munasinghe M, Osman-Elasha B (2009) International scientific congress climate change: global risks, challenges & decisions—synthesis report. Technical report, International Alliance of Research Universities
Robalino-López A, Mena-Nieto Á, García-Ramos J-E, Golpe AA (2015) Studying the relationship between economic growth, CO_2 emissions, and the environmental Kuznets curve in Venezuela (1980–2025). Renew Sustain Energy Rev 41:602–614

Saucedo-Acosta EJ (2013) Europe 2020 strategy and eco-innovation. In: Rullán S, Saucedo-Acosta EJ (eds) Essays on innovation. University of Veracruz Ed, Xalapa, pp 145–164

Schuschny AR (2007) El método DEA y su aplicación al estudio del sector energético y las emisiones de CO_2 en América Latina y el Caribe. CEPAL, Santiago de Chile

Sun J (2005) The decrease of CO_2 emission intensity is decarbonization at national and global levels. Energy Policy 33:975–978

Tapio P (2005) Towards a theory of decoupling: degrees of decoupling in the EU and the case of road traffic in Finland between 1970 and 2001. Transp Policy 12:137–151

United Nations Environment Programme (, UNEP,) (2012) UNEP year book 2012: emerging issues in our global environment. UNEP, Nairobi

Vehmas J, Malaska P, Luukkanen J, Kaivo-Oja J, Hietanen O, Vinnari M, Ilvonen J (2003) Europe in the global battle of sustainability: rebound strikes back? Advanced sustainability analysis. Publications of the Turku School of Economics and Business Administration, series discussion and working papers, 7

Yamaji K, Matsuhashi R, Nagata Y, Kaya Y (1991) An integrated system for CO_2/energy/GNP analysis: case studies on economic measures for CO_2 reduction in Japan. Workshop on CO_2 reduction and removal: measures for the next century. International Institute for Applied Systems Analysis, Laxenburg

Zhang Z (2000) Decoupling China's carbon emissions increase from economic growth: an economic analysis and policy implications. World Dev 28:739–752

Zhou P, Ang B (2008) Decomposition of aggregate CO_2 emissions: a production-theoretical approach. Energy Econ 30:1054–1067

Zhou P, Ang BW, Poh KL (2006) Slacks-based efficiency measures for modeling environmental performance. Ecol Econ 60(1):111–118

Zhou P, Ang BW, Poh KL (2008) Measuring environmental performance under different environmental DEA technologies. Energy Econ 30:1–14

Zhou P, Ang B, Han J (2010) Total factor carbon emission performance: a Malmquist index analysis. Energy Econ 32:194–201

Political Risk on the Belt and Road

David Morris

Abstract China's programme for inter-regional economic connectivity, the Belt and Road Initiative (BRI), will develop new trade routes and production chains linking predominantly developing world economies with the Chinese market, making a unique contribution to global economic development but disrupting power relativities. At the same time, problems with debt servicing, corruption and a range of other political risks such as the role of Chinese state-owned enterprises have emerged in some BRI partner countries and with some projects. These have encouraged an increasingly negative commentary, particularly following the shift of the US rhetoric since 2017, characterising China as a strategic competitor. Conventional geopolitical, realist and liberal internationalist analysis appears to have reached foregone conclusions that the BRI will generate zero sum benefits to China and costs to others, yet there is a significant research gap in empirical case studies of what is actually taking place on the BRI. To date, firms engaged in BRI projects have been overwhelmingly Chinese, but it is likely that there will be future internationalisation of BRI projects and firms (and governments) will need to assess the full range of political risks of participation. Political risks are non-market risks that may affect business outcomes. While most political risk analysis has usually taken place at the national (country) level or at the firm (project) level, this paper utilises a political risk framework to identify political risks generated by the BRI at the geopolitical and trans-national level, as well as at the country and project levels. Under each of these categories, this paper discusses how risks are constructed, assesses available evidence, agency of stakeholders and identifies where further empirical investigation and theoretical development are required.

Keywords China · Infrastructure · Geopolitics · Trade · Investment · Political risk

D. Morris (✉)
Corvinus University, 1093 Budapest Fővám tér 8, Budapest, Hungary
e-mail: david@davidmorrisprojects.com

A. Horobet et al. (eds.), *Business Performance and Financial Institutions in Europe*, Contributions to Economics, https://doi.org/10.1007/978-3-030-57517-5_10

1 Introduction

China's new programme for inter-regional economic connectivity, the Belt and Road Initiative (BRI), will develop new trade routes and production chains linking developing world economies with the Chinese market, making a unique contribution to global economic development but disrupting power relativities. At the same time, problems with debt servicing, corruption and a range of other political risks such as the role of Chinese state-owned enterprises have emerged in some BRI partner countries and with some projects. These have encouraged an increasingly negative geopolitical commentary, particularly following the shift of the US rhetoric since 2017, characterising China as a strategic competitor. Understanding political risks of the BRI, therefore, involves multiple dimensions including at the geopolitical level, as well as at the country and firm levels.

To date, firms engaged in BRI projects have been overwhelmingly Chinese, but it is likely that there will be future internationalisation of BRI projects and firms (and governments) will need to assess the full range of political risks of participation. While most political risk analysis has usually taken place at the national (country) level or at the firm (project) level, the BRI is a program with international reach. Its infrastructure connectivity projects across the developing world and beyond seek to re-shape the international economic and therefore geopolitical environment. This ambitious programme generates risks for both governments as well as internationalised risks for firms beyond the scope of traditional national or project-level political risk categories.

Political risk refers to non-market risks that may affect business outcomes as a result of changing political, security, social, cultural, environmental or other factors. These are risks that require strategies for understanding, mitigation, management or sometimes avoidance by firms investing in foreign business environments but are also important for governments which promote outward foreign investment or seek to attract inward foreign investment. Political risks apply in specific spatio-temporal business environments with multiple variables across all dimensions and are therefore not amenable to general theory. Rather, political risk is more developed amongst practitioner consultants than in academia, with the practices of governments and firms tending to utilise area studies specialists and multiple sources of expertise to understand the multi-disciplinary factors at play in particular business environments at particular times (Simon 1984).

There is not yet a general theory of political risk for the BRI, and this paper does not propose one, but discusses risks in three broad categories: geopolitical, country-level and project-level. Under each of these categories, this paper discusses how risks are constructed, assesses available evidence, agency of stakeholders and identifies where further empirical investigation and theoretical development is required.

The first section of this paper provides a background to the geopolitical shift out of which the BRI has emerged, which is important for the discussion of geopolitical and indeed country and project risks below.

The second section of the paper provides an introduction to the BRI itself and discusses the initiative as indeed a domestic risk mitigation strategy for China, including to address its geopolitical imperatives and constraints; extend and diversify economic cooperation; and assist Chinese firms and the broader economic transformation of China. It is important to understand these domestic drivers in any analysis of political risks because the BRI seeks to integrate developing economies with the Chinese market.

The third section of the paper examines the geopolitical "China threat" that is becoming dominant in the English-speaking narrative about the BRI by assessing a number of case studies from recent years, about which the discourse has focused on fears of growing Chinese geopolitical power including claimed "debt traps".

While foreign investment and infrastructure investment in particular always entail risk, with major infrastructure projects often requiring government guarantees, many of the countries on the BRI corridors are in addition particularly high-risk business environments with varying degrees of poor governance, high levels of corruption and in some cases serious security threats. The fourth section of the paper discusses these country risks, examining a number of recent case studies.

The fifth, and shorter, section of the paper raises potential project risks in a largely theoretical discussion, as this is a category of political risk in which there is much rumour and stereotyping about Chinese firms, including state-owned enterprises in particular, but very limited study of practical, real-world case studies and is therefore an area that would benefit from further research.

Finally, some conclusions are drawn about how political risks on the Belt and Road might be managed.

2 Background

After four decades of domestic reform and internationalisation of its economy, China has become a major global power and contributor to global growth. The scale and competitiveness of its export industries, its market for imports, its capital investment capabilities and its centralised Party State make it a formidable player in the world economy, currently ranked second to the USA in economic size.

China's elevation to the front rank in trade and investment has occurred against the backdrop of a decline in confidence in other major powers as the USA and Europe, in particular, suffered financial crisis and ongoing political crises in the first decades of the twenty-first century. Importantly, the prevailing discourse on China has shifted from the first decade and a half of the century, when it centred upon awe at China's rapid economic development, to a new geopolitical focus on how China's rise poses a threat to the global balance of power.

Launched at what may prove to have been a peak of optimism about China's economic rise, in 2013, the BRI comprises a network of projects to develop new trade routes and production chains linking the growing and globalising Chinese economy predominantly with the developing world. If successful, the initiative will contribute to shifting the Centre of Economic Gravity closer to China (Chohan 2018). Consistent with the (early twenty-first century) discourse on China's impressive economic rise, the BRI was in its foundation stage often characterised as an original contribution to the challenge of global economic governance, focused on building new infrastructure and capabilities primarily in the developing world to enhance global economic integration, at a time when the developed world appeared to be turning inwards and retreating from the exuberant globalisation of recent decades.

More than one hundred nations, mostly in the developing world, have signed up to participate in the initiative, for new Chinese-funded infrastructure projects. As China's relative power grows, and as the discourse has switched in recent times to fear of a "China threat", the BRI is however increasingly being interpreted by Western powers as a geopolitical disruption. At the same time, problems with debt servicing characterised as "debt trap diplomacy", allegations of corruption and a range of other political risks such as the role of "opaque" Chinese state-owned enterprises have emerged with a number of projects in the first six years of the initiative. Much of the discourse has been however theoretical and not well-grounded in empirical studies, partly because of the ambiguity around what constitutes a BRI project which, as will be discussed below, has become an umbrella term for a wide range of enlarged Chinese international economic activity.

Whether the benefits of the BRI projects will be evenly shared or will accrue disproportionately to China will be an important area for future study. It is too early to tell, after only six years since the initiative was launched. Whether it will complement or strengthen the liberal, globalising trend towards more open trade and investment or whether it will come to represent one side of a new economic divide is something only future researchers will be able to determine. The BRI does, nonetheless, promise important new economic development and internationalisation opportunities, in particular for developing countries. On the other hand, it is clear that BRI projects in high-risk locations for investment and infrastructure development raise new and diversified risks and that these are distributed between China and its partners.

3 The Belt and Road as Domestic Risk Mitigation

For China, the initiative represents in itself a giant risk mitigation strategy with several elements. First, it seeks to reassure the world about China's peaceful rise, offering "new silk roads" for development, supporting China's claim to be a leading advocate of globalisation by integrating developing countries into global production chains and trade routes through new aid, finance and investment. Second, it strengthens China's geo-economic position, deploying China's surplus capital, capacity and infrastructure expertise to build a wider network of new, inter-dependent economic partners, further internationalising Chinese firms and potentially the Chinese currency over time (Chohan 2018). Third, investing in production chains will support China's ambitious domestic restructuring towards a higher value consumption economy, by shifting lower value production to lower cost partners in integrated supply chains at the same time as building new infrastructure and connectivity to support market development in under-developed Western China (Leandro 2018). Fourth, it is also a diversification strategy, to build supply chains from a wider range of sources than those on which China currently relies and to grow and build logistical links to new markets for Chinese exports.

The BRI is promoted by the Chinese government as an open platform of inter-regional connectivity to foster economic cooperation. It is theoretically open to developed as well as developing nations to partner on Belt and Road projects, although to date the participating firms have been overwhelmingly Chinese. Utilising Chinese capital and expertise at its core, it envisages investment in infrastructure connectivity, policy coordination, unimpeded trade, financial integration and people-to-people links (State Council of the People's Republic of China 2015; National Development and Reform Commission 2015).

From a previously low-key role in providing aid, finance and investment to the developing world, China is now shifting gear, to play a leading role in financing and building developing world infrastructure and connectivity to major markets. The new focus of the Belt and Road includes projects in Central Asia, South Asia, Southeast Asia, Africa, Central and Eastern Europe and recently extended to the South Pacific and the Arctic.

It is a qualitative shift for Chinese firms to finance, plan and construct major projects in high-risk, developing country environments. Nevertheless, some of these projects were underway before the BRI was articulated and have been retrospectively badged as falling within the initiative, including major projects in Sri Lanka, Pakistan and Kazakhstan. Since the unveiling of the initiative, virtually all Chinese-funded and implemented infrastructure projects in the developing world have been brought under its banner, including industrial estates, railways, ports and energy projects across Eurasia and the Pacific and Indian Oceans.

There has been significant criticism of BRI projects, which was perhaps inevitable in the first years of the initiative. Government aid programs and investments by even the most seasoned global corporations can often fail, be poorly designed and executed or be captured by corruption or clientelism. China's large-scale investments are just as likely to include failures as those of other countries and perhaps more so, given the significant cultural differences and earlier position on the experience curve for the government and Chinese firms in many destinations. By bringing a large number of projects under the one initiative, China has perhaps inadvertently opened the door for any failed projects to upset the reputation of the entire initiative.

The BRI is nevertheless larger than any of its constituent projects and must be understood as part of the new discourse around China in the world. The "Belt and Road" branding appears to be an attempt to shape the narrative around China's rise, to maintain the focus on bilateral and regional platforms for trade and investment development—geoeconomics rather than on geopolitics. The language of the BRI is carefully crafted around "win-win" mutual benefits, all of which resonates with developing world partners that are more familiar with major powers that seek to impose values and conditions on financing for development. It builds upon China's successful development approach of investing in infrastructure and opening China to international trade, offering other countries the platform for them to find their own path to development.

At a global level, the initiative positions China as providing economic leadership in addressing the massive gap in financing infrastructure in the developing world. The umbrella of the BRI has been rhetorically extended to include the grants and interest-free loans for projects provided by the Chinese State, concessional loans provided for infrastructure projects by the Exim Bank of China and commercial finance from the China Development Bank. At the same time, China has sponsored the creation of new multilateral financing vehicles, the Asian Infrastructure Investment Bank and the New Development Bank, as well as a Silk Road Fund.

4 Geopolitical Risks

The geopolitical narrative that has developed in the West in recent years describes the BRI as a grand strategy for maritime and land route domination by China, using subsidised finance and disproportionate scale to develop infrastructure and relationships across vast swathes of the world to impose its will, including for future potential projection of military power. The narrative goes that China is trapping developing nations in debt that will be impossible to repay, laying the groundwork for Chinese economic and political domination and potential seizure of strategic assets (Hart and Johnson 2019). This narrative has developed at the same time as China has been militarising islands in the South China Sea, using mass detention as social engineering in Xinjiang and sharpening its rhetoric on unification with renegade Taiwan. It is therefore understandable that geopolitical analysts may conflate a range of Chinese actions, combined with the authoritarian nature of the Chinese Party State, with the BRI to construct a "China threat" to the global order. Before assessing the evidence for this narrative in relation to the BRI, any discussion utilising a geopolitical frame requires an outline of China's geopolitical imperatives and constraints.

China is a rising power, but it is a constrained power. Unlike the British Empire or the USA before it, China does not and cannot enjoy dominance of the sea and is surrounded by strategic rivals. To grow and prosper, China must trade with the world, both to import resources and other goods for its huge domestic market as well as to export goods to the world. To do so, it must have access to maritime trade routes. Yet the Chinese perception is that the global and regional hegemon, the USA, with military bases across the Pacific and around the world, has the capacity to interdict China's trade. China, therefore, has a geopolitical imperative to expand its options, by developing new sea trade routes, as well as new land routes that will bring the added benefit of strengthening links to resource-rich Central Asia by developing—and potentially stabilising—China's troubled Western regions. The scale of the Chinese economy allows it to simultaneously develop new trade routes in all directions, including to Southeast Asia, South Asia and beyond.

The rise of China, including its rapid growth in military capabilities (Lague and Lim 2019), will certainly disrupt existing power relativities, strengthening China's geopolitical position. Based on the historical experience of previous rising powers, it is understandable that observers expect with the development of new trade routes will come demands to keep them secure by building bases and other platforms for the Chinese military to defend its economic interests and to protect its people overseas, which may explain unsubstantiated claims, for example, that China planned a military base in tiny, non-aligned Vanuatu (Wroe 2018a, b). In 2017–2018, the USA abandoned its decade-long policy of constructive engagement with China and embraced a new doctrine of strategic competition, manifested in the 2017 US National Security Strategy and 2018 Defence Strategy. The BRI is therefore firmly positioned within the contemporary geopolitical rivalry between China and the USA. In a landmark speech on China at the Hudson Institute in 2018, US Vice President Pence accused China of using "debt diplomacy" to expand its influence globally, citing in particular "pressure" to deliver a Sri Lankan port "directly into Chinese hands" which "may soon become a forward military base for China's growing blue-water navy" (Pence 2018).

Sri Lanka's Hambantota port is the singular project that has drawn most attention by critics. It is regularly used to make a generalised case that China has geopolitical designs to trap nations in debt and then to seize strategic assets such as ports in the event that the host country fails to make debt repayments. Closer investigation of the case does not appear to support the generalised claims. In this case, the former Sri Lankan government borrowed funds from China to build the Hambantota port with an agreement that it would be constructed by state-owned China Harbour Engineering Company. A mix of commercial and preferential borrowings from China for a series of related projects comprised about ten per cent of Sri Lanka's total debt (Weerakoon and Jayasuriya 2019). When Sri Lanka proved unable to service a series of debt agreements, China and the Sirisena government negotiated a 99-year joint venture concession over the port and adjacent land for an industrial park with the majority share awarded to one of China's leading port operators, China Merchants Port Holdings Company. Western media reports present "Chinese" control of the port as a geopolitical win for China.

There is no evidence, however, that the Chinese operator plans to convert the port to a military base as might be inferred from the geopolitical commentary. Notably, the first warship to visit the port since the change in port governance was Japanese (Orchard 2018). Indeed, Sri Lanka's public-private partnership agreement for China Merchants to operate the port included a specific condition that the port cannot be used for military purposes (Weerakoon and Jayasuriya 2019).

The agency of Sri Lanka in development of the port and associated industrial zone, as a political show pony project, has been overlooked in most commentary. Zhang (2019) notes that the Sri Lankan government remained committed to the project yet only Chinese firms demonstrated the capability to construct the port and integrate it with a new industrial development strategy to link it to new trade routes. Further, China Harbour had patiently built its reputation in Sri Lanka long before the Hambantota port project, by successfully implementing aid projects and bidding for local projects, as well as volunteering to help rebuild damaged fishing ports after the 2004 tsunami. According to Zhang, the Sri Lankan government approached the firm to progress the Hambantota port, which other firms from India had decided not to pursue. Equally, China Merchants, which subsequently took over the Hambantota Port, had been a major investor in Sri Lanka for years prior, including a successful expansion of Colombo port.

Commentators such as Lee (2018) construct a geopolitical "debt trap" narrative, in which the debt burden of countries such as Sri Lanka makes them client states of China, that will over time amass political leverage through its firms' control of international supply lines. This appears, at least so far, as too simplistic, however, given the complexity of each BRI project and the multiple actors involved. Zhang (2019) notes the importance of agency on the part of governments that engage with China. Both China and major BRI partners such as Pakistan and Malaysia are carefully reassessing projects that were ambitiously developed in recent years, to more realistically scale them and to ensure affordability as well as fitness for purpose.

A Rhodium study (Kratz et al. 2019) of forty cases of Chinese lending to 24 countries over a decade found no evidence of "debt trap diplomacy" but rather that China had agreed to about US$50 billion of debt rescheduling, often on favourable terms to borrowers.

While the Western "debt trap diplomacy" discourse appears to have over-reached, the Chinese-led discourse that the BRI will be a stabilising geopolitical force, aiding development and greater economic cooperation between the nations along its trade routes, may also be too simplistic. Significant geopolitical risks may indeed accrue to China, which may find itself and its interests caught in the middle of conflicts and disputes along new land-based trade routes which will change the shape of local economies and raise new political challenges. Southeast Asia, Central Asia and other regions encapsulated by the BRI contain deep strategic rivalries and internal divisions, for which few outlets of public expression and representation are available, and China and local Chinese business communities could conceivably become the targets of alienated populations in the future. The geopolitical stakes—both risks and opportunities—are therefore particularly high for China as well as for the world.

Another important component of the geopolitical discourse is the frame of "influence", representing concerns that China's growing economic reach will extend not only hard military and other capabilities but also "soft power" and political influence over a wider range of international partners and clients, which would generate its own risks for non-Chinese firms seeking a level playing field. A recent US government assessment describes how Chinese influence over BRI partner countries will "shape their interests to align with China's" (US Department of Defence 2018). Often conflated with geopolitical power, "influence" naturally follows from economic integration and subsequent familiarity. The more developing nations receive aid and investments from China, and the more these are matched by leadership dialogue and people-to-people links, China will accrue more "soft power". In particular, if Chinese aid and investments support economic development, it is likely China's reputation as a development partner will grow. With greater influence, it might be supposed China will lean on its partners to support its firms over those of third countries, for example. The Chinese Party State can certainly lean on its own firms to support state interests and the more Chinese firms become active in international markets, the more influence will inevitably accrue to the Chinese state. This is an area that will require careful analysis on a case-by-case basis and should form the basis of further research and theoretical development.

It remains unclear what kind of geopolitical impact the BRI and therefore what new form of inter-regional relationships it will come to represent over time. If the motivations and practices are primarily about addressing China's geopolitical imperatives and constraints, it might be expected in conventional geopolitical thinking that China will use its scale and influence to pursue its interests over the interests of others, undermining the international system by building a rival system of dependence on China as hub and Chinese influence over trade, investment, finance, policy coordination and people to people exchange. The scale of China and its potential power tends to encourage this analysis. On the other hand, if China develops a new geoeconomic-focused approach, or "win-win" in Chinese jargon, the BRI may complement and strengthen the international system by deepening interdependence and embed new platforms for trade, investment, finance, policy coordination and people to people exchange for mutual benefit. This would be consistent with the way other East Asian economies sought new kinds of regional economic cooperation as they internationalised, which complemented globalisation. The liberal optimism about bringing China into the international system through membership of the World Trade Organisation in 2001 appears to have evaporated in recent years, but it is too early to make predictions and it is helpful to examine evidence relevant to today's conditions rather than view China through frames developed for previous rising powers.

5 Country Risks

Foreign investment and infrastructure investment in particular always entails risk, with major infrastructure projects often requiring government guarantees. Many of the countries on the BRI corridors are particularly high-risk business environments with varying degrees of poor governance, high levels of corruption and in some cases serious security threats.

The greatest country risk is the sovereign risk that countries along the Belt and Road may not be able to make debt repayments. This is not only a geopolitical issue (as discussed above) but is a significant exposure for China as creditor. Its financial institutions have generally advanced funds in US dollars given the inadequate internationalisation so far of the Chinese renminbi (RMB). The new capitalisation injected into the China Development Bank, the China Export-Import Bank and the Silk Road Fund in 2014, to fund BRI projects, as well as capital for multilateral lending institutions, the Asian Infrastructure Investment Bank and the New Development Bank, all comprised US dollars, although the Chinese government is seeking to increase RMB denominated loans (Carrai 2018).

A chorus of commentators attribute blame to the Chinese funders for high debt levels rather than reflect on the agency of debtors. As a typical example of English language media discourse, the Murdoch media referred in a syndicated story to "Chinese lending practices" that risked "crushing" poor countries "under unaffordable levels of debt", yet conceding China was indeed seeking to learn from best practice, working with multilateral development banks and countries such as the UK (Aldrick 2019).

Some of the countries included in the BRI now have high levels of indebtedness to Chinese institutions. Others do not. China itself is exhibiting high levels of debt after a decade of expansionary policies. This is a new risk environment in which developing countries may be ill-prepared if a new global financial shock occurs in the short to medium term. Asset and real estate bubbles that have emerged from the flow of funds to China and other emerging economies will face adjustment (Zhang 2018). These are all risks that are less to do with the BRI itself than macro-economic policies in an uncertain international economic environment.

It might reasonably be assumed that debtor countries seeking to renegotiate debt terms with Chinese financial institutions risk negotiating from a position of weakness. Yet an examination of the experience to date is that, as the Rhodium study cited above found, a significant number of debtor countries have been able to achieve rescheduling of debt or even conversion of debt to grant aid. Ethiopia's repayments for a problematical railway project were deferred from ten to thirty years (Pilling and Feng 2018). Tonga, which became highly indebted to after taking out two concessional infrastructure loans, convinced China to defer repayments for a further five years beyond its initial five-year grace period (Dornan and Brant 2014). In most cases, China has tended to offer a grace period of five to seven years before repayment periods of fifteen to twenty years begin, typically at around two per cent interest. It remains to be seen how China may exercise leverage over governments in financial distress in future and whether this is a risk to Chinese funding institutions or a geopolitical opportunity for the State.

Further, the Belt and Road includes many operating environments which are characterised by poor local governance, inadequate security, inconsistent rule of law, lack of policy and project coordination capacity, inadequate infrastructure and labour skills, amongst other risks, all of which are challenges for successful project implementation and outcomes. Regardless of the BRI, these are environments in which corruption and clientelism, opaque and conflicting state and stakeholder interests, political instability and even threat of conflict and law and order problems may exist. Investing in states without strong institutions and good governance is both a risk and a calculated opportunity, given Chinese confidence in their own model of development. Typically, only major resources and energy investors are prepared to take on high-risk environments (in expectation of high returns), but these are now being matched by Chinese infrastructure firms.

Some high-profile projects have failed, such as the US$4 billion Addis Ababa-Djibouti freight railway, because of poor planning, underuse and power shortages, which cost the China Export and Credit Insurance Corporation (Sinosure) losses of around US$1 billion (Ng 2018).

The Chinese government and Chinese firms are demonstrating with the BRI a level of confidence in their ability to operate in challenging environments that may bring significant future costs. Equally, receiving states often welcome Chinese finance for infrastructure investment and its more flexible conditions and processes, compared with other international sources of finance. Vanuatu Foreign Minister, Ralph Regenvanu, echoed a common refrain amongst developing nations when he referred to China's "less stringent processes for getting large infrastructure projects implemented" (Regenvanu 2019).

Nevertheless, Chinese firms which have dominated BRI projects to date are taking on serious risks. Attempts to manage and mitigate these risks by Chinese firms tend to be coordinated through the active role played by the Chinese government in BRI projects. Like other major powers, China has a global network of embassies actively gathering information to better understand the economic operating environment in each country. Following collection of such information, government-to-government agreements are negotiated to determine the BRI projects for which the host government is seeking financing. In theory, these are aligned with the national development plans of the host countries and local governments might be expected to collaborate with Chinese partners to reduce country risks.

In practice, major country risks are difficult to mitigate. Adaptation to local conditions is more likely, with all of its attendant risks of corruption, poor project implementation and outcomes. These will vary by country. Dornan and Brant (2014) demonstrate, through a comparison of Pacific Island countries, the difference in project outcomes as a result of the diversity in governance. In Tonga, two Exim Bank loans were negotiated directly by government ministers and expert government agency advice was either ignored or not sought. A substantial component of Tonga's first loan, provided to fund rebuilding the capital's downtown district following riots in 2006, was diverted to building a wharf and a palace extension for the king. The relevant government agency was unable to enforce its preferred Australian construction standards on a road project funded by the second loan. By contrast, in Samoa, no such concerns about quality or outcomes from Chinese-financed projects have been noted, which Dornan and Brant ascribe to a well-functioning system of transparent processes for decision making.

Corruption risks also vary across different operating environments. While the Chinese government has embarked in recent years on a highly visible anti-corruption drive, it is difficult to demonstrate whether corruption risks are being successfully managed in BRI projects. The high cost of many projects would appear to indicate that corruption remains widespread. Anecdotal discussion suggests that where projects are renegotiated after changes of ministers or of governments, that corruption is being recycled and the Chinese companies are being extorted repeatedly in some instances. While it is impossible to find such evidence on the public record, the reduction in costs by one-third of the Malaysian East Coast Rail Link following the 2018 change of government suggests prices had been artificially inflated (Ng 2019).

Security risks have been major problems for some BRI projects. In Pakistan, more than forty workers on China Pakistan Economic Corridor projects have been killed by militants, requiring the host government to provide paramilitary security forces to allow the projects to proceed (Feigenbaum 2017). Other threats of terrorism and sabotage have become problems for Chinese projects in Central Asia and Africa (Saltskog and Clarke 2019).

In a time of uncertainty about the future of multilateral trade liberalisation, BRI projects may face future risks if host countries do not implement efficient border trade facilitation or behind the border regulatory reform to ensure the success of trade-enhancing projects (Waters 2018), although China is engaged in active trade diplomacy with its BRI partners to manage these risks.

When disputes arise over project implementation or when projects fail, as is inevitable, the legal systems of host countries will be tested and another key area of active Chinese engagement to manage such risks is the development of agreed dispute resolution mechanisms. Many of China's bilateral investment agreements are out of date and may not adequately protect investors (Lai and Lentner 2018).

Country risks need to be assessed on a case-by-case basis. The generalised risks discussed above will tend to be more prevalent in weakly governed BRI partner countries. Further research on BRI implementation in well-governed partner countries and projects with multiple project partners will help to demonstrate variation, as well as to delineate best practice. Singapore, for example, a longstanding strategic partner for China in trade and investment, has become financing hub for a significant number of BRI projects, including China Construction Bank issuing BRI infrastructure bonds in Singapore dollars and Singapore's United Overseas Bank collaborating with Shanghai Pudong Bank on BRI opportunities (Belt and Road Advisory 2018). Japan has also indicated it will partner with China in developing Thailand's rail network, although it has stopped short of framing such cooperation as under the BRI. While the Chinese government may be attractive to poorly governed partner countries because of the lack of conditions applied to project finance, more internationalised projects in future may be able to exert more influence to manage and mitigate country risks.

6 Project Risks

BRI projects are characterised to date by Chinese funding, project management and construction, often by state-owned enterprises employing significant Chinese labour and contracting Chinese suppliers, all of which are understood by the Chinese government and key Chinese stakeholders to provide risk mitigation. Chinese construction companies, after all, have a proven track record. As noted above, Chinese firms tend to operate with coordinated Chinese government leadership, mediated by Commercial Counsellors in Chinese embassies.

For recipient governments and domestic stakeholders, as well as potential third country firms, however, Chinese firms, particularly those in their early internationalisation, may not be familiar with local operating environments and expectations, delivering what might be perceived as poor-quality construction or creating and suffering from culture clash by inadequate communication and closed shop operations. Chinese firms appear still to suffer from a low "legitimacy" factor as latecomers to globalisation (Zhang 2019). A significant backlash has sometimes become evident, as demonstrated in recent elections in Malaysia and Pakistan (Balding 2018).

Further, Chinese state-owned enterprises, in particular, are often perceived as acting uncompetitively and unfairly backed by Chinese state financing, undermining the local competitive environment or even exerting political influence (Yin 2018). Chinese firms, whether state-owned or private sector, work closely with the Chinese funding institutions and, in most cases, there is no formal tender process as might be expected in Western governance models. For government-funded projects, firms are selected through a Chinese government decision-making process that is not transparent to external observers. Key national funding institutions, the Exim Bank and China Development Bank, which have mandates to support Chinese firms, make funding for projects conditional on the use of Chinese firms. By contrast, the new multilateral financial institutions created by China in part to support BRI, the Asian Infrastructure Investment Bank and National Development Bank, have no such requirements (Carrai 2018) and should, in time, facilitate more co-financed and joint venture projects under the BRI umbrella. This should help to spread risk and open projects up to a broader set of experienced international partners operating at high global standards. In the meantime, Chinese firms face their own risks in ensuring quality implementation and can easily become the target of government or community criticism when projects do not progress as anticipated or simply for being Chinese and perceived as favouring Chinese interests and employing predominantly Chinese labour.

Complex infrastructure projects anywhere in the world are prone to scope creep, project redesign, construction delays, cost blowouts and other problems. In Asia, high-profile Korean and Taiwanese high-speed rail projects have failed, for example (Kotani et al. 2018). Yet Chinese-funded and implemented projects badged under the BRI are often depicted as being particularly prone to problems. Chinese firms, although rapidly developing expertise and competitive advantage, are still in the early phase of internationalisation and commonly exhibit poor planning, inadequate due diligence and understanding of local conditions as well as characteristically low levels of transparency. Chinese firms tend to enter markets on the basis of government-to-government agreements and often pay insufficient attention to feasibility studies, cost-benefit analysis and building broader stakeholder and community support for their presence. This is arguably related to cultural factors and is consistent with Chinese investor behaviour even in mature, developed (non-BRI) markets (Nicholas and Yang 2017).

Furthermore, BRI projects are prone to relatively more problems because China is funding projects in high-risk environments that the Bretton Woods financial institutions have shown little enthusiasm to fund. Feigenbaum (2017) notes that China is the number one investor in five of the ten riskiest countries and that Chinese state-owned enterprises, underwritten with government financial guarantees, appear to have a higher threshold for risk than the international norm. Chinese authorities and financial institutions have nevertheless recently strengthened risk assessment processes.

Perceptions that Chinese state-owned enterprises are subsidised may also constitute a political risk to Chinese firms tendering for projects, if governments come under geopolitical or political pressure to find reasons to discriminate against Chinese firms. In Croatia, for the first time in the European Union a Chinese firm bid for and won a tender to construct a bridge, yet the process was characterised by international media as likely unfair underbidding (Santora and Surk 2018). The unsuccessful Austrian bidder failed in its appeal against the tender and Croatia has proceeded with the project, but in the current geopolitical climate it is likely there will be more push-back against Chinese state-owned enterprises in tender processes. In Greece, for example, where numerous projects have received Chinese concessional finance, the European Commission has raised concerns, in particular in the energy sector (Bastian 2019). European ambassadors reportedly wrote an internal report in 2018 warning that the BRI gives subsidised Chinese companies an unfair advantage and warned that European firms could fail to compete if China is not pressured to adhere to European standards of transparency in public procurement, as well as environmental and social standards (Heide et al. 2018).

Over time, internationalising Chinese firms may adapt and develop strategies that will be well suited to local conditions and therefore mitigate risks. More joint venture or other partnership agreements with local and international firms should reduce risks through joint problem solving and knowledge transfer (Lorenzoni and Lipparani 1999). In the meantime, however, are Chinese firms bringing to BRI projects standards and actions that are encouraging corruption and bringing poor net benefits to local communities? This is the criticism levelled by commentators such as Lee (2018) who describes Chinese deals as "opaque" and "rigged from the start". This is closely connected to the country risks above of operating in business environments with poor governance. In theory, in each host country the local government has full sovereignty to impose operating rules including tender processes and construction standards. In some operating environments, ministers appear to welcome dealing directly with Chinese firms to strike deals behind closed doors. Little wonder in such cases the outcomes do not always address the development needs of their constituencies. The lack of evidence on the public record about the deficiencies of such cases makes it difficult here to demonstrate such behaviour but rumours abound.

7 Observations and Conclusion

Whether the benefits of the BRI will be evenly shared or will accrue disproportionately to China will be an important area of future study. It is too early to tell, after only six years since the initiative was launched, and given the ambiguity around what constitutes a BRI project and measurement of success. On the other hand, it is clear that the BRI raises a range of risks and that these are distributed between China and its partners. Further, for firms the political risks to be analysed, assessed and managed are not only at the project or country level, but must include a careful investigation of geopolitical risks. Foreign firms will need strategies for understanding and partnering with Chinese state-owned enterprises as well as Chinese private firms with close links to the Party State, in addition to strategies for each third-country business environment.

While the BRI signifies a new phase of China's internationalisation, it appears the geopolitical narrative has over-reached, and therefore obscured the complexity of implementation and agency in each specific country and project. China does not (at least yet) have geopolitical power to impose a grand strategy on the developing world, although it does have significant resources to build influence and, with willing partners, build new infrastructure and trade routes. The BRI undoubtedly has the potential to address China's geoeconomic and geopolitical imperatives. Whether it can also meet the needs of its (often asymmetrically weaker) partners warrants future study. It is important to carefully assess the evidence of the dominant narrative, as there is a diverse range of country partners in Belt and Road projects, and likely future non-Chinese firms, which have their own agency and will assess the balance of benefits and costs and develop risk management strategies according to their own interests.

The initiative has been marked by many high-profile government announcements but not all of the advertised projects have progressed. Others are proceeding but sometimes more by feeling the way than any clear design, making it difficult and undesirable to draw generalised conclusions. On the Chinese side, there is a great diversity of project implementation. Ang (2018) notes that Chinese firms and bureaucrats may even be making mistakes in implementing projects because of their enthusiasm to please those in the state hierarchy, including grouping increasing numbers of aid and investment projects under the BRI banner, regardless of their contribution to providing important new infrastructure and connectivity. Anyone familiar with China would recognise the confusion, duplication, best intentions, clumsy execution and uncoordinated communication that might well ensue. Further case study analysis will be required to observe these phenomena.

In recognition of the problems in BRI project implementation to date, there is now an important debate underway in China about "fine tuning" projects, learning from the mistakes of the first five years and ensuring BRI projects are more market-oriented, sustainable and "win-win" for all participants. This is within a broader push to focus outward flows of investment to projects with sound business cases, at the same time as China's efforts to stem flows of cash to developed countries for trophy real estate and other purchases. The Chinese government recently initiated a review of freight train route development to Europe, one of the central concepts of the BRI, to manage risks of over-expansion. While the new routes reduce the time required for transport of goods, they face complex customs clearance hurdles. Subsidies to support the early development phase are now being reduced requiring a new focus on efficiency and lower operating costs (Wang 2018).

The powerful NDRC, which oversees the BRI, as well as the financing institutions, will need to take a greater look at political risk. While one of the attractions for developing countries of Chinese finance has been its lack of conditionality, unlike the conditionality (often unsuccessfully) imposed by the Bretton Woods institutions (Carrai 2018), it may be that the institutions funding BRI projects will need to apply stricter guidelines around debt levels, governance standards and even greater transparency to ensure successful future projects.

One of the most prospective steps that China and its firms could take to improve both perceptions and implementation of BRI projects would be to partner with third countries and to seek more co-financing with multilateral development banks. This would help address concerns about project design, transparency in tendering and governance accountability. Whether through partnerships or deepened experience, it might be expected that Chinese projects will over time converge with international standards. However, further observation of Chinese government strategy and Chinese project governance is required before reaching such a conclusion, as it is also possible that China will develop confidence in its "exceptionalism" as a development partner and seek to bring others under its own development model rather than adapting to international norms. Such a model might utilise market elements but maintain a top-down "managed" approach aligned with political objectives, bringing us back to the geopolitical discussion. At the end of the day, the Chinese Party State is not like any other Great Power and may well behave differently. Whether that is to be preferred to previous Great Powers or feared may well vary according to whose shoes the observer is walking in.

At the Second Belt and Road Forum, a meeting of government leaders in Beijing in 2019, Xi Jinping pledged to pursue the BRI with diversified finance and for shared benefits, according to internationally accepted rules, standards and best practices to ensure debt sustainability, combat corruption and ensure green growth (Shi and Cai 2019).

Undoubtedly, the BRI represents an opportunity for countries that have otherwise struggled to develop, with hopes of multiplier effects from new infrastructure and connectivity to drive new industry development, trade and investment. It does not have to be a debt trap, if projects are well designed and executed. Indeed, it may yet prove to be a platform to help countries avoid poverty traps. For decades, aid flows have often had the opposite effect of their benign intention, trapping countries in dependence and encouraging outward migration of talent. To develop, capital formation and infrastructure investment are necessary, which require debt but also adequate returns on investment over the medium to long term for all parties. To bring returns, the political risks, at the country and firm levels, must be managed as the highest priority.

References

Aldrick P (2019) China turns to UK for advice on world aid. The Australian. Available via: https://www.theaustralian.com.au/world/the-times/china-turns-to-uk-for-advice-on-world-aid/news-story/fa292d43fb52ae77d4a212390db967ba. Accessed 16 Apr 2019

Ang Y (2018) Needed for China's Belt and Road: a roadmap. Bloomberg. Available via: https://www.bloomberg.com/opinion/articles/2018-09-27/china-s-belt-and-road-initiative-is-a-campaign-not-a-conspiracy. Accessed 28 Sept 2018
Balding C (2018) Why democracies are turning against Belt and Road: corruption, debt, and backlash. Foreign Affairs. Available via: https://www.foreignaffairs.com/articles/china/2018-10-24/why-democracies-are-turning-against-belt-and-road. Accessed 24 Oct 2018
Bastian J (2019) European fault lines and Chinese crossroads. ReconnectingAsia.csis.org. Available via: https://reconnectingasia.csis.org/analysis/entries/european-fault-lines-and-chinese-crossroads/. Accessed 9 Jan 2019
Belt and Road Advisory (2018) Singapore is China's top Belt and Road partner. Available via: https://beltandroad.ventures/beltandroadblog/singapore. Accessed 18 Nov 2018
Carrai M (2018) It is not the end of history: the financing institutions of the Belt and Road Initiative and the Bretton Woods System. In: Chaisse J, Górski J (eds) The Belt and Road Initiative: law, economics, and politics. Brill Nijhoff, Boston, pp 107–145
Chohan U (2018) What is one belt one road? A surplus recycling mechanism approach. In: Chaisse J, Górski J (eds) The Belt and Road Initiative: law, economics, and politics. Brill Nijhoff, Boston, pp 205–219
Dornan M, Brant P (2014) Chinese assistance in the Pacific: agency, effectiveness and the role of Pacific Island government. Asia Pac Policy Stud 1(2). https://doi.org/10.1002/app5.35
Feigenbaum E (2017) Risky business, Chinese style. Macropolo.org. Available via: https://macropolo.org/risky-business-chinese-style/. Accessed 21 Sept 2017
Hart M, Johnson B (2019) Mapping China's global governance ambitions. Americanprogress.org. Available via: https://www.americanprogress.org/issues/security/reports/2019/02/28/466768/mapping-chinas-global-governance-ambitions/. Accessed 28 Feb 2019
Heide D, Hoppe T, Scheuer S, Stratmann K (2018) EU ambassadors band together against Silk Road. Handelsblatt. Available via: https://www.handelsblatt.com/today/politics/china-first-eu-ambassadors-band-together-against-silk-road/23581860.html?ticket=ST-337240-ncDS4iOfbaTyVkMH2DkT-ap5. Accessed 17 Apr 2018
Kotani H, Suzuki J, Yamada K (2018) Catalyst or catastrophe? Lessons from Asia's high-speed rail failures. Nikkei Asian Review. Available via: https://asia.nikkei.com/Business/Business-trends/Catalyst-or-catastrophe-Lessons-from-Asia-s-high-speed-rail-failures. Accessed 14 Oct 2018
Kratz A, Feng A, Wright L (2019) New data on the "debt trap" question. The Rhodium Group. Available via: https://rhg.com/research/new-data-on-the-debt-trap-question/. Accessed 29 Apr 2019
Lague D, Lim B (2019) Special report: China's vast fleet is tipping the balance in the Pacific. Reuters. Available via: https://www.reuters.com/article/us-china-army-navy-specialreport/special-report-chinas-vast-fleet-is-tipping-the-balance-in-the-pacific-idUSKCN1S612W. Accessed 30 Apr 2019
Lai H, Lentner G (2018) Paving the Silk Road BIT by BIT: an analysis of investment protection for Chinese infrastructure/projects under the Belt & Road Initiative. In: Chaisse J, Górski J (eds) The Belt and Road Initiative: law, economics, and politics. Brill Nijhoff, Boston, pp 250–283
Leandro F (2018) The OBOR global geopolitical drive: the Chinese access security strategy. In: Chaisse J, Górski J (eds) The Belt and Road Initiative: law, economics, and politics. Brill Nijhoff, Boston, pp 83–106
Lee J (2018) China's Trojan ports. The American Interest, vol 14, no 4. Available via: https://www.the-american-interest.com/2018/11/29/chinas-trojan-ports/. Accessed 29 Nov 2018
Lorenzoni G, Lipparini A (1999) The leveraging of interfirm relationships as a distinctive organizational capability: a longitudinal study. Strateg Manag J 20(4). Available via: https://www.jstor.org/stable/3094214?seq=1
National Development and Reform Commission, Ministry of Foreign Affairs and Ministry of Commerce of the People's Republic of China (2015) Vision and actions on jointly building Silk Road economic belt and 21st century maritime Silk Road. Available via: https://reconasia-production.s3.amazonaws.com/media/filer_public/e0/22/e0228017-7463-46fc-9094-0465a6f1c

a23/vision_and_actions_on_jointly_building_silk_road_economic_belt_and_21st-century_maritime_silk_road.pdf. Accessed 28 Mar 2015
Ng E (2018) Botched Chinese railway project in Africa is a warning to belt and road investors. South China Morning Post. Available via: https://www.scmp.com/business/banking-finance/article/2170549/botched-chinese-railway-project-africa-warning-belt-and. Accessed 29 Oct 2018
Ng E (2019) Malaysia says revised China deal shows costs were inflated. AP News. Available via: https://apnews.com/6b0446f8fbdd4992a3c8ad64c1bcb7fb. Accessed 15 Apr 2019
Nicholas A, Yang X (2017) The license that matters: beyond foreign investment review board approval for Chinese investment in Australian agriculture and agribusiness. Available via: https://powelltate.com.au/wp-content/uploads/2017/05/PT-Report_SP_FINAL.pdf
Orchard P (2018) What's at stake in Sri Lanka's government shake-up. Geopolitical Futures. Available via: https://geopoliticalfutures.com/whats-stake-sri-lankas-government-shake/. Accessed 31 Oct 2018
Pence M (2018) Vice President Mike Pence's remarks on the administration's policy towards China. The Hudson Institute. Available via: https://www.whitehouse.gov/briefings-statements/remarks-vice-president-pence-administrations-policy-toward-china/. Accessed 4 Oct 2018
Pilling D, Feng E (2018) Chinese investments in Africa go off the rails. Financial Times. Available via: https://www.ft.com/content/82e77d8a-e716-11e8-8a85-04b8afea6ea3. Accessed 5 Dec 2018
Regenvanu R (2019) "The China alternative" symposium. Vanuatu Daily Post. Available via: https://dailypost.vu/news/the-china-alternative-symposium/article_eb9f9d3a-2b2d-5cfb-b1d2-6d3a57fd2050.html. Accessed 2 Mar 2019
Saltskog M, Clarke C (2019) The little-known security gaps in China's Belt and Road Initiative. The National Interest. Available via: https://www.rand.org/blog/2019/02/the-little-known-security-gaps-in-chinas-belt-and-road.html. Accessed 18 Feb 2019
Santora M, Surk B (2018) For China, a bridge over the Adriatic is a road into Europe. The New York Times. Available via: https://www.nytimes.com/2018/10/11/world/europe/china-croatia-bridge-adriatic-sea.html. Accessed 11 Oct 2018
Shi J, Cai J (2019) Xi Jinping makes plenty of promises on Belt and Road plan, but can China deliver? South China Morning Post. Available via: https://www.scmp.com/news/china/diplomacy/article/3007972/xi-jinping-makes-plenty-promises-belt-and-road-plan-can-china. Accessed 28 Apr 2019
Simon J (1984) A theoretical perspective on political risk. J Int Bus Stud 15(3). Available via: https://www.jstor.org/stable/154279?seq=1
State Council of the People's Republic of China (2015) Action plan on the Belt and Road Initiative. Available via: https://english.www.gov.cn/archive/publications/2015/03/30/content_281475080249035.htm. Accessed 30 Mar 2015
US Department of Defense (2018) Assessment on U.S. Defense implications of China's expanding global access. Available via: https://media.defense.gov/2019/Jan/14/2002079292/-1/-1/1/EXPANDING-GLOBAL-ACCESS-REPORT-FINAL.PDF. Accessed 20 Dec 2018
Wang Y (2018) Govt to assess railway links to Europe. China Daily. Available via: https://www.china.org.cn/business/2018-10/17/content_66611081.htm. Accessed 17 Oct 2018
Waters J (2018) "Unimpeded trade" in Central Asia—a trade facilitation challenge. In: Chaisse J, Górski J (eds) The Belt and Road Initiative: law, economics, and politics. Brill Nijhoff, Boston, pp 375–400
Weerakoon D, Jayasuriya S (2019) Sri Lanka's debt problem isn't made in China. East Asia Forum. Available via: https://www.eastasiaforum.org/2019/02/28/sri-lankas-debt-problem-isnt-made-in-china/. Accessed 28 Feb 2019
Wroe D (2018a) China eyes Vanuatu military base in plan with global ramifications. The Sydney Morning Herald. Available via: https://www.smh.com.au/politics/federal/china-eyes-vanuatu-military-base-in-plan-with-global-ramifications-20180409-p4z8j9.html. Accessed 9 Apr 2018
Wroe D (2018b) Vanuatu PM defends China deals but vows to oppose any new foreign military base. The Sydney Morning Herald. Available via: https://www.smh.com.au/politics/federal/van

uatu-pm-defends-china-deals-but-vows-to-oppose-any-new-foreign-military-base-20180412-p4z96m.html. Accessed 13 Apr 2018

Yin W (2018) The role of Chinese state-owned investors and OBOR-related investments in Europe: the implications of the China-EU BIT. In: Chaisse J, Górski J (eds) The Belt and Road Initiative: law, economics, and politics. Brill Nijhoff, Boston, pp 284–314

Zhang Y (2018) Globalization has reached a turning point. China Daily. Available via: https://global.chinadaily.com.cn/a/201809/29/WS5baeb230a310eff303280217.html. Accessed 29 Sept 2018

Zhang H (2019) Beyond 'debt-trap diplomacy': the dissemination of PRC state capitalism. China Brief 19()1. The Jamestown Foundation. Available via: https://jamestown.org/program/beyond-debt-trap-diplomacy-the-dissemination-of-prc-state-capitalism/. Accessed 5 Jan 2019

Printed by Printforce, the Netherlands